THE NEW WHITEHALL SERIES
No. 11

The Ministry of Agriculture, Fisheries and Food

THE NEW WHITEHALL SERIES

is prepared under the auspices of

THE ROYAL INSTITUTE OF PUBLIC ADMINISTRATION

and is edited on its behalf by Sir Robert Fraser, OBE

*The purpose of the series is to provide
authoritative descriptions of the present work
of the major Departments of Central Government*

Already published

1. THE HOME OFFICE (*reprinted*)
2. THE FOREIGN OFFICE (*reprinted*)
3. THE COLONIAL OFFICE
4. THE MINISTRY OF WORKS
5. THE SCOTTISH OFFICE
6. THE MINISTRY OF PENSIONS AND
   NATIONAL INSURANCE
7. THE MINISTRY OF TRANSPORT AND
   CIVIL AVIATION
8. THE MINISTRY OF LABOUR AND
   NATIONAL SERVICE
9. THE DEPARTMENT OF SCIENTIFIC AND
   INDUSTRIAL RESEARCH
10. HER MAJESTY'S CUSTOMS AND EXCISE

In preparation

THE TREASURY

INLAND REVENUE

THE AIR MINISTRY

THE POST OFFICE

THE MINISTRY OF HEALTH

THE ADMIRALTY

THE NEW WHITEHALL SERIES

No. 11

The Ministry of Agriculture, Fisheries and Food

SIR JOHN WINNIFRITH

KCB

Permanent Secretary to the Ministry

LONDON · GEORGE ALLEN & UNWIN LTD

NEW YORK · OXFORD UNIVERSITY PRESS INC

PRINTED IN GREAT BRITAIN
in 10 on 11 point Times Roman type
BY C. TINLING AND CO. LTD
LIVERPOOL, LONDON AND PRESCOT

PREFACE

THIS book follows the general plan of the New Whitehall Series. Part I gives a broad conspectus of the work of the Ministry of Agriculture, Fisheries and Food today, and an account of its development and expansion during its comparatively short history.

The second, and by far the longest part of the book describes the Ministry's work in detail. The account is not comprehensive, but I hope that those topics have been selected which are likely to be of most interest to the general reader and the student of public administration.

The third part of the book describes the headquarters and local organization of the Ministry and various 'common service' divisions.

Inevitably as time goes on, the Ministry's functions and the way in which they are discharged will change. No organization can remain static, if it is to adapt itself to changing needs, and the Ministry may well evolve as considerably in the future as it has in the past. This book has, of course, been written before the outcome of the negotiations on this country's application to join the Common Market is known. Decisions on this issue may well have a profound effect on agricultural policy, and therefore on the Ministry's organization.

The text has been compiled very largely through the efforts of my colleagues, who deserve any credit there may be for this record of the Ministry's work.

A. J. D. WINNIFRITH

January, 1962

CONTENTS

CONTENTS

PART I

Introduction and History

CHAPTER I

The Ministry Today

THIS book describes in some detail the present-day activities of the Ministry of Agriculture, Fisheries and Food. This introductory chapter outlines briefly the general scope and extent of these activities.

Two points should be made clear at the outset. The first is that the agricultural, fishing and food industries are amongst the most highly developed and progressive commercial activities in the country. Any notions that modern agriculture is managed by country yokels wearing smocks and with straw in their hair should be cast aside. The discovery and rapid development of successive technical improvements in farming and fishing make the production methods of a decade ago as stale as yesterday's newspaper. Indeed many, even perhaps the bulk, of the national problems reaching the administrators' desks are the product not of an out of date and stagnating industry but of an industry improving the volume and efficiency of production too rapidly to be absorbed in the free market at prices which are realistic to the producer. Hence the need for a battery of price and market support mechanisms, described later in the book, to protect individual producers from the full effect of their collective achievements.

The second, and allied, point is to dispel at an early stage any misconceptions that the activities of the Ministry are confined to domestic issues of little general interest. Minor domestic issues such as the regulations governing the composition of ice-cream can be relied upon to promote a storm of controversy when undergoing their periodic inspection by Parliament. And some of the more peripheral activities of the Department are of considerable interest to wide sections of the community—for instance, the attempts by the National Stud to breed the winner of next year's Derby, or the preparation of the Ordnance Survey maps produced originally as one of the instruments for opening up the Highlands and preventing another '45, but now in more widespread use by the weekend motorist and country rambler. But the main operations of the Ministry are more clearly related to the problems of agriculture, fishing and the food industries, and range from laboratory investigations of microscopic diseases to international agreements on a world-wide scale. A brief summary of these operations will give a bird's-eye view of the extent of the Ministry's activities before the details of what is done in individual divisions and branches is read in the later chapters.

Perhaps the place to start this résumé is the administration of farm subsidies and the annual farm price review which, although a relative newcomer to the scene, brings the Ministry into prominence each year in Parliament and the national Press. Before the last war, a series of *ad hoc* schemes were introduced to support the prices and to assist in the marketing of the more important farm products. The advocates of a completely *laissez-faire* economy saw the thin end of the wedge in the mid-twenties when government support was provided temporarily for the infant industry of sugar beet production in this country. Nothing can be as permanent as a temporary scheme, and further measures were taken during the 1930's to support other commodities suffering severely from the prevailing agricultural depression—as serious and damaging as its predecessor in the eighties. A number of statutory marketing boards were established to improve the marketing of farm products. Also wheat production was assisted by the introduction of the Wheat Act in 1932; later in the decade other agricultural commodities were assisted in one way or another. But many of these actions were essentially piecemeal palliatives to particularly hard-pressed sections of the industry.

During the war, agriculture had to be given the means of saving the nation from starvation and all these measures were submerged in controls and price regulations for nearly all the products of United Kingdom farms, with the Government acting as the sole buyer of many commodities. The lesson learned during the war that it was in the nation's interest to support agriculture in general and not only particular commodities within the industry resulted in the Agriculture Act of 1947. This was introduced 'for the purpose of promoting and maintaining, by the provision of guaranteed prices and assured markets for the produce mentioned in the First Schedule to this Act, a stable and efficient agricultural industry capable of producing such part of the nation's food and other agricultural produce as in the national interest it is desirable to produce in the United Kingdom, and of producing it at minimum prices consistent with proper remuneration and living conditions for farmers and workers in agriculture and an adequate return on capital invested in the industry'.

These could have been no more than fine phrases, but in fact they have provided a charter for the whole agricultural industry. It is the interpretation of these phrases, in the rapidly changing circumstances from year to year, which takes place during annual discussions each February. At these discussions the Government and representatives of the farmers examine the economic condition and prospects for the agricultural industry, after which Ministers determine the appropriate types and levels of support prices for the coming year.

The student of economics as well as the student of public administration can learn much from the operation of these price support methods. This is not the place to argue the case for or against support as such—although it should be mentioned that agricultural support programmes are not peculiar to this country; they can be found in practically all the advanced economies in the world. But accepting that price supports of some sort are to be adopted, the ingenuity of some of the methods used to reconcile government intervention with the classical economists' concept of a free market economy should bring a gleam to the eye of the student of such affairs.

Price guarantees, of varying degrees of complexity, are in operation for all the more important commodities. In addition, the Government provides a whole miscellany of production grants and subsidies for such operations as ploughing up old grassland or liming and draining the land to improve the productivity of farms. These production grants and subsidies have gradually increased in importance and, in recent years, they have totalled about one-third of the total government subvention to agriculture. The multiplicity of the schemes administered by the Department—financial assistance for the improvement of farm buildings and for the making of silos; for the maintenance of hardy breeds of sheep and cows in certain designated hill farming areas; for comprehensive farm improvement schemes in hill areas; for the rearing of calves for beef production, and so on—as well as the research, advisory, educational, and other activities, demonstrates an important aspect of its work. The Ministry has not merely to administer Acts of Parliament but it also has to be active in suggesting and initiating schemes to assist in the development of the industry in the national interest.

The detailed operation of these various price support schemes and other forms of assistance to agriculture is described in later chapters. The main point to note at this stage is that the administration of these schemes accounts, directly and indirectly, for a substantial proportion of the resources of the Ministry. Most of these activities are relatively new types of functions for a government department, and they have brought farmers into very close day-to-day contact with officials.

A farmer today would scarcely believe how little his grandfather was affected by the activities of the old Board of Agriculture. His grandfather had, indeed, to inform the Board if any of his stock showed signs of the cattle plague or various other contagious diseases. Once a year he filled in a very simple census form to give the acreage of his crops and the number of his stock. The Board was brought in to regulate certain relationships in land tenure. For the rest, the Board meant little to him for good or ill. It did little to interfere in his affairs. It equally did little to cure his troubles in the great agricultural depression of the eighties.

Today the farmer may complain that the Ministry concerns itself too closely with his affairs, that its officials come too often to his farm; but at least he will agree that with this development has come a very considerable concern to support him and to provide him with help to run his farm profitably. For a generation or more, the Ministry has set out by positive measures to promote and encourage an efficient and prosperous agricultural industry. And as one of the main methods to secure this objective it has established a system of financial support designed to guarantee a reasonable return to the grower.

The Government has also invested heavily in agricultural research to extend the basic knowledge of agricultural phenomena and in advisory work to disseminate as widely and as rapidly as possible the results of research and experiment. The progenitors of modern agricultural research, 'Turnip' Townshend, Coke of Holkham and Robert Bakewell, to mention some of the household names of agricultural history, were essentially practical innovators trying to improve the techniques of husbandry. It was not until the mid-nineteenth century that Lawes and Gilbert at Rothamsted established a research station to undertake organized and continuous field experiments. Since then, the cost of agricultural research has extended far beyond the potentialities of private funds; and the Government, through the Agricultural Research Council, now finances a variety of research activities throughout the country to investigate subjects ranging from fundamental research on virus diseases of crops to finding better and quicker ways of milking dairy cows. The Agricultural Research Council, however, is responsible to the Agricultural Research Committee of the Privy Council, and not directly to the Minister of Agriculture, Fisheries and Food. Whilst the more fundamental or 'pure' research is undertaken under the auspices of the ARC, the Ministry directly finances a broad programme of applied research on specific problems relating to livestock, plant health and plant varieties of immediate concern to farmers and growers. It also has a series of experimental farms and horticultural stations to act as a sort of half-way house between the research stations and commercial farms.

Technical advice to farmers is provided by the National Agricultural Advisory Service, established in 1946, as a comprehensive service throughout England and Wales to take the place of the pre-war advisory facilities provided by county councils and agricultural colleges. In addition to giving technical advice on how much fertilizer to apply to grassland, the composition of rations for fattening pigs and so on, the NAAS also advises farmers on ways of improving the profitability of their holdings—an advisory activity unheard of in grandfather's day and at first treated with some scepticism by the more traditionally-minded farmers. Indeed, in recent years a scheme has been introduced whereby financial grants to small farmers have been coupled with advice to improve the standards of farm management. The financial assistance depends upon the farmer's willingness to adopt a long-term plan designed to improve the profitability of his farm business.

Some of the oldest activities of the Ministry have been related to the control of animal and plant diseases and pests. The Government, working closely with other authorities and with farmers, has been combating pests and diseases since the mid-nineteenth century; but continued vigilance is still needed to prevent widespread and severe damage to farm crops and animals. The Colorado beetle and foot-and-mouth disease are perhaps the best known trouble-makers, since the radio and national Press immediately inform the whole country when fresh outbreaks occur. The control measures to deal with these are described in a later chapter, and only one point need be mentioned here. The speed and thoroughness of the action taken when an outbreak of foot-and-mouth disease is suspected would be commendable even in a book of thriller fiction. And the meticulous care taken to trace precisely the origin of each fresh outbreak would win the approval of Sherlock Holmes himself.

Most of the work on the control of animal and plant diseases is, however, of a more routine nature. A persistent effort over a number of years has virtually eliminated bovine tuberculosis from the herds of this country—an achievement of the greatest service to the health of the nation. A close watch is maintained at all ports of entry on produce which may be harbouring pests and diseases which would be harmful to British agriculture. In addition, international agreements have been made with many countries for the routine inspection of farms supplying plants and other produce for international trade to certify that certain specified diseases and pests are absent.

The work of infestation control is occasionally helped materially by some natural phenomenon, as when myxomatosis wiped out almost the whole of the rabbit population in the mid-1950's. On the other hand, new diseases appear from time to time which require firm and immediate action to prevent their rapid spread throughout the country. Fireblight of fruit trees is a recent example. The emergence of these new problems demonstrates that the control of nature is no easy task, and seems to ensure that civil servants, by their

B

successes in controlling existing diseases, do not find themselves without a job.

Together with the control of pests and diseases, some of the oldest activities of the Ministry have been associated with livestock improvement. This was an obvious development from the efforts of the early nineteenth century improvers to breed more productive strains of animals. As elsewhere in modern life, science has superseded crude observations and control in the field; and now a variety of research programmes and testing stations are devoted to the scientific improvement of livestock.

Older still than the Ministry's assistance in livestock breeding has been government intervention in matters affecting the inclosure of common lands, the contractual relationships between landlord and tenant, and the provision of allotments for 'the labouring poor'. Nowadays, a much wider range of activities relating to land and land use are undertaken by the Ministry. The Agricultural Land Service offers advice and guidance in the field of estate management similar to the farming advice given by the NAAS.

Legislation regarding the relationships between landlord and tenant is important in a country where about one-half of the farmers, many of them in a small way of business, rent the whole or part of their farms. An efficient tenant needs some degree of security of tenure whilst, on the other hand, a landlord needs protection from the hazards to his capital investment resulting from poor farming. The necessary legislation and its administration require adjustment from time to time to keep in step with developments in the science and practice of agriculture.

One responsibility of the Minister illustrates how deep into the past go the roots of land tenure. The Minister is Lord of the Manor of the sole surviving village practising the mediaeval system of open or three-fold husbandry—at Laxton in Nottinghamshire. Incidentally, the pumps of a small oilfield can be seen operating within a few miles of this village: a sign of twentieth-century development adjacent to the timeless traditions of agriculture.

The commercial economy of the present-day has brought problems far removed from these traditions. Land development for buildings, roads, quarrying and suchlike activities is the concern of other government departments and local authorities. But the Ministry is naturally much involved to see that when country land has to be used for development the worse and not the better land is taken. A special case is the problem of reconciling the interests of agriculture and re-afforestation in hill and upland areas. This function is shared between the Ministry and the Forestry Commission and requires a nice judgement to balance the numerous interests involved. The

Ministry is also involved in the restoration of land torn asunder by opencast workings for coal, ironstone, sand and gravel. And, continuing the work of many centuries to remove surplus water from the land, it is active in promoting schemes to improve land drainage and water supply to farms.

Some of the activities already mentioned have important international implications, and questions of international trade and commercial policy account for a considerable part of the work at headquarters. The problems of the Caribbean sugar producer, the New Zealand dairy farmer and the Danish pig producer are brought forcefully to the notice of the Ministry. International agreements are in force regulating world trade in sugar and wheat to provide a reasonable degree of price stability. Discussions with certain Commonwealth countries exporting food to the United Kingdom take place regularly to reconcile as far as possible domestic agricultural policy and the agricultural policies of the exporting countries. Various international bodies such as the Food and Agriculture Organization of the United Nations are also actively supported by the Ministry—which provides expert advice both in policy formation and in the execution of specific programmes.

Enough has been said to give some indication of the widespread activities of the Ministry in the field of agriculture. A number of substantial areas of work have not been mentioned. Regulations governing the wages and conditions of employment of agricultural workers; orders controlling the purity of seeds and the sale of fertilizers and animal feedingstuffs; the work involved in administering the Agricultural Marketing Acts under which a number of marketing boards have been established, are just some of the other activities in this field. But the purpose of an introductory chapter is to introduce the reader to the scope of the contents, rather than to summarize the whole book. It only remains, therefore, to describe the other main fields of interest—the food industries and fishing.

Any division of the Ministry's activities into 'food' and 'agriculture' is largely arbitrary since much of the work in the agricultural field is closely related to the provision of wholesome food to the consumer. But there are some activities related almost wholly to protecting the interests of the consumer and these may, for convenience, be described as the 'food' side of the Ministry.

This side of the Ministry's work has, of course, contracted substantially when compared with the elaborate system of controls and rationing in force during and immediately after the 1939–45 war. These war-time activities are described briefly in the historical chapter with references to the more detailed descriptions published elsewhere. However, the Ministry still maintains up-to-date plans for safeguarding food supplies in the event of war or peace-time civil emergencies. It is also concerned in the watch maintained by governments to safeguard the nation's food from harmful effects which may arise incidentally from the use of atomic energy.

The prevention of fraud by adulterating food and drink necessitates detailed regulations specifying the contents of particular foods and the descriptions given to certain foods when advertised or sold. The Food and Drugs Act, 1955, is the present culmination of centuries of intervention by government. The Minister of Health and the Minister of Agriculture, Fisheries and Food jointly administer many of the powers available under this Act. The work, which is undertaken in close consultation with the manufacturing and distribution trades, and with other interested bodies, is typical of so much government administration. The protection given to the consumer is generally taken for granted. It is only when some national controversy flares up that the public realizes the extent of government protection against unscrupulous trading.

Two commodities which are the particular concern of the Ministry are meat and milk. For meat, the Government aims to maintain adequate facilities, humane conditions and high standards of hygiene in slaughter-houses. In addition, regulations are in force for the inspection of all meat supplies, whether home-produced or imported.

Similarly, regulations are needed to ensure that the production and distribution of milk is hygienic. Thus, inspectors regularly visit dairy farms to check that the methods of milk production are hygienic and conform to certain standards. The treatment of milk before retail sale is also subject to regulations, with the Ministry and local authorities sharing the statutory responsibilities.

Food research is another activity with which the Ministry is concerned in collaboration with other scientific bodies. Accelerated freeze-drying, a major advance in the dehydration of foods, was developed by the research staff of the Department until the process was sufficiently well advanced to be adopted by private industry both at home and abroad.

In addition to these specific measures to safeguard and improve the nation's food supply, more general aspects of nutrition are the concern of the Ministry. The nutritive value of new foods is evaluated, and by means of the National Food Survey an eye is kept on the level of nutrition of the more vulnerable categories of the nation.

Finally, in fisheries the work of the Department covers a wealth of interest and action—too much action indeed during the recent controversy over Icelandic fishing rights. But even in less strenuous times there are many activities of great interest in the two divisions concerned with all kinds of marine life.

The catching of whales in the Antarctic is subject to conservation rules laid down in an international whaling convention. These rules are enforced by Government inspectors travelling with all whaling expeditions to check that the limits to the number and size of whales which may be caught are not exceeded. Further international agreements are in force to conserve deep-sea fisheries and to control fishing vessels on the high seas. But attempts in recent years to reach international agreement on the limits of coastal waters under national jurisdiction have so far proved abortive.

The impression must not be given that the whole of the Fisheries Department is engaged in international affairs. Many domestic issues of importance occupy the time of many of the staff. The Government's role in assisting in the development of modern fishing fleets has expanded considerably in recent years. The White Fish Authority, financed by a levy on white fish, has been established with wide powers to assist the industry. Similarly, the Herring Industry Board undertakes a number of activities to help that side of the industry. The administration of various subsidies and grants to the fishing industry is also the responsibility of the Department.

Salmon and freshwater fishing provide interest, exercise and frustration for a surprisingly large number of anglers. Legislation to conserve stocks and to regulate fishing rights has been in force for centuries; and the Department keeps a general watch on the administration of the current regulations by River Boards. It does not, however, provide any advisory service for the unsuccessful angler. But it does undertake research, at sea, at fishing ports, and even in the basement at Ministry headquarters, to help solve the problems of the fishing industry and to promote improvements.

The general picture, then, is of a Ministry with a very wide range of activities supporting the three great industries with which it works. In the course of the last half-century the functions of the Ministry have changed beyond recognition when compared with those of the old Board of Agriculture. Most of the old duties persist, but to them have been added a range of tasks covering innumerable facets of the industries. The way in which those functions have grown is symptomatic of the way in which central government has extended its relations with industry. Those functions and the services which Parliament has said shall be provided are now very considerable. That is why it needs a longer chapter to set out the work and a long book to plough the whole field.

CHAPTER II

The Ministry in History

AGRICULTURE AND FISHERIES

IT was not until 1889 that government responsibilities for agricultural questions were combined in one Department, the Board of Agriculture. A previous Board of Agriculture had, however, been established nearly a hundred years earlier.

The latter part of the eighteenth century was a period when remarkable developments were taking place in the practice and science of crop and animal husbandry in Great Britain. Progressive landowners and farmers like Coke of Holkham, 'Turnip' Townshend and Robert Bakewell were introducing new techniques in the growing of crops and the breeding of livestock. The general interest aroused among leading agriculturists by these developments found expression in a resolution which Sir John Sinclair, Bart., a Scottish landowner of quite amazing versatility and energy, submitted to the House of Commons in 1793 in the following terms—

'That an humble Address be presented to His Majesty, entreating, that His Majesty would be graciously pleased to take into his Royal consideration the advantages which might be derived, by the Public, from the establishment of a Board of Agriculture and Internal Improvement.

'Humbly representing to His Majesty, that, though in some particular districts, improved methods of cultivating the soil are practised, yet that, in the greatest part of these kingdoms, the principles of agriculture are not yet sufficiently understood, nor are the implements of husbandry, or the stock of the farmer, brought to that perfection of which they are capable . . .'

The resolution was passed and the Board or Society for the Encouragement of Agriculture and Internal Improvement was constituted by Royal Charter.

This was not really a government department, but a Society supported by an annual grant of £3,000 from the Exchequer. Sir John Sinclair was the first President, and Arthur Young, editor and to a large extent author of the monthly *Annals of Agriculture*, was the Secretary. King George III, himself an active farmer who had contributed some articles to Young's *Annals* under the name of his shepherd at Windsor, 'Ralph Robinson', became Founder and Patron of the Board.

The activities of the Board included the issue of county reports which provided an authoritative account of the state of agriculture throughout the country, the publication of volumes of 'communications' on agricultural questions, including one on so modern a topic as the conversion of grass to arable land, the establishment of a small experimental farm, the arranging of lectures on agricultural chemistry by Sir Humphry Davy and the promotion of the first national agricultural show at an exhibition of livestock held at Aldridge's Respository, St Martin's Lane.

The withdrawal of the exchequer grant in 1820 after the retirement of Sir John Sinclair and Arthur Young led, however, to the winding up of the Board in 1822. Its true successor was the Royal Agricultural Society of England, founded in 1838, and not the Ministry.

Over the next fifty years however the Government created several statutory bodies to deal with various aspects of agriculture which can be regarded as the ancestors of the present Ministry. First of all three bodies of Commissioners were set up between 1836 and 1841 to deal with particular questions of land tenure, namely the commutation of tithe, the inclosure of common land, and the enfranchisement of copyhold land. In 1822 they were all merged in a single Land Commission for England responsible to the Home Secretary.

The other forerunner of the Ministry of Agriculture was the Cattle Plague Department, established in 1865 to deal with a serious epidemic of the cattle plague known as rinderpest which had broken out in that year. The Department started as a branch of the Home Office but was transferred to the Privy Council in 1866, and four years later its title was changed to the Veterinary Department. Armed with statutory powers for the slaughter of affected animals the Department succeeded in stamping out rinderpest in a couple of years and continued in existence to deal with a series of Acts for the control of other animal diseases and insect pests. In 1883 it took over from the Board of Trade responsibility for the publication of the annual agricultural statistics and changed its name to the 'Agricultural Department'; the statistics continued to be collected by the Department of Inland Revenue.

The 1880's were a difficult time for British agriculture, and the Government was frequently urged to bring under a single Minister all its functions relating to the industry.

This it did in the Board of Agriculture Act of 1889. To the new Board were transferred the powers and duties of the Land Commissioners, and those of the Privy Council under the Contagious

Diseases (Animals) Acts and the Destructive Insects Act, 1877; to these were added responsibility for the Ordnance Survey (transferred from the Commissioners of Works and Public Buildings), for the collection and preparation of agricultural (and forestry) statistics and for agricultural (and forestry) research and education. The Board consisted on paper of many high officers of State such as the Lord President of the Council, the Principal Secretaries of State and the First Lord of the Treasury—a form of departmental control which followed the precedent of the Board of Trade. The Board however never met, and its powers were exercised by the President.

In 1903 an Order in Council transferred to the Board the responsibilities of the Commissioners of Works and Public Buildings for the Royal Botanic Gardens, Kew. In the same year the title of the Board was altered by Statute to 'Board of Agriculture and Fisheries' and it took over the powers and duties of the Board of Trade relating to salmon, freshwater and sea fisheries in England and Wales.

Eight years later the establishment of a Board of Agriculture for Scotland relieved the Department of its functions north of the Border, except those relating to the control of animal diseases and general responsibility for the Ordnance Survey.

The outbreak of the First World War did not lead immediately to any significant change in the work or organization of the Department, for government policy was still based on the findings of the Royal Commission on the Supply of Food and Raw Materials in time of War of 1904–5, that barring a grave naval disaster, not only was there no risk of a total cessation of our supplies but no reasonable probability of serious interference with them. In the early days of the war in fact there was no serious shortage of food. The announcement however of Germany's policy of unrestricted submarine warfare, together with the poor harvest of 1916, led to the establishment at the beginning of 1917 of a separate Food Production Department within the Board of Agriculture and Fisheries, with a Director-General directly responsible to the President.[1]

To a large extent this Department operated locally through county agricultural executive committees consisting of landowners, farmers, workers and others locally interested in food production. To the committees, for example, were delegated powers to issue directions for the ploughing and cultivation of land and to take possession of land that was not properly cultivated and farm it themselves. Contrary to practice in the 1939–45 war, most of the members of committees

[1] The story of the Food Production Department has been told by its Deputy Director-General, Sir Thomas Middleton, in *Food Production in War*, a volume in the Economic and Social History of the World War, Oxford University Press, 1923.

were appointed by the county council and only a minority by the Minister.

After the armistice the Government decided that there was no longer need for a separate Food Production Department, and its remaining functions were absorbed by the Board early in 1919. In the same year the Board became a Ministry. This change was not in fact proposed by the Government or the Board itself, and was brought about by a Private Member's amendment to a Bill primarily concerned with other matters. The establishment of the Forestry Commission in the same year relieved the Department of its statutory responsibilities for forestry matters.

In the twenties the Ministry remained a comparatively small and static department though concerned with a wide variety of matters, such as the control of pests and diseases, the development of agricultural research and education, the settlement of a large number of ex-service men on the land (largely through the county councils), and the unification of the very heterogeneous collection of bodies concerned with arterial drainage in the catchment boards and drainage boards constituted under the Land Drainage Act, 1930.

In the late twenties and early thirties, however, the work of the Department expanded quite considerably. The main reason for this was decisions of government to introduce measures to safeguard farmers' incomes in the great depression in agricultural prices which occurred in the late twenties and early thirties as part of a general world-wide slump in commodity prices. These measures could be regarded as the counterpart of the comprehensive protective tariff system for industry which was introduced in 1932 and reversed this country's traditional free trade and non-protectionist policy. For a wide range of fruits, vegetables and other horticultural produce tariff protection was granted. This was a matter primarily for the Import Duties Advisory Committee, but the Ministry was concerned both in supplying the Committee with information and in discussions with the Board of Trade, Treasury and other departments on the action to be taken on the Committee's reports.

Other means of protection with which the Department was more directly involved were adopted for other agricultural products, such as quota restrictions on imports of bacon, hams and other meat and subsidies or price insurance schemes for wheat, cattle, milk manufactured into butter and cheese and finally for sheep. The beet sugar subsidy had been introduced in 1925, but for a ten-year period on a diminishing scale, and it was only in 1936 that this was put on a permanent basis by an Act which caused much work for the Department at the time in the arrangements for the amalgamation of the beet-sugar manufacturing companies and the establishment of a statutory Sugar Commission. Special bodies such as the Wheat Commission and the Cattle Committee (later the Livestock Commission) were also set up to administer certain other subsidies, working under the supervision of the Agricultural Ministers and Departments.

Another cause of additional activity for the Department was the report of the Linlithgow Committee on the Distribution and Prices of Agricultural Produce[1] which sparked off a variety of measures for improving both the preparation of agricultural produce for market and also the marketing arrangements themselves. These included the development of the National Mark Schemes for the grading of home-grown produce, and the Agricultural Marketing Acts of 1931 and 1933, which enabled producers, subject to safeguards for the consumer and the public interest, to control the marketing of their produce through statutory marketing boards.

Marketing boards were accordingly established for hops, milk, pigs, bacon and potatoes. Both the preliminary work leading up to the establishment of such boards, including surveys of existing marketing arrangements, and in many cases the setting up of reorganization commissions to prepare draft marketing schemes, and work arising from the activities of the boards once established, added to the Department's tasks.

The Food Production Campaign 1939–45

It was not until the third year of the First World War that the Government had found it necessary to take any drastic steps for increasing home food production (or indeed for controlling the distribution of food).

By contrast, defence planning in the late thirties assumed that in any future major war supplies of food from overseas would be restricted by shortage of shipping and foreign currency and that an immediate effort would be called for to increase home food production.

Some of the steps taken went beyond mere planning. For example, a scheme was introduced in 1937 to subsidize the spreading of lime and basic slag on agricultural land so as to build up the inherent fertility of the soil. A reserve of agricultural tractors was laid in, and key men were earmarked for the proposed county war agricultural committees. Thus as soon as war broke out the whole organization of the Department was changed, less urgent questions were shelved, and senior officers started to put in hand a big campaign for increasing food production. No separate Food Production Department was established on this occasion.

[1] Final Report. Cmd. 2008 of 1924.

This is not the occasion for telling in any detail the story of that food production campaign, which is described in Sir Keith Murray's volume on *Agriculture* in the Official History of the Second World War, United Kingdom Civil Series, (HMSO and Longmans, Green & Co. 1955). Some reference, however, is necessary to the local administrative machinery, including in particular the war agricultural executive committees, especially as this has a very direct bearing on the present local organization of the Department (see Chapter XVIII).

The Ministry itself in its London headquarters (or in the offices in Blackpool and Bournemouth to which the bulk of the staff were sent for the duration of the war) necessarily had the task of settling production policy objectives and of negotiating with other departments to see that agriculture as a whole had its fair share of the available supplies of manpower, agricultural machinery, fertilizers and animal feedingstuffs. In translating the paper plans of Whitehall into concrete action on some 300,000 farms, however, the Department was well aware that it would have to cope not only with the wide diversities of farming practice which were the inevitable result of the differences of soil and climate in various parts of the country, but also with the innate conservatism of the British farmer and his suspicion of any advice from anyone outside his own neighbourhood.

This suspicion of the outsider was nothing new. Lord Ernle in his *English Farming, Past and Present* tells us of a Mr Pringle, a retired army surgeon, who in 1756 or thereabouts introduced the drilling of turnips on his estate near Coldstream in Berwickshire. His crops were superior to those of the neighbouring farmers, but none of them followed his example. A few years later, however, a farmer named William Dawson did the same thing on his farm at Frogden in Roxburghshire. 'No sooner did Mr Dawson (an actual farmer) adopt the same system, than it was immediately followed, not only by several farmers in his vicinity, but by those very farmers adjoining Mr Pringle, whose crops they had seen for ten or twelve years so much superior to their own.'[1]

The solution adopted, as in the First World War, was for the Minister to appoint county war agricultural executive committees consisting of local farmers, landowners, representatives of agricultural workers, and others locally interested in food production. To these committees the Minister delegated a wide range of powers under the defence regulations to cultivate and direct the use of any agricultural land and to prevent its use for other purposes, to terminate the tenancies of land in respect of which such directions had not been complied with, and to take possession and to terminate

---

[1] J. Bailey and G. Culley: *General view of the Agriculture of the County of Northumberland*. 3rd Edition (1805), p. 102.

tenancies of any land not cultivated in accordance with the rules of good husbandry (subject only to the Minister's prior consent being obtained before a committee took possession of any land or terminated a tenancy). Farmers could be required by committees to plough up grassland and to grow given acreages of various crops, clean out their ditches and drains, apply adequate quantities of fertilizers, and so on.

Though there were in the background powers of compulsion under defence regulations it was comparatively seldom that they needed to be invoked.

'Those concerned with the planning of the production policies . . . willingly acknowledge and give due credit to the lead given in persuasion by the thousands of members of the County War Agricultural Executive Committees and their Sub Committees. That these men should be trusted by their fellow-farmers and that their advice should be followed was an essential part of the war-time plans; the measure of their success was the increase that was achieved with a minimum of compulsion. County quotas were worked out largely on the basis of what the members of the Committees thought to be possible, adjusted subsequently by the central authorities. Production programmes for individual farms, and even for individual fields, were worked out between the farmers and the Committee members and a balance was struck between the needs of the country and the practical consideration of the circumstances of each farm and farmer . . . The instances where the ultimate sanctions of compulsion were necessary were infinitesimal in number compared with the number of changes in cropping and livestock production that were brought about by the generous advice and persuasive powers of the farming members of the Executive, District and Parish Committees. They often accomplished what could not have been done by the expectation of higher returns, compulsion or the withholding of supplies. Understanding, experience, patience, confidence and goodwill were required for this work and they were not lacking.'[1]

Some mistakes, of course, were inevitably made from time to time. Thus in the early days of the war one committee found that, through reliance on out-of-date maps, they had served directions on a farmer to plough up the main line of the Great Western Railway. The farmer, in writing to draw attention to this, said he would do his best but felt he must point out that the embankment at this point was rather steep.

The committees also had a wide range of other tasks, including the local administration of various grant and subsidy schemes, such

[1] Sir Keith Murray. *Op. cit.* pp. 308-9.

as those for field drainage and the ploughing up of grassland, the carrying out under contract of field drainage work as well as ploughing and other services requiring machinery that smaller farmers at that time might not possess, the organization of mobile labour gangs for hiring out to individual farmers, the local administration of the schemes for the rationing of feedingstuffs and fertilizers, and the provision of goods and services on credit.

Much of the detailed work of the committees was delegated either to various sub-committees dealing with such questions as labour, machinery, land drainage, technical development, etc., or to district committees consisting for the most part of prominent and progressive local farmers on whom fell much of the work of dealing with individual farmers.

Each county committee had an Executive Officer as its chief official. The majority of these had previously been employed by the county council either as the County Agricultural Officer responsible for local agricultural education and advisory services or as County Land Agent. The Executive Officer and other staff were essentially employees of the committee and not of the Ministry and were not civil servants. One of the Ministry's land commissioners, a professional officer with land agency qualifications, was, however, attached to each county committee to advise them on the exercise of the powers delegated by the Minister. The Land Commissioner's approval was required for the exercise of the more important of the functions of the county committees, including the dispossession of tenants and taking possession by requisition of land and buildings.

What in fact did the campaign (together with the parallel efforts in Scotland and Northern Ireland) achieve? The Ministry's index figure of net output of agriculture in the United Kingdom, i.e. after deducting the value of imported feedingstuffs, store stock and seed, was, in the peak year of 1943/44, 25 per cent above pre-war.[1] This increase, in the words of Sir Keith Murray, 'must be credited to the additional effort of farmers and agricultural workers and to their willingness and ability to adopt new systems and techniques of farming'.[2] This increase was achieved notwithstanding the loss of some 800,000 acres of agricultural land to the Service Departments and a reduction in the effective labour force. In terms of calories the achievement is even more striking. In a final quotation from Sir Keith Murray—

'By 1918/9, the peak of the effort resulting from the First World War, the net output of calories had been increased by about 24 per

[1] Fifteen per cent net increase, if from the gross increase of 25 per cent is deducted the increased use made by agriculture of the products of other industries —machinery, fuel, fertilizers and lime.
[2] *Op. cit.* pp. 243-244.

cent, compared with the years before the war; in the Second World War, the same increase had been achieved by the second harvest of the war and by 1943/4 this increase had been quadrupled.[1]

Post-war Developments

The machinery and measures which had been introduced during the First World War for securing an increase in home food production were dismantled fairly soon after the armistice. The separate Food Production Department, for example, was wound up in March, 1919, and the guaranteed prices for cereals provided by the Corn Production Acts were withdrawn in 1921.

At the end of the war in 1945, however, the prospect of a world shortage of food for many years, combined with the need to husband our depleted reserves of foreign exchange, pointed the need for government action to ensure a continued high level of food production, a policy to which all the main political parties subscribed.

The post-war Labour Government accordingly decided soon after they came into office to continue the system of county committees which had proved so successful during the war. The wartime committees had been established under defence regulations and their life was essentially limited, but the Agriculture Act, 1947, established a permanent system of county agricultural executive committees charged with the duty of promoting agricultural development and efficiency to whom the Minister could delegate any of his functions relating to agriculture. Members of the committees continued to be appointed by the Minister but the majority were now chosen from lists submitted respectively by the National Farmers' Union, the Country Landowners' Association and the Farmworkers' Unions. In practice a large proportion of the members of the old war agricultural executive committees continued to serve as members of the new county committees. The staffs of the committees became civil servants employed by the Minister and attached by him to the committee—a change of very considerable significance.

In their early days the new committees were called on to assist in a considerable expansion of home food production. In August, 1947, for example, as one of the measures to correct the country's adverse balance of payments position the Prime Minister, Mr Attlee, announced a programme designed to increase the net agricultural output of the United Kingdom by £100 million, or 20 per cent, over the next five years, representing an increase to 50 per cent above pre-war. In 1952 the Conservative Government increased this 'target' figure for net output to 'at least 60 per cent above pre-war', a figure which has now been reached.

[1] Op. cit. p. 244.

The new county committees continued broadly the work of the war agricultural executive committees. It was only to be expected, however, that in the course of time some of the committees' activities would dwindle or disappear whilst others would become more important.

Even by 1947 the power to require the ploughing up of land or its cropping in a particular way had lapsed. Committees continued to have the power to place under supervision farmers and landowners who were disregarding the rules of good husbandry or good estate management, and in the last resort, and with the Minister's approval, to dispossess them (though this latter power was now subject to the right of appeal to an independent Agricultural Land Tribunal). The use of these disciplinary powers became increasingly difficult and out of line with current public opinion as time went on, and following criticisms in the report of the Committee, under the chairmanship of Sir Oliver Franks, on Administrative Tribunals and Inquiries[1] these powers were repealed in the Agriculture Act, 1958.

Another development was the decision, in 1954 (following the report[2] of an investigation by Sir Andrew Clark, QC, into the conduct of various officials of the Ministry and others who had been dealing with the disposal of farm land at Crichel Down, in Dorset) to sell as much as possible of the agricultural land acquired by the Government which was at that time under the management of the Agricultural Land Commission.

The work of the county committees again was reduced by the disappearance of such measures as the rationing of animal feeding-stuffs and the ending of the need for mobile labour gangs, whilst trading services, such as the machinery service, were gradually reduced in extent and scope over the course of the years. On the other hand efficiency in production was becoming increasingly important and this meant extra work for county committees in other directions, particularly in the promotion of technical development to be described later on in Chapter V.

Government action to maintain and increase efficiency in home food production called for a strong corps of scientific and technical officers to service the county agricultural executive committees, to provide advice to farmers and landowners, and to assist in local administration of various of the Department's schemes for improving the standard of agricultural efficiency.

In pre-war days county councils, with grant aid from the Ministry, had provided an advisory service to farmers as well as vocational instruction for young people. Counties were grouped into some

[1] Cmnd. 218 of July, 1957.   [2] Cmd. 9176.

thirteen 'provinces' in each of which there was a University Agricultural Department or an Agricultural College to which had been attached a number of specialist advisory officers in various branches of agricultural science, such as chemistry, entomology and dairy bacteriology; the salaries of these advisory officers were normally defrayed by the Ministry and they were not expected to do more than a very limited amount of teaching. The county staffs under a County Agricultural Organizer were the general practitioners to whom a farmer could first turn for advice whilst the advisory staff at the provincial centres were the specialists to whom the county staffs could refer the farmer who needed something outside the daily run of advisory work.

During the war most of the county and provincial staffs were seconded for service with the county war agricultural executive committees for both advisory and other work. The post-war development of the agricultural education and advisory services had been reviewed by a committee under the chairmanship of the Rt Hon Lord Justice Luxmoore which reported in 1943.[1] The Government decided that after the war there should be one advisory service for the whole of England and Wales directly employed by the Ministry, and the National Agricultural Advisory Service, whose work is described in Chapter V, was established accordingly in October, 1946. This was followed in 1948 by the establishment of the Agricultural Land Service which provides a technical advisory service on questions of land management and land use as well as performing other services for the Ministry which call for professional land agency qualifications.

FOOD

The First Ministry of Food

There have been two Ministries of Food, each essentially a wartime creation.

In the first two years of the First World War the purchase and distribution of food was to a large extent left in the hands of private industry free from government control, and adequate supplies were available for all. In the early days of the war the Board of Trade was given powers which in fact it never used to requisition stocks of food that were being unreasonably withheld. The Board also in the early days of the war issued lists of recommended retail prices for various provisions prepared by an Advisory Committee of retail traders, but these were soon discontinued.

Difficulties with particular foods were dealt with *ad hoc*. Before the war two-thirds of our sugar supplies had come from Austria-

[1] Cmd. 6433.

Hungary, and a Royal Commission on the Sugar Supply quite independent of the Board of Trade was appointed with executive powers to purchase, sell, and control the delivery of sugar on behalf of the Government. The Board of Trade became responsible for purchasing imported meat for the Army, and secret purchases of wheat were made by private buyers on government account.

Rising food prices combined with the threat of the resumption of unrestricted submarine warfare by Germany led to the appointment at the end of 1916 of Lord Devonport as Food Controller (i.e. Minister of Food), at the head of a Ministry of Food which absorbed the Food Department of the Board of Trade which had recently been established.

It would be inappropriate to recount here in any detail the story of the activities and achievements of the first Ministry of Food; that has been done by Sir William Beveridge (now Lord Beveridge) in his volume on *British Food Control* in the Economic and Social History of the World War.[1] But eventually the Ministry were buying practically all imported foods, as well as home produced supplies of meat and potatoes. Sugar, meat, butter, margarine, lard, tea and jam were eventually all rationed, and price controls imposed on a far greater number of foodstuffs.

The Inter-War Years

Once fighting ceased and food became gradually more plentiful the Government no longer felt the need for a separate Ministry of Food. The last of the rationing schemes for sugar came to an end in November, 1920, and the first Ministry of Food came to an end on March 31, 1921, its few remaining powers and duties being transferred to the Board of Trade.

The remaining Ministry of Food staff retained at the Board of Trade were engaged mainly in winding up Ministry of Food activities, including in particular the settlement of accounts and compensation claims. The Board of Trade also retained the services of the Divisional Food Commissioners (some fifteen covering Great Britain), local persons of standing and independent of the food trade, who had supervised the local administration of rationing and other food control measures. Under their new name of Divisional Food Officers they provided a cadre for a regional organization to safeguard food supplies in the event of strikes or other peace-time emergencies. They took charge, for example, of the local arrangements for food distribution in the General Strike of 1926. The contacts which the Divisional Food Officers maintained with local authorities and with the food

[1] Oxford University Press, 1928.

C

trade were to prove of great value when the time came to plan food control measures for a future war.

There was also a small amount of legislation for the protection of the consumer, such as the Sale of Tea Act, 1922, which prescribed standards of quality and made sales by net weight compulsory.

In accordance with the recommendation of the Royal Commission on Food Prices[1] a Food Council was appointed in 1925 with the duty of investigating and reporting to the President of the Board of Trade on complaints about the supply or price of articles of food for general consumption. The Council had no executive powers and could only rely on the publicity given to their reports. For example they promulgated a scale of maximum prices for bread based on the price of flour, but this was by no means universally observed; enquiries which the Council made in July, 1938, showed that in 39 per cent of a sample of towns in England and Wales bread prices were in excess of the recommended scale.

The Second Ministry of Food

The first Ministry of Food was not established until the third year of the war and had hurriedly to improvise its food control arrangements.

By contrast the outbreak of the war in September, 1939, had been preceded by several years of intensive planning, on the hypothesis that shortages of supplies of foreign currencies and of shipping, to say nothing of the possible damage to ports and railways by aerial attack, might require drastic food control measures on the outbreak of war.

In December, 1936, a Food (Defence Plans) Department was established within the Board of Trade under the direction of Sir Henry French, seconded from the Ministry of Agriculture and Fisheries, who was subsequently to become Permanent Secretary to the Ministry of Food for the whole of the war. This Department was charged with the duty of formulating 'plans for the supply, control, distribution and movement of food (including feedingstuffs for livestock) during a major war with a view to ensuring that the food supplies of the United Kingdom are maintained and distributed in all eventualities, including aerial attack'.

Sir William Beveridge had concluded his account of the first Ministry of Food, referred to above, by saying: 'The account that has been given here of these particular experiments, long as it may seem, is no more than a surface gleaning of the archives. There forms and circulars, reports and instructions, schemes and counter-schemes and plans for another war, all so many monuments of toiling ingenuity, lie mouldering gently into dust and oblivion—lie buried,

[1] Cmd. 2390 of 1925.

please God, for ever.' This hope was not to be realized. In fact the records of the first Ministry of Food proved of inestimable value in planning for the second.

By the time that war broke out in September, 1939, detailed plans had been worked out, which could be put into operation forthwith, for controlling the purchase and distribution of the most important foodstuffs, and the key men had been selected for work in the Ministry of Food as trade directors and advisers.[1] Ration books had been printed and distributed and reserves of sugar, wheat and whale oil had been purchased. Mr W. S. Morrison (as he then was), who as Chancellor of the Duchy of Lancaster had been responsible for food defence plans from the previous April, was appointed Minister of Food at the outbreak of war and the Food (Defence Plans) Department became the Ministry of Food.

The wartime work of the Department has been told in detail by Mr R. J. Hammond in his volumes on *Food* in the History of the Second World War: United Kingdom Civil Series, (HMSO and Longmans, Green & Co.). [Volume I, 1951; *The Growth of Policy*. Volumes II and III, 1956 and 1962: *Studies in Administration and Control*.] A shorter account is given in the official booklet *How Britain was fed in war time: Food Control 1939–1945*, (HMSO, 1946). Mr Hammond has also written a rather shorter book *Food and Agriculture in Britain 1939–1945: Aspects of Wartime Control*, (Stanford University Press, Stanford, California, 1954), which reviews the work not only of the Ministry of Food but of the Agricultural Departments.

In view, especially, of the existence of these works no attempt will be made here to tell in any detail the story of wartime food control or to show how the Ministry of Food became the world's largest trading organization with an annual turnover of the order of £1,000 million per annum and administered schemes for the price control and rationing of most of our food (including the points rationing scheme, which had no counterpart in the First World War). By the latter years of the war, food imports were reduced to half the pre-war figure—11 million tons instead of 22 million tons. This reduction was only made possible as the result both of increased home food production, and of rationing and other control over the distribution of all important foods.

Whilst the war was at its height the Ministry had foreseen that the

[1] Lord Woolton tells us in his Memoirs that in March, 1939, he was invited to become Area Meat and Livestock Officer designated with responsibility for 'the collection and slaughter of livestock, and the wholesale and retail distribution of meat'. The Food (Defence Plans) Department cannot be accused, in this instance at any rate, of failing to aim high.

immediate effect of the end of hostilities would be to increase rather than to diminish the seriousness of our food problem, since food would then have to be found for the countries in Europe and in Asia which at that time were occupied by the enemy. By the end of 1943 as Mr Hammond records[1] the Coalition Government had decided to secure its forward supplies of imported foodstuffs by entering wherever possible into long term contracts with overseas suppliers for as much as four years ahead. In the event the difficulties in obtaining food immediately after the war were aggravated by the sudden withdrawal of Lend-Lease supplies, though this was subsequently mitigated by the American dollar loan.

During the war it had been the boast of the Ministry of Food that there had never been occasion to ration the two 'filler' foods—bread and potatoes—but the world shortage of wheat in 1946 led to the rationing of bread and flour, for a period of two years, and the failure of the crop in 1947–48 necessitated a scheme for rationing potatoes as well.

On November 7, 1945, the Minister of Food announced[2] that the Ministry of Food would be retained as a separate and permanent Department to implement the Government's policy of ensuring that adequate supplies of food necessary for health were available to all members of the public at reasonable prices and of raising the standard of nutrition of the people.

It is easy now to forget how tight food supplies continued to be for a number of years after the war. Rationing of butter, margarine and meat did not finally end until 1954, and the world shortage of fat and of meat led the Government to embark on large scale enterprises for the growing of groundnuts in East Africa and for the production in Queensland, Australia, of maize (Sorghum) to be fed to pigs.

Amongst the achievements of the Ministry was the provision of the foods needed by the more 'vulnerable' sections of the community, particularly nursing and expectant mothers and their young children. Lord Woolton, who no doubt carried with him memories of what he had seen in his undergraduate days at the Ancoats Settlement in what was then one of the worst slum areas of Manchester, tells in his Memoirs that as Minister of Food 'I determined to use the powers I possessed to stamp out the diseases that arose from malnutrition, especially those among children, such as rickets. The health of the children of today is the reward of that policy.'

In accordance with this policy expectant mothers and young children were assured of a pint of milk a day at a special cheap rate, or free, according to means, at a time when the rest of the nation

[1] *Food and Agriculture in Britain*, pp. 216-217.
[2] H. C. Deb. (1945), *c*. 1284.

might be getting only a quarter of a pint at the full price; they were
also entitled to special allowances of oranges, dried eggs, fruit juices
and cod liver oil. It used to be said in the Ministry of Food that they
could get anything out of the Minister for what were vulgarly
referred to as the 'preggies'. The Minister himself was much
touched by the number of photographs which mothers used to
send him of their babies who had benefited from these extra
rations, though his pride was sometimes tinged with embarrass-
ment when mothers wrote on the photographs 'One of Lord
Woolton's babies'.

More generally, the war left the nation much more 'food conscious',
and the National Food Survey started during the war and now
continued provides information not previously available on the food
budgets of all classes of the community, including especially vulnerable sections, such as old age pensioners.

The extent to which the leaders of the food trades worked in or
with the Ministry of Food was another war-time development with a
peacetime sequel. When such men went back to their old firms after
the war, it was only natural that they and their old Department
should keep in touch with one another thus helping to preserve
greater mutual understanding between the Government and the
food industry.

THE MINISTRY OF AGRICULTURE, FISHERIES
AND FOOD

By 1953 the present and prospective volume of work of the Ministry
of Food was running down quite rapidly, and food rationing was
expected to end by about the middle of 1954.

On the other hand, it was clear that under any government the
volume of 'food' work would be considerably greater than it had been
before the war. First of all the Ministry of Food was operating the
various schemes for providing the farm price guarantees under the
Agriculture Act in free market conditions (described in greater detail
in Chapter IV). These included deficiency payments schemes for
cereals and fatstock, continued government buying and selling of
eggs pending a decision whether there was to be a producer marketing
board, and trading in surplus potatoes which meant considerable
work for the Department even when the Potato Marketing Board
took over the actual trading operations. Although some of this work
had its counterpart in that of the pre-war Wheat Commission, Livestock Commission, etc., its volume and complexity was now considerably greater.

Then there were the long term contracts for purchase of food from overseas, such as meat from Australia (until 1967) and copra and coconut oil from the south-west Pacific (up to the end of 1957) and commitments under the Commonwealth Sugar Agreement to purchase considerable quantities of sugar for at least a further eight years. Again, the Department was responsible for future policy on slaughter-houses and also the food side of Food and Drugs legislation.

Furthermore, although rationing had ended it was clear that for many years the Government would be concerned with the effect of food imports on our balance of payments. Food defence plans would need to be kept up to date, and strategic stocks of food would have to be maintained and managed. The Government must also be in a position to safeguard supplies of food in civil emergencies, such as transport strikes and floods.

Thus there was clearly going to be a considerable amount of permanent 'food' work but perhaps hardly enough to require a separate department.

There were, therefore, two possible courses. The Ministry of Food could be amalgamated with the Ministry of Agriculture and Fisheries, some of the work dealing with Scottish Agriculture being transferred to the Secretary of State. Alternatively the Ministry of Food's work could be split between a number of departments broadly on the pre-war lines, e.g. the Board of Trade might take over responsibility for food defence plans, imports and overseas questions; the Agricultural Departments home agriculture questions, including the implementation of the price guarantees; and the Health Departments matters such as food hygiene and slaughter-houses.

Weighty arguments could be advanced in favour of either course. On the one hand, for example, it was urged that there ought to be 'a Minister free to speak for the consumer' and that this would no longer be possible if 'the rump of the Ministry [of Food] was swallowed up in the Ministry of Agriculture'.[1] On the other hand it was argued that it would make for easier handling of the government relationships with the farming industry if the Minister in charge of them had a responsibility covering all the main aspects of food problems—production, importation, manufacture, distribution, etc.

The attentive student of the Official Histories of Food and Agriculture in the last war and of contemporary references in newspapers and other periodicals can hardly fail to catch fairly frequent echoes of keen controversy between the two departments and it would be idle to suppose that the occasions for such controversy diminished in the subsequent post-war years. It was argued that if one Minister and one department were responsible for looking after the interests

[1] *The Economist*, October 9, 1954, p. 108.

both of the farmer and fishermen and of the consumer it should be easier for them to take a balanced view.

On grounds of administrative convenience and efficiency the arguments seemed all in favour of amalgamation of the Ministry of Food with the Ministry of Agriculture and Fisheries, rather than splitting its work up between a number of departments and in particular allocating a substantial section of it to the Board of Trade.

The burden falling on the President of the Board of Trade and his senior officials at that time was already one of the heaviest in Whitehall. Any appreciable addition to the responsibilities of the Board of Trade was therefore undesirable, whilst the combination of the Ministry of Food with the Ministry of Agriculture and Fisheries, after allowing for the reduction of overlap and the other economies resulting from amalgamation, could be expected to result in a department of approximately the same size as the Board of Trade. Again, if the work of the commodity divisions of the Ministry of Food were divided between several departments much work would be needed to reassemble them if it ever became necessary again to have a separate Ministry of Food, say in a future war.

After considering the alternatives the Government came down in favour of amalgamating the Ministry of Food with the Ministry of Agriculture and Fisheries. Certain of the functions of the Department in Scotland, such as local administration of cereals, fatstock and milk guarantees, were to be taken over by the Department of Agriculture (and it was subsequently decided to transfer to the Health Department a limited amount of work on food hygiene and welfare foods).

This decision was announced in October, 1954. Before the actual amalgamation could take place a great deal of work had to be done on the detailed organization of the new Department, entailing as it did the combination in one branch or division of work previously done in separate commodity divisions of the two departments, to say nothing of the fusion of 'common service' divisions, such as Establishments, Finance, Legal and Information. Detailed negotiations and discussions with the two Departmental Whitley Council Staff Sides were needed on all questions of assimilation of the practice of the two Ministries where any divergence existed. All these matters were eventually settled to an extent sufficient to enable the amalgamation to be effected (by an Order in Council under the Ministers of the Crown [Transfer of Functions] Act, 1946) in April, 1955, as originally planned. In this interim period the then Minister of Agriculture and Fisheries (Mr Heathcoat Amory, as he then was) also doubled the office of Minister of Food as a preliminary to becoming Minister in charge of the combined Department.

The amalgamation, coinciding as it did with the run-down of old Ministry of Food work, inevitably meant dislocation and some personal inconvenience to many who had to be assigned to new duties, but all this was in the main cheerfully accepted.

PART II

The Work of the Ministry

CHAPTER III

The Farm Subsidies and the Annual Price Review

THIS chapter deals with the present system of exchequer grants and price support schemes for agriculture associated with the annual farm price review, which in 1960/61 accounted for over 80 per cent of the expenditure of the Ministry and of the Department of Agriculture and Fisheries for Scotland, or a total of approximately £263 million; the figure for 1961/62 will be considerably higher. The various schemes which the Department now administers to provide the guaranteed prices for farm produce will be described in the next chapter.

Before the war the Ministry and the Department of Agriculture for Scotland administered either directly or through statutory commissions a variety of government subsidies for different farm products. First in time was the sugar-beet subsidy, originally introduced in 1925 for a ten-year period to assist the establishment of an infant industry but subsequently made permanent. Next were the payments to wheat growers under the Wheat Act, 1932, administered by a Wheat Commission and financed not from the Exchequer but by the consumer through a levy on home-milled and imported flour. Subsequently subsidy schemes were introduced for cattle and sheep (administered by a Livestock Commission), milk, barley, oats and bacon pigs. The various schemes under different Acts of Parliament grew up in a piecemeal fashion, and there was no machinery for looking at the level of the different subsidies from time to time in the light of the financial position of the farming industry as a whole.

During the war these piecemeal schemes had lapsed and the farmer's returns were assured either by the purchase of his produce by the Ministry of Food or its agents at prices fixed in advance or by the Ministry fixing the prices at which private traders could buy. Any loss which the Ministry of Food incurred on the resale of its purchases formed part of the 'food subsidies'. In war-time when food was scarce and rationed there was no natural market price for much of it, and as increases in the controlled retail prices were deliberately restricted as part of the government's policy of stabilizing the cost of living it was impossible to say how much of the Ministry's trading loss represented a subsidy to the farmer and how much a subsidy to the consumer.

The Agriculture Act, 1947, gave statutory sanction for continuing in peacetime a comprehensive system of guaranteed prices and assured markets for the principal agricultural products, namely milk, fatstock (cattle, sheep and pigs), eggs, cereals (wheat, rye, oats and barley), potatoes and sugar beet (wool was subsequently added to the list). For the time being guaranteed prices and assured markets continued to be provided by government purchase of the farmers' produce. Between 1952 and 1954, however, the control and rationing of food ended, and the Ministry of Food for the most part ceased to purchase and trade in food. It therefore became necessary to find means of implementing these provisions of the Agriculture Act, 1947, other than through State trading and in accordance with government policy of avoiding as far as possible interference with the free play of the market.

The schemes devised for the various commodities are described in the next chapter. Most of them are based on the idea of the deficiency payment. The principle of this in its simplest form is that the farmer sells his produce on the free market for the best price he can get, and the Government then, if necessary, makes a payment to all producers of an amount sufficient to bring their *average* return up to the guaranteed or standard price. This can be illustrated by a simple hypothetical example. Suppose that the guaranteed price for wheat is 28s per cwt. and that the average of the prices of all the recorded wheat sales in the country is 25s a cwt. What would be the position of three farmers, the first of whom has sold his wheat at 20s, the second for 25s and the third for 30s per cwt? Under the system the Government would make a payment to all growers on their sales of wheat at a uniform rate equal to the amount by which the average price falls short of the guaranteed price—in the above example a payment of 3s a cwt. In the three cases taken the first farmer would get, in all 23s a cwt.—20s from the market and 3s from the Government. The second who sold at the average price would get, in all, 28s a cwt., while the third would get 33s a cwt.

Under this system, which now applies to fatstock as well as cereals, the farmer gets the full benefit of any improvement in his market return which he can secure from producing a good quality article and studying the needs of the market, since the price he gets can only have an infinitesimal effect on the average price realized by all producers. On the other hand, in so far as the average price is increased as a result of farmers generally improving the quality of their produce and their marketing methods and the guaranteed price remains unchanged the Exchequer benefits from the reduction in the rate of deficiency payment.

The Government also announced that it would be their policy in appropriate cases to make use of producers' marketing boards in the administration of the price Guarantee Schemes.[1] The present price guarantee arrangements for milk, eggs, wool and (in Great Britain) potatoes are in fact all operated through producer marketing boards and are again all based on the principle of the deficiency payment, i.e. of bringing the average return for all eligible produce up to the guaranteed level. In the arrangements for eggs and for milk manufactured into products such as cheese, butter and milk powder the Government and the marketing board share in agreed proportions the amount by which the average price realized by the board exceeds or falls short of a certain target figure, so as to give the board an incentive to obtain the best possible return.

Wool and sugar-beet are the two commodities for which the farmer still gets a fixed price settled in advance.

One consequence of the deficiency payment system is that the cost of the guarantee payments in any year will depend to a large extent on world prices and supplies of cereals, meat, etc. which affect the price which farmers over here can get for their produce and hence the rate of deficiency payment. It is thus impossible to estimate accurately in advance the amount of money that the Exchequer will need to find for implementing the price guarantees in any year, and in some years a large supplementary estimate may be required while in others there may be substantial savings. This is an inevitable consequence of any arrangement which in effect insures farmers to a large extent against fluctuations in world market prices.

In addition to providing price guarantees for the farmers' produce, the Government during and since the war has been making various 'production grants' to farmers and landowners to encourage operations such as the ploughing up of grassland and the liming and drainage of agricultural land with a view to increasing output and efficiency.

A list of the current agricultural subsidies, including the price guarantees, is given in the following table, together with their cost in 1960/61. The table also shows where an account of any particular price guarantee scheme or subsidy can be found in this book. The table does not include the improvement grants for horticulture (see Chapter X) which cost about £100,000. (See pages 46 and 170.)

The Department of Agriculture and Fisheries for Scotland administer most of these price guarantees and production grants in that country. There are a few, however, distinguished in the table by a reference, which the Ministry of Agriculture, Fisheries and Food administers for the whole of the United Kingdom. These are the price guarantee schemes administered by agricultural marketing

[1] *Decontrol of Food and Marketing of Agricultural Produce*, para. 4. Cmd. 8989.

THE AGRICULTURAL SUPPORT SUBSIDIES, 1960/61

	Expenditure £million	Page in this book where a description of the subsidy, etc. is given
I. IMPLEMENTATION OF PRICE GUARANTEES		
Cereals—		54
Wheat and Rye	18·1	
Barley	33·6	
Oats and Mixed Corn	11·7	
	63·4	64
Eggs (hen and duck)[1]	22·5	59
Fatstock—		
Cattle	12·3	
Sheep	13·9	
Pigs	20·0	
	46·2	
Milk (excluding school and welfare milk)	10·8	66
Wool[1]	2·6	62
Potatoes[1]	5·7	68
Total I	151·2	
II. FARMING GRANTS AND SUBSIDIES		
General Fertilizers Subsidy[1]	32·2	154
Lime Subsidy[1]	8·7	155
Ploughing Grants	10·9	88
Field Drainage Grants (tiling, moling and ditching)[2]	2·7	137
Water Supply Grants[2][3]	0·8	143
Grants for Improvement of Livestock Rearing Land[3]	1·5	114
Marginal Production Assistance Grants[2]	1·0	88
Bonus Payments under the Tuberculosis (Attested Herds) Scheme[2]	9·0	100
Calf Subsidy	17·6	92
Hill Sheep[3] and Hill Cattle Subsidies	5·3	92
Silo Subsidies	0·9	90
Grants for Farm Improvements[2]	7·8	116
Grants to Small Farmers	5·9	86
Grants to Rabbit Clearance Societies[2]	0·2	106
Total II	104·5	
Total I and II	255·7	
Administrative costs applicable to the foregoing expenditure	6·1	
III. OTHER SERVICES		
Arrangements for the benefit of agricultural producers in Northern Ireland financed from the UK Exchequer	1·1	75
TOTAL COST OF AGRICULTURAL SUPPORT	262·9	

[1] MAFF administers for the whole of the United Kingdom.
[2] Does not extend to Northern Ireland.
[3] These grants, and those for tile drainage, do not count as 'relevant production grants' for Annual Review purposes—see page opposite—since (apart from the Hill Sheep Subsidy) they are normally paid to the landlord and not the tenant of agricultural land. They do not therefore normally come within the ambit of the Price Review discussions.

boards which cover the whole of Great Britain or the United Kingdom as the case may be, and also the lime and fertilizer subsidies.

The table also shows certain grants which do not extend to Northern Ireland (though in some cases there are roughly corresponding provisions under Northern Ireland legislation).

The cost of the price guarantee for sugar-beet is met by the purchasers of sugar (through the Sugar Board levy) and not by the Exchequer. Accordingly it is not included in this table. Nor is the effect of protective tariffs on the price of fruit, flowers and vegetables.

THE FARM PRICE REVIEW

So much for the system of financial support for agriculture. It remains to describe how the level of support is varied and determined from time to time.

In the course of the last war the Government established a procedure for fixing farm prices each year after discussions with the Farmers' Unions of the United Kingdom. This became known as the Annual Farm Price Review, and the Agriculture Act, 1947, continued it on a statutory basis. The review gives the Government each year an opportunity of consulting with the producers on the economic condition and prospects of the industry. In the light of this review and taking into account the interests of the consumer and the taxpayer as well as the interests of those engaged in the industry, the Government determines for the coming year the level of the guaranteed prices and also of the 'relevant production grants' towards the costs of various farming operations, such as the lime and fertilizer subsidies and the ploughing grants. These determinations also are a guide to the industry as to the lines on which production can most usefully be developed in the national interest.

Under the 1947 Act minimum prices for livestock and for livestock products (i.e. milk, eggs and wool), were also fixed for up to four years ahead. These did not prove as effective as had been hoped as a long term guarantee, and following discussions between the Government and the Farmers' Unions in 1956 revised arrangements were agreed which gave farmers a greater degree of assurance on the future level of the guaranteed prices. These were set out in a white paper, *Long Term Assurances for Agriculture*,[1] and subsequently implemented by Part I of the Agriculture Act, 1957. Under the new arrangements the guaranteed price for any review product could not be reduced by more than 4 per cent in any year, and for livestock and livestock products the total price reduction was not to exceed 9 per cent over any period of three years. The new arrangements also

[1] Cmnd. 23.

provided that the 'total values of the guarantees' could not be reduced by more than $2\frac{1}{2}$ per cent in any year plus any decrease, or minus any relevant increase in costs on review commodities since the last annual review. The 'total value of the guarantees' is calculated by multiplying the current guaranteed price of each product by the current quantity of output qualifying for the guarantee and adding to this total the value of the 'relevant production grants'.[1]

It had also been open to the Farmers' Unions to ask for a 'Special Review' as a sequel to a sudden and substantial alteration of their costs between annual reviews (such as an increase in the minimum agricultural wage) with a view to securing compensatory increases in the guaranteed prices. Such reviews tended to become an annual event, and the 1956 agreement limited the circumstances in which a special review could be held, and there have so far been no special reviews since that date.

The price guarantees and most of the production grants apply to the whole of the United Kingdom; therefore the conduct of the annual reviews and the subsequent price determinations are a matter for the three Agricultural Ministers, namely, the Minister of Agriculture, Fisheries and Food, the Secretary of State for Scotland, and the Home Secretary as the Minister at Westminster responsible for agriculture in Northern Ireland. There is a separate Minister of Agriculture in the Government of Northern Ireland, with whose Department the Ministry normally deals direct on day to day questions affecting Northern Ireland agriculture, although the Home Office are brought into the consideration of any important policy issues.

The procedure laid down by the Agriculture Acts falls into two distinct parts. The Agricultural Ministers are required first of all to review each year 'the general economic condition and prospects of the agricultural industry', consulting in the process 'such bodies of persons as appear to them to represent the interests of producers in the agricultural industry' (in practice the National Farmers' Union of England and Wales, the National Farmers' Union of Scotland and the Ulster Farmers' Union).[2] The Ministers then in the light of their conclusions from this review decide what changes, if any, there shall be for the ensuing year in the level and basis both of the guaranteed prices and of the various production grants.

[1] For example, if the total value of the guarantees is £1,200m., and in the year preceding the review costs have gone up by £10m. the total reduction may not exceed £30m., minus £10m. = £20m.

[2] Before the review opens, it is customary for officials of the Department to have discussions also with the Country Landowners' Association and with the trade unions of the agricultural workers.

In practice the future level of the guaranteed prices and of the production grants is discussed fully with the Farmers' Unions. Constitutionally, however, it is incorrect to refer to this process of consultation as 'negotiations'. The fact that the process is often so described no doubt arises from the Government's desire to ascertain whether the determination they considered necessary in the national interest can be reconciled with the views of the NFUS.

The review discussions are conducted on the Government side by officials of the three Agricultural Departments (i.e. the Ministry, the Department of Agriculture and Fisheries for Scotland and the Ministry of Agriculture for Northern Ireland), but all the preparations for the review and reports to Ministers on the issues involved and on the progress of the discussions are the responsibility of an 'Official Team' consisting of officials of the three Agricultural Departments and of the Treasury, other departments being brought in as necessary. The Official Team is presided over by the Permanent Secretary or a Deputy Secretary of the Ministry, and includes the Under Secretaries responsible for the various commodity divisions, Economics and Statistics and External Relations, together with the Chief Scientific Adviser (Agriculture), the Principal Finance Officer and the Welsh Secretary. Altogether, therefore, a high proportion of the senior staff of the Ministry is involved in the review discussions, as is only right in view of the importance of the issues which come up, both in the preparation for the review and in submitting reports to Ministers in the course of the review, often at very short notice, in order to obtain their instructions for the next round of talks with the farmers.

The purpose of the price guarantees was defined in Section I of the Agriculture Act, 1947 as being to promote and maintain 'a stable and efficient agricultural industry capable of producing such part of the nation's food and other agricultural produce as in the national interest it is desirable to produce in the United Kingdom, and of producing it at minimum prices consistently with proper remuneration and living conditions for farmers and workers in agriculture and an adequate return on capital invested in the industry'. This obviously raises a number of questions. How much of our requirements of beef, wheat, eggs, etc. is it desirable to produce at home at any time? There is room for a variety of opinions, and any intelligent assessment must take into account such issues as the cost to the Exchequer, the volume and prices of supplies available from overseas, our commercial relationships with overseas countries, and the external balance of payments position; again, what at any time are the minimum prices consistent with the requirements of the Act at which the desired volume of output can be achieved?

D

To enable the 'general economic conditions and prospects of the agricultural industry' to be studied a variety of statistical material is required for the review. Much of this is assembled and examined before the review starts by the economists of the Agricultural Departments and of the Farmers' Unions, who are generally able to agree on the relevance and degree of reliability of the various figures, though some issues may have to be left over for the main review discussions. Much of the statistical material relevant to the review is included in the white paper now issued after each review under the title *Annual Review and Determination of Guarantees*.[1] It includes estimates of the aggregate net income of the industry, and its distribution by type and size of farms, changes in costs such as transport and labour costs since the previous review; a comparison between farm incomes and other classes of income; and the size of the subsidy bill in total and for the different commodities and production grants.

Another preliminary to the review is the consideration by the commodity divisions of the Ministry and the Official Team of any changes in the arrangements for the various price guarantee and production grants. In an extreme case this might mean the complete recasting of the basis of a scheme (such as the change in the form of the potato guarantee which took place in 1959) which would normally require discussion with the Farmers' Unions and other interests involved outside the review. On the other hand, it might be a simple amendment of one detail of the scheme (known as a 'basis point'), such as an alteration of the maximum weights of fat sheep on which guarantee payments may be made.

When all this material has been considered and digested by the Official Team they prepare their recommendations to Ministers on the production objectives and the general lines of price policy.

When the instructions of Ministers have been received the review discussions start (normally early in February) with the farmers' representatives, consisting of the Presidents and other chief officers and officials of the three Farmers' Unions.

After discussing any proposed changes in the guarantee schemes, the meeting exchanges views on the statistical data about the general trends of profits and costs in the industry; for example, what trends are revealed by the figures of farm income? The Departmental representatives then make a statement about the Government's production policy, giving a broad indication of the way in which the Government would like to see the production pattern developed. This leads on to a review of all the relevant factors, such as production trends and consumption requirements, world market prospects, the cost of the various subsidies, the trend of profits in the industry as a

[1] For 1961, Cmnd. 1311.

whole, changes in production costs and the industry's productivity, overseas trading relations, and the national economic situation.

The white paper published after each review gives some indication of the relative importance which is attached to these various considerations in any year. Some, such as aggregate net income and aggregate cost changes, have particular relevance to the general level of Exchequer support to be afforded to the industry, whilst others may be thought by the Government (or the farmers) to indicate the need for changes in the level of guaranteed prices for particular products or in various production grants. The respective weight to be attached to the various factors may vary from year to year; there is no formula for computing automatically what the level of guarantee and production grants should be in any particular set of circumstances.

One incidental feature of this empiricism is that it has become possible to present statistics which are subject to appreciable margins of error, and even to extend some of the statistical material into the realm of forecast and speculation, without risk of their being used as a yardstick for reading off a result. Thus it has become possible to combine a procedure for determining guarantees with what is, in the words of the Act, 'a review of economic conditions and prospects', i.e. a review of all aspects that can be displayed factually .

In the closing stage of the review the discussions are concentrated on the detailed changes in the guaranteed prices and production grants which are finally settled by Ministers after they have considered the views expressed by the Farmers' Unions during the review, which will often have concluded with a meeting between the Agricultural Ministers themselves and the leaders of the Farmers' Unions.

These decisions are then set out in the white paper, which also contains a statement of the Government's production and guarantee policies, as well as a summary of some of the main statistical data considered at the review.

These annual reviews, although they are only one of the many activities of the Ministry, are certainly one of the most important. The same is probably true of the year's work of the National Farmers' Union. This is mainly because of the large sums of money involved in changes in the total value of the guarantees, which may amount to as much as £20 or £30 million in any year. In terms alike of the difference which the outcome of the review may make to the livelihood of the farmers, the political position of the Ministry and the balance of the national accounts, it focuses an immense amount of interest and concern. It follows that the conduct of the review demands considerable preparation over several months, perhaps even calling for a searching examination of major aspects of agricultural policy, and a great concentration of effort during its progress each February and March. Moreover, the regular annual timing of the review produces one of the effects of an annual Budget—that some matters which might otherwise be settled at intervals during the year tend to become drawn into its orbit. In short, the review has become the occasion for some of the most concentrated and important thought and action falling to the Ministry during the year.

CHAPTER IV

The Agricultural Guarantees

THIS chapter describes schemes introduced under the Agriculture Acts of 1947 and 1957 to provide guaranteed prices and assured markets for the principal agricultural products—cereals, fatstock, wool, eggs, milk, potatoes and sugar-beet. It demonstrates how a general principle—that of deficiency payments—can be implemented to meet the widely differing requirements of individual commodities. In meeting these requirements the guarantee schemes set out to provide not only price supports but also, either directly or indirectly, assured markets and encouragement for orderly marketing. In the guarantee schemes for some commodities, however, the deficiency payments principle is either absent or present in a modified form for a variety of reasons which will be explained. The chapter also deals with some closely related subjects: the organization for investigating suspected cases of subsidy fraud, the special grants for Northern Ireland agriculture and the alternative form of State support—tariff protection—provided for horticulture.

Although the various guarantee schemes differ considerably in detail, they all attempt, as far as is reasonably practicable, to satisfy the following conditions—

1. There should be the minimum of interference with freedom of marketing, and the farmer (or a marketing board acting on his behalf) should have the fullest incentive to get the best possible return from the market by producing goods of the quality and variety that purchasers are wanting.
2. The scheme should not be unduly costly to administer, and should not interfere more than is really necessary with the farmer's methods of selling his produce or with the normal practices of the trade.
3. Payments should relate to actual produce, and there should be adequate precautions against frauds such as claiming subsidy twice on the same goods or claiming improperly on goods not originating in the United Kingdom.
4. It should be possible to lay down and enforce minimum standards for the quality of the produce that is to get the guarantee, and there should be no encouragement to produce low grade stuff with the primary object of earning subsidy.

5. In accordance with general government policy[1] producers' marketing boards are used in appropriate cases in the administration of the schemes.

CEREALS

The Wheat Act of 1932 was the first legislation to provide for deficiency payments on a farm crop. The scheme was administered by a Wheat Commission and not by the Agricultural Departments. The Commission consisted of representatives of growers of wheat, flour millers, flour importers, dealers in wheat and consumers (including a representative of bakers) with an independent chairman and vice-chairman, all appointed by the Agricultural Ministers. The finance for the deficiency payments and the cost of administration was provided by a levy, known as a quota payment, imposed on all flour milled in the United Kingdom or imported into the United Kingdom. During the war and post-war period of control the Commission's powers were in abeyance, but it was not formally dissolved until after the present deficiency payments scheme financed by the Exchequer had been introduced.

The present deficiency payments schemes for the various cereals described in this chapter have been in force with minor changes since the 1954 harvest. In England and Wales they are administered by a headquarters branch of the Ministry known as the Cereals Deficiency Payments Unit. The Ministry of Agriculture for Northern Ireland acts as the Ministry's agents in administering the schemes in that country. In Scotland, the schemes are administered by the Department of Agriculture and Fisheries for Scotland, who have the full responsibility for their operation there. This account of how the schemes work is written primarily in terms of England and Wales; the procedure in Scotland and Northern Ireland is similar in all essentials.

The guaranteed prices for wheat, rye, barley and oats are determined and announced after the price review for the crops to be harvested later in the same year. For rye and oats a single guaranteed price applies throughout the season. But in order to promote orderly marketing of wheat, and in particular, to encourage farmers to hold their wheat off the market during the harvest peak, the cereal year (July–June) is divided into five separate accounting periods and the basic guaranteed price for wheat converted into a scale of rising seasonal standard prices, one for each period. Thus for 1961 the scale began at 24s 6d per cwt., rising to 29s 6d to give an average of 26s 11d. The deficiency payment on wheat is calculated separately for each period on the basis of prices realized by growers for wheat

[1] *Decontrol of Food and Marketing of Agricultural Produce*, Cmd. 8989, para. 4.

delivered (after sale) in that period. Similarly, to avoid market gluts of barley during the autumn, the 1961 review white paper announced the Government's decision to provide for a higher average rate of payment to barley growers who deliver barley after sale in the later months of the cereal year than to those who deliver their crop earlier.

A grower wishing to claim cereal deficiency payments must first apply to the appropriate Department for registration, giving particulars of all the farms he is occupying. The one registration covers all the guaranteed cereal crops.

Deficiency Payments on Wheat and Rye

For these crops, the deficiency payments to individual farmers are based on the quantity of grain marketed. As in the pre-war scheme, a grower of wheat claims deficiency payments on the basis of a certificate, countersigned by a merchant authorized by the Agricultural Ministers, that the grower has sold millable or potentially millable wheat for delivery off his farm. The sale is usually made to the authorized merchant who certifies it, but authorized merchants can also certify sales to other buyers. Each certificate must show the name and address of the grower, his registered number, the name and address of the buyer, the quantity of wheat sold, the price and the dates of sale and dispatch. Before issuing a certificate, the authorized merchant must satisfy himself that the wheat is of millable or potentially millable quality and condition as defined in the scheme. Special certificate forms have to be completed in certain circumstances —for example, where wheat certified as potentially millable needs to be dried after sale to make it of millable quality (when 4 per cent is deducted from the weight delivered off the farm to arrive at the weight on which deficiency payment is payable) or when wheat is to be redelivered to the grower for use as seed.

Completed wheat certificates are sent, usually by the authorized merchant on behalf of the grower, to the Cereals Deficiency Payments Unit. At the end of each seasonal accounting period, the Unit calculates the average price per cwt. realized for millable wheat delivered (after sale) in that period for the whole of the United Kingdom. This price is deducted from the appropriate seasonal guaranteed price to arrive at the rate of deficiency payment for the period. (Prices paid for potentially millable wheat are not included in the calculated average price.) The Unit then issues payable orders to growers against wheat certificates for that period.

Officers of the Ministry's regional and divisional organization carry out checks to guard against abuse of the scheme. For example, every grower who claims a deficiency payment must make a return of his acreages of each cereal. Each return of wheat acreage is compared with the total of wheat sales by that grower shown on wheat certificates. The yield of wheat per acre so obtained and the yield known to be general in the area concerned are compared and if a grower's total certified sales of wheat indicate a suspiciously high yield per acre, special enquiries are made. In addition, a percentage of growers' claims are selected for routine enquiries.

Officers of the Cereals Deficiency Payments Unit also make periodic visits to the offices of authorized merchants to ascertain how they, in practice, operate the scheme and to see that it is working smoothly. Special checks are made to see that deliveries (after sale) of wheat which requires drying to bring it to millable condition are certified on the appropriate form as potentially millable wheat, so that the 4 per cent deduction will be applied, or that, where the sale has been certified as one of millable wheat, the weight shown on the certificate is the dried weight ascertained after drying.

Following the practice of the Wheat Commission, the Agricultural Ministers appoint Local Wheat Committees consisting of growers, corn merchants and flour millers to assist in the administration of the scheme. There are forty-eight Local Wheat Committees in England and Wales, five in Scotland and one in Northern Ireland. The committees advise the Departments on the appointment of authorized merchants, and are available to advise authorized merchants on points arising in connection with the scheme, if requested to do so by the appropriate Department. The committees also hear and determine appeals by growers against the refusal of an authorized merchant to issue a wheat or rye certificate.

Deficiency payments for rye are made on the basis of rye certificates and the administrative arrangements are similar to those for wheat. The only major difference is that there is no seasonal scale of standard prices for rye. The rate of deficiency payment, therefore, cannot be finally determined until the end of the cereal year. An advance payment on account of the final deficiency payment is, however, made about half-way through the cereal year if market prices and prospects are such as to justify it.

A central Wheat and Rye Deficiency Payments Advisory Committee advises the Agricultural Departments on the detailed arrangements for operating deficiency payments on wheat and rye. This Committee includes representatives of the growers, corn merchants, flour millers and animal feedingstuff manufacturers. The Committee is invariably consulted on the seasonal scale of guaranteed prices for wheat and on advance payments for rye.

It will be apparent that the wheat and rye schemes have all the features of the classical deficiency payments system as set out at the beginning of the previous chapter. For wheat and barley there is also an incentive to spread marketing over the year. These deficiency payments schemes indirectly provide an assured market for farmers' grain, because without loss to farmers market prices can fall to the point where all offers are absorbed. In addition however the flour milling industry has in each year since 1954/55 given an undertaking to the Minister to use its best endeavours to absorb not less than one and a quarter million tons of home-grown wheat during the cereal year. So far the millers have been able to fulfil this undertaking in every year, except 1958/59 when the poor milling quality of the crop made it impossible for them to do so.

Deficiency Payments on Barley, Oats and Mixed Corn

The arrangements for these crops differ from those for wheat and rye inasmuch as the deficiency payments are based not on the quantity of grain marketed but on the acreage grown for harvesting as grain. About 15 to 20 per cent of the barley crop and over 80 per cent of the oats and mixed corn crops are normally retained on the farm of origin for animal feed. If deficiency payments for these crops were to depend on sale, much of this grain would be drawn on to the market solely to enable the growers to claim deficiency payments on it. This would tend to depress market prices and increase the deficiency payments. For these reasons the acreage basis has been preferred for these crops.

A grower wishing to claim deficiency payment on barley, oats and mixed corn makes a return by July 31st of the acreages of these crops which he is growing for harvesting as grain in that year. A proportion (in 1961/62, about half) of these claims are checked by an inspection by field officers from the divisional office. These inspections are made not only to check that the acreages claimed are being grown, but also to see that the rules of good husbandry are being followed. The majority of any reductions in claims are agreed by the growers while the field officer is on the farm. If, however, a field officer's report leads the divisional office to amend an acreage claim and reduce or withhold payment without the grower's agreement, the grower is informed and given an opportunity to make representations to the county agricultural executive committee. If the committee uphold the grower the matter is referred to the regional controller who will if necessary discuss the case with the committee. If he is unable to reach agreement with them the case is referred to headquarters for a final decision.

When these claims have been checked, and amended where appropriate, forms are prepared on which growers declare either that they have harvested their crops or that they have been brought to the state of being available for harvesting. These declaration forms are normally sent out in October to growers for completion and return to the divisional office.

Claim forms and growers' declarations provide no particulars of realized prices for sales of barley and oats. These are calculated for deficiency payment purposes from the weekly returns made by merchants and other dealers in grain at selected towns in Great Britain under the Corn Returns Act, 1882, and from similar returns made by market reporters and merchants in Northern Ireland. These returns relate only to that proportion of each crop which is put on sale in the selected towns but they provide a reliable guide to actual prices realized on average by growers for all sales.

The average realized price for the season for each crop so derived is deducted from the guaranteed price for the season. This price deficiency is then converted to an acreage basis by multiplying it by an average yield of merchantable grain per acre. (The yields of harvested grain for the past five years are averaged, and an allowance of $7\frac{1}{2}$ per cent deducted for tailings and waste to arrive at the average merchantable yield.) Each grower's return of acreage harvested or available for harvesting is then multiplied by the deficiency payment per acre, and payment made on this basis for barley and oats. The deficiency payment per acre of mixed corn (mixtures of various cereals and possibly pulses such as peas and beans grown together for animal feed) is based upon the rate for oats.

The final rate of deficiency payments on barley and oats cannot be calculated until the end of the season. If, however, market prices and market prospects justify this, advance payments on account of the final payment are made to growers in December and January.

As in the case of wheat and rye, there is a Barley and Oats Deficiency Payments Advisory Committee which advises departments on the administration of deficiency payments for these crops. The committee includes representatives of the growers and users of barley and oats, and is invariably consulted on whether there should be advance payments on these crops, and if so at what rate these should be made.

The deficiency payments scheme for barley, oats and mixed corn satisfies the main requirements for a deficiency payments scheme in that it provides an incentive to the growers to secure the best price in the market. Where the producer does not sell his crop the return is independent of the quality of the crop, but the Department requires to be satisfied that the rules of good husbandry have been followed in the growing of the crop. Since most of the oats and mixed corn are retained for stock feed on the farms where they are grown, there is no need for the scheme to provide an incentive to spread sales over the season. But in recent years there has been a tendency for an undue proportion of the barley crop to be marketed soon after harvest. Accordingly, the barley scheme has been modified somewhat to provide a financial incentive to sell barley later in the season rather than at harvest time.

As for wheat and rye a guaranteed market is provided indirectly because without loss to growers market prices of barley and oats can fall to the point where all offers are absorbed. In addition the manufacturers of compound animal feedingstuffs undertake each year to use as much home grown barley as they can, provided its price, quality, condition and continuity of supply are satisfactory.

FATSTOCK

The price guarantees for fat cattle, fat sheep and fat pigs resemble those for wheat and rye described in the previous section, inasmuch as they are deficiency payments calculated so as to bring the average return of producers over the year as a whole up to a guaranteed price, whilst leaving the individual producer with every incentive to get the best return he can from the market.

The fatstock guarantee scheme is, however, even more complicated than the cereal guarantees, and no attempt will be made here to set out all the details, for which the reader is referred to the annual booklet issued by the three United Kingdom Agriculture Departments entitled *The Fatstock Guarantee Scheme* (HMSO).

The most important ways in which the fatstock guarantees differ from the wheat and rye schemes are—

1. The standard prices for fat cattle and fat sheep vary from week to week, instead of every two or three months (as for wheat) or only once a year (as for rye). This is a consequence of seasonal variations in cost of production and level of marketing. It is necessary, for example, to provide higher standard prices for the smaller supplies of winter-fed cattle marketed in the spring than for the larger numbers of grass fed stock marketed in the autumn. Each scale of weekly standard prices is constructed so that the average for the whole year (April–March) is equal to the guaranteed price.

2. There is no similar seasonal variation in the standard price for fat pigs: but since feedingstuffs are by far the biggest item of expense in the raising of a fat pig, the standard price of pigs is related to a basic feedingstuffs ration and adjusted up or down each week as the feed prices change. In this way, producers are protected against a rise in feed prices, whilst the Exchequer gets the benefit of any fall. Also, following the 1961 Price

Review, the arrangements have been introduced whereby the standard price is linked to a particular level of production and is automatically increased as supplies in prospect fall below the predetermined level, or reduced as they exceed it. The deficiency payments scheme is thus used to counteract the well-known pig cycle, with a view to limiting the fluctuations in supplies which have bedevilled this branch of farming for so long.

3. The market price used in calculating the rate of guarantee payment for animals sold in a particular week is the average for an eight-week period starting five weeks before the week of sale; for the first four weeks actual prices are taken, and for the remaining four weeks estimated prices. This is done so that the producer is not completely insulated from week-to-week fluctuations in market prices, and he has an incentive to keep his beasts from the market in a week when market prices drop substantially. If the average were calculated solely from prices during the week of sale then, if market prices were temporarily depressed in any week, producers might still be tempted to send forward their animals, knowing that the low market price would be made up to the standard price for that week by means of a high rate of deficiency payment.

4. On the other hand, one of the purposes of the guarantees is to protect producers from violent fluctuations in market prices. Consequently, there is a further provision for a 'stabilizing adjustment' to the rates of guarantee to ensure that average returns to producers for the week do not differ from the standard price by more than a certain amount either way. This can moderate the effect of the eight-week average if prices are subject to a particularly violent fluctuation in any week. In other words, the scheme is designed to encourage producers to get the best possible price from the market, but at the same time they are protected from the more violent market fluctuations.

5. The final rate of guarantee payment on animals sold in a particular week is calculated early in the following week. Accordingly producers get one final payment in respect of each sale within a matter of a few weeks, instead of having to wait some considerable time as is the case with cereal deficiency payments.

6. The subsidy claim is based not on a sale certified by an authorized merchant but on the 'presentation' of the beast or its carcase at the time of sale at an approved 'certification centre' which may be either a fatstock auction market, a bacon factory or a slaughter-house. The presenter of an animal is not necessarily the man who reared it; it may be an organization such as the Fatstock Marketing Corporation acting on behalf of

producers, or a wholesaler, butcher or dealer, who has bought the animal at a price inclusive of any guarantee payment.

About three-quarters of the fat cattle, two-thirds of the fat sheep and 30 per cent of the fat pigs in this country are sold at auction markets. All fatstock auction markets of any size (487 in England and Wales) are, therefore, recognized as liveweight certification centres; where there is more than one firm of auctioneers at a market there is usually a separate centre for each firm, and in this way the total number of centres at the end of 1960 was brought up to 588. The Ministry appoints the auctioneer as Certifying Officer with the duty of seeing that fatstock presented for certification are duly weighed, that all certified stock are permanently marked as a precaution against double payment of subsidy, that their weights are recorded and that payment certificates are completed and despatched to Ministry headquarters. Ministry Fatstock Officers attend the certification centre to see that only eligible animals are certified, and that those which reach the prescribed standards are placed in the correct guarantee classes.

When an animal is sold by private treaty instead of by auction the seller can still get the guarantee payment by taking it to the certification centre and getting it certified and marked. The prices realized at private treaty sales are not, however, brought into the calculation of the weekly average price for the purpose of calculating the rate of guarantee payment, since it is impossible to check any prices returned for such sales (which only form a small proportion of total liveweight sales) as surely as those realized at public auction.

There are two kinds of certification centre for carcases sold by deadweight and not liveweight, i.e. sold 'on the hook' and not 'on the hoof'. First of all there are the bacon factories approved for this purpose, which account for roughly 40 per cent of total pig sales. Then there are other slaughter-houses approved as deadweight certification centres for cattle, sheep and pigs. The Ministry's own Fatstock Officers act as certifying officers at all these centres. They determine whether the carcases are eligible for the guarantee, they mark the carcases to show that they have been certified (as a precaution against double payment of subsidy) and they complete the payment documents. Prices paid at bacon factories are included in the calculation of the average weekly price but those at other slaughter-houses are not, again because prices at those slaughter-houses cannot be adequately checked.

There are a certain number of centres which are approved only for the certification of pigs, and here the certification may be done by the local authorities' meat inspectors, as determining the eligibility of fat pigs does not require the same amount of specialized knowledge and skill as for cattle and sheep. There were at the end of 1960 in England and Wales 627 deadweight centres for all classes of stock, 73 for pigs only and in addition 166 approved bacon factories.

One difficulty which had to be overcome in the early days of the scheme was the shortage of officers qualified to undertake the grading of animals at deadweight centres. The War Office abattoir at Aldershot is now being used for regular courses of basic training for technical staff from all over the country.

The Certifying Officer, whether at a liveweight or deadweight centre, is responsible for sending to the Ministry at Guildford details of the beasts certified, together with the names and addresses of the presenters. The calculation each week of the average market price of fat cattle, fat sheep and fat pigs and the subsequent calculation of the guarantee payment on all sales and the production of the necessary payable orders is an immense task which has to be completed quickly to enable producers to receive their guarantee payments within a reasonable period after the sale of the beasts. The work is done on an electric computer by the Data Processing Division of the Finance Department at Guildford (see Chapter XVII).

WOOL

In the guarantee schemes we have described so far, namely those for cereals and for fatstock, the deficiency payments are made to the individual producers, who sell their produce on a free market. We now turn to the guarantee arrangements for three other products, namely, wool, eggs and milk which (subject to any exemptions provided in the relevant marketing schemes) are sold on behalf of the producers by marketing boards,[1] which to this extent are monopoly sellers.

The deficiency payments here are made to the appropriate marketing board which, incidentally, reduces considerably the number of staff the Department needs for administering the guarantee; instead of having to pay a host of individual producers the Ministry has only to check and settle a comparatively few claims from the marketing boards. The guarantee arrangements are in each case governed by a financial agreement between the Ministry and the board and relate to the average return to the board instead of that to individual producers.

The present arrangements for wool are essentially the same as those which have operated since the Wool Marketing Scheme came into

[1] For a general account of the agricultural marketing boards, see Chapter X.

operation in 1950. The basis of the marketing scheme (which incidentally does not extend to skin wool, i.e. wool taken from the carcase of
the sheep after it is slaughtered) is that producers consign their wool
to merchants who collect, grade, handle and store it as agents of the
British Wool Marketing Board. The board then arranges for the
wool to be sold by auction, and the Ministry (subject to the provisions
governing the Special Account mentioned below) pays the board
whatever may be necessary to bring the total return for the wool up
to the guaranteed price. The guaranteed price, as with milk and
eggs, includes an allowance for the board's administrative and
marketing expenses.

The payment to the Wool Board is a straightforward deficiency
payment, in contrast to the profit and loss sharing arrangements for
milk and eggs which provide an incentive for the marketing boards
to obtain the best possible prices from the market. What assurance
therefore can there be that the board is selling the home clip to the
best advantage, thus minimizing the call on the Exchequer? First of
all the facts that the wool is sold by auction and that there is a wide
and competitive demand for this produce is at any rate *prima facie*
evidence that the board could not get an appreciably better return
than that actually achieved under the present arrangements.

Secondly, the Government's general policy on the level of the wool
guarantee as laid down in various annual review white papers is
'that taking one year with another the wool guarantee should not
require continuing Exchequer payments' and that 'if the guarantee
arrangements are to work effectively the guaranteed price should not
remain continually above the market price'. This does not mean that
there should be no subsidy, but rather that there ought not to be
continuing payments year after year. The guaranteed price has in
fact exceeded the realization price for the British clip in every year
since 1950, but a day may well come when the board will be getting
no guarantee payment, and if the board had not devised and maintained satisfactory methods for selling the wool to best advantage it
would be the producers who would then suffer.

There are two special features about the wool guarantee arrangements which should be mentioned. The first arises from the fact that
at the time that the marketing scheme first came into operation in
the autumn of 1950 it was foreseen that a large surplus would be
realized on the clip of that year in view of the abnormally high level
to which wool prices had risen as a result of the Korean War. It was
accordingly agreed that the Wool Board should open a 'Special
Account' into which they would pay 90 per cent of any profits from
the sale of the clip in any year; conversely any loss which the board
might make after paying producers the guaranteed price was to be

defrayed in the first place from any funds in the Special Account before calling on the Exchequer for an advance. In the event a surplus of no less than £16·3 million was realized on the 1950 clip out of which £14·6 million was paid into the Special Account and this sufficed to meet the deficit on the next five years' operations without any call on the Exchequer.

The second special feature of the wool arrangement is that the exact price the producer will get for his wool is settled and announced in advance. The board publish each year a schedule of prices for different varieties and grades of wool designed to give an average price equal to the guaranteed figure less expenses of administration. In practice, of course, the actual average works out at a slightly different figure owing to the impossibility of forecasting with complete accuracy the relative quantities of the different kinds of wool that will be produced.

EGGS

The eggs guarantee is now operated through the British Egg Marketing Board, which was established in 1957.

To obtain the guarantee the producer must sell his eggs to the marketing board through an egg packing station. These are privately-owned establishments, many being run co-operatively by egg producers themselves, which were an essential part of previous war-time and post-war guarantee schemes. The packing station acts as the agent of the board in collecting the eggs from the producer, examining them for any faults (the guarantee only covers first quality eggs weighing not less than one and a half ounces), grading them by weight and then packing them for distribution. The packer is also responsible for paying the producer at not less than the minimum price prescribed by the board. For these services the packing station receives an allowance from the board.

Many packing stations in fact also act as first hand distributors and wholesalers, and they have an option to purchase from the board as many of the eggs they have packed as they wish at the price at which the board itself is selling currently to wholesalers. In practice the packing stations purchase the greater part of the eggs for their own trade, although a substantial quantity (say 10 per cent on average for the country as a whole) are left with the board for disposal.

The price guarantee is, as with wool, a collective guarantee to the board and not to the individual producer, and is implemented by a deficiency payment to the marketing board. The board, however, is not dealing with a stable commodity such as wool but with a perishable article whose price can fluctuate considerably with the levels of supplies coming on the market. Considerable judgement and skill must therefore be exercised by the board in such matters as deciding when to divert surplus supplies into the manufacture of products such as frozen egg to prevent an undue weakening in the market for fresh eggs. Accordingly there is a profit and loss sharing arrangement to give the Egg Board an incentive to obtain the best return it can from the market. It operates as follows.

At the beginning of each year (April–March), Ministers estimate the average selling price that the board will obtain for eggs during the year. (In practice, this estimate is an average of previous years' prices rather than a forecast of actual prices.) If the guaranteed price to the board is, say, 4s 0d per dozen then the difference between this price and the estimate of the board's selling price, say, 3s 0d—i.e. 1s 0d per dozen—would be the provisional flat rate of subsidy for the year (which, like the guarantee payments for fat pigs, is subject to periodic adjustment in accordance with changes in the price of poultry feedingstuffs).

If, however, the board is able to 'beat bogey' by realizing a higher price than the estimate then it retains about one-half of the 'profits' which it uses to increase the price to the producers or for any other purpose it thinks fit. Some of the remaining 'profits' are allocated to a Statutory Reserve Fund used towards meeting losses in other years, and the Government gets the remainder.

On the other hand, if the prices actually realized are lower than the estimate then the board and the Government share the burden of this 'loss', if it cannot be met from the Statutory Reserve Fund. There is an additional proviso that the Government will accept a greater share of the 'loss' if market prices drop substantially below the estimate.

In other words, if the board is able to 'beat bogey' it will have additional funds to put into reserve or to pass on to producers. But if the board is unsuccessful in obtaining the estimated price for its eggs then it will have to reduce the payments to producers, or alternatively draw on any funds available in its reserves. A similarity in concept between this guarantee and the fatstock guarantee may be noted. In each case producers (either as individuals or acting collectively through the board) have incentives to get the best possible price from the market. But provision is also made (by means of the stabilizing adjustment or the additional proviso mentioned above) for the Government to protect the industry from a sudden and substantial decline in market prices.

This account of the guarantee arrangements has been written in terms of hen eggs. The guarantee for the comparatively small quantity of duck eggs operates in a similar manner, although with some differences in detail and in particular with an appreciably lower level of guaranteed price.

The validity of the board's claim on the Ministry is essentially dependent on the accuracy of the returns which the egg packing stations make to the board of the numbers of eggs they are handling under the guarantee arrangements. The Egg Board therefore maintains a team of travelling auditors to inspect the books, records and stocks at egg packing stations, and this is supplemented as necessary by test checks by the Ministry's own internal audit staff.

MILK

The wool and the egg guarantees are each implemented through a single marketing board which covers the whole of the United Kingdom. For reasons dating from the pre-war arrangements for the marketing of milk there are by contrast five separate milk marketing boards, one covering England and Wales, three more which between them cover most of Scotland, and a fifth for Northern Ireland. For simplicity this account of the way in which the milk guarantee works is written primarily in terms of the Milk Marketing Board (MMB) for England and Wales. The position with the Scottish Boards and the Northern Ireland Board is not essentially different.

There are a number of important differences between the milk guarantee and those for other products. These differences arise largely because there are alternative markets for milk. The greater part of our milk production goes to the remunerative market for liquid consumption. What we do not drink, however, must be sold at lower prices for manufacture into products such as milk powder, butter and cheese. If total milk production is to be adequate to meet the requirements of the liquid market day by day then over the year as a whole there must in any event be a 'necessary surplus' of the order of 20 per cent of liquid consumption going to manufacture, since cows naturally produce more milk in summer than in winter consumption does not vary much throughout the year.

All farmers, unless they retail their milk themselves, are required to sell their milk to the marketing board which then acts as a monopoly seller of that milk, charging different prices according to the use to which the milk is put. The board uses the receipts from the sale of the milk, together with the guarantee payment from the Exchequer, to pay farmers each month a uniform 'pool price' for their milk. Farmers who retail their own milk have to pay a levy to the board.

The present operation of the guarantee arrangements is governed by two main considerations of government policy. First of all the consumer is now required to pay a price for his milk sufficient to cover the guaranteed price to the boards on the quantity of milk sold for liquid consumption, together with the margins allowed for distributing that milk and the cost of the 'necessary surplus' referred to above. Secondly, for some years appreciably more milk has been produced in the United Kingdom than the quantity needed to ensure adequate supplies for the liquid market throughout the year, and accordingly there can be no question of encouraging any further increase in production so long as this would only lead to still more milk going into the much less remunerative manufacturing market.

The details of the guarantee calculations are complicated but the following account gives the broad outline.

Each year after the price review Ministers fix for each of the five milk marketing boards a guaranteed price related to a specified quantity of milk known as the standard quantity. Broadly each board receives the guaranteed price on its standard quantity, but for anything above this only the average price obtained for milk sold for manufacture.

The standard quantities were originally equal to the estimated total sales off farms for each board area for the year immediately preceding April 1, 1954, when the present arrangements came into force. Ministers have agreed that it is right that milk boards should be rewarded for the success of their efforts to increase the consumption of liquid milk, and so the standard quantity for each board is now adjusted every year by the amount by which the board's liquid sales have increased (or decreased) in the immediately preceding calendar year by comparison with the year before.

As part of the arrangements for implementing the guarantee the Minister under a financial agreement with the board specifies the prices at which the board sells milk for liquid consumption and the allowances which it pays to distributors for various services such as heat-treatment. In addition, in order to safeguard the interest of consumers and the Exchequer, in the absence of a free market and of competition from imports, the Minister prescribes maximum retail prices under powers now conferred by the Emergency Laws (Repeal) Act, 1959, so, in effect, determining the retail margin. (Distributive margins and allowances are determined on the basis of information on current costs of distribution collected regularly from the industry.) Milk is now the only foodstuff subject to direct government price control. It has already been explained that the retail price is sufficient to yield to producers the guaranteed price for liquid sales plus the necessary reserves. Since, broadly, there is no deficiency payment in milk in excess of the standard quantity that is sold for manufacture, it follows that the Ministry's payment to the board is principally on account of milk included in the standard quantity which is in excess of liquid sales and the necessary reserve. Mainly because of higher retail prices, which are now determined on the basis described above, the total Exchequer payment for the United Kingdom as a whole is now of the order of £10 million a year as compared with a figure of the order of £75 million some ten years or so ago. Thus the consumer of liquid milk rather than the taxpayer now shoulders the greater part of the cost of the milk guarantee. (But now see note, p. 78.)

On milk in excess of the standard quantity the board gets broadly only what it can realize from its sale for manufacture. Ministers have agreed, however, that the board should have an incentive to get the best price it can for all the milk it sells for manufacture, whether within the standard quantity or in excess of that. Accordingly at the beginning of each year the Minister estimates the average price which the board is likely to obtain for milk sold for manufacture. If the board succeeds in 'beating bogey' and gets a higher average price it retains half the benefit, and the Exchequer gets the other half by way of reduction in the guarantee payment; conversely if the actual price is below the estimate, the Ministry makes good half the difference.

These arrangements therefore provide the Milk Marketing Board with incentives both to increase the amount of milk sold for liquid consumption and also to get the best price it can for the remainder that has to be sold for manufacture. In so far as milk is produced in excess of the standard quantity the overall average return to the board (and accordingly the price it can pay the producer) is reduced below the guaranteed level. This reduction is of the order of a half-penny a gallon for every 50 million gallons of excess for the United Kingdom as a whole.

POTATOES

Sir William Beveridge, writing of the experience of the Ministry of Food in the First World War said, 'As a producer of problems for Food Controllers, the potato has no rival in the vegetable or the animal world.[1] The accounts which Mr R. J. Hammond gives of the experience of the Ministry of Food in the Second World War,[2] show that what Sir William Beveridge described as 'this puckish vegetable' gave no less trouble in the Second World War. It has proved equally difficult to devise a satisfactory guarantee scheme for potatoes in peace-time.

[1] Sir William Beveridge: *British Food Control*, Oxford University Press, 1928, p. 153.
[2] *Food*. Volume II: *Studies in Administration and Control*, HMSO and Longmans, Green, 1956, pp. 105 et seq., and *Food and Agriculture in Britain*, 1939-41, Stanford University Press, California, 1954, pp. 79 et seq.

The reasons why the potato has caused so many headaches in peace-time as in war-time are that the yield of potato crop per acre as well as the acreage can vary very considerably from year to year, that the demand for potatoes for human consumption is highly inelastic (that is to say, that you cannot increase consumption appreciably by reducing the retail price), that it is difficult to find alternative markets for a surplus, and that the crop cannot be carried over for use in the following year.

These conditions of considerable fluctuations in yield per acre from year to year coupled with inelasticity of demand were the main reason for the introduction of the Potato Marketing Scheme for Great Britain in 1934. The essential feature of the pre-war scheme was that the Potato Marketing Board had the power to prescribe acreage quotas and also the minimum size of potato that could be sold for human consumption. It is in any case the usual practice to 'dress' the potato crop for market by putting it over a sieve or 'riddle' so as to separate out the small potatoes or 'chats' (normally used for stock-feed), and the Potato Marketing Board regulated the supplies for the ware market, i.e. of potatoes for human consumption, by varying from time to time the size of the mesh to be used in the riddle. In a year of high yield, therefore, the board would prescribe a relatively large riddle to keep more potatoes off the ware market and so maintain the price.

During the 1939–45 war the Potato Marketing Board's activities were suspended. Potatoes were the crop which yielded the greatest amount of food measured in calories per acre, and the Government encouraged the planting of a larger acreage mainly by guaranteeing fixed prices for all potatoes of a standard suitable for human consumption, the Ministry of Food acting as a buyer of last resort at the guaranteed price.

This arrangement was continued with some modification after the war as the means of providing the guarantee to potato growers under the Agriculture Act, 1947. In 1955 the Potato Marketing Board was reinstated, and acted as agent of the Ministry of Agriculture, Fisheries and Food and the Department of Agriculture for Scotland in purchasing at the appropriate guaranteed support prices all potatoes of suitable standard offered to it which producers in Great Britain could not sell or use themselves. Potatoes that were surplus to the requirements of the ware market were either processed or sold raw for stockfeed after being dyed or left to rot on the farm if no economic outlet could be found for them. The Ministry re-imbursed the Potato Board for 95 per cent of the loss which it incurred on these trading operations. The Ministry of Agriculture for Northern Ireland acted as agents of the Ministry in that country which is not covered by the Potato Marketing Board, and were reimbursed for losses incurred on similar support operations.

This scheme, however, proved unsuitable as a permanent means of implementing the guarantee to producers when there was no longer a shortage of food. The fact that growers were given an assured market for all their ware potatoes at the guaranteed price discouraged the Board from exercising its powers to use the riddle as a means of regulating the volume of supplies coming on to the ware market in Great Britain in a year of surplus, and thus reduce the burden on the Exchequer. The scheme involved rigid scales of support prices in the United Kingdom varying only according to season and region, which bore little relation to prices in a free market and tended to encourage an uneconomic pattern of production which was unsuited to normal peace-time conditions. It was also open to abuses which it was difficult to detect.

Accordingly the Government decided to introduce a fundamentally different type of guarantee scheme for the crops of 1959 and subsequent years based on the deficiency payment principle. Under the new scheme the average growers' price realized for main crop potatoes sold for human consumption each year is calculated by the Agricultural Departments on the basis of returns obtained from licensed potato merchants through the Potato Marketing Board and the Ministry of Agriculture for Northern Ireland and checked as necessary by inspection of the merchants' records by the Government and Potato Marketing Board's audit staff. If this average price is lower than the guaranteed price for that year then the Exchequer provides for the benefit of the growers what is in effect a global deficiency payment of an amount calculated by multiplying the price deficit by the tonnage of potatoes sold for human consumption. Seven-eighths of the total payment goes to the Potato Marketing Board who can use it in whatever way it thinks fit for the benefit of growers in Great Britain, and the remaining one-eighth goes to the Ministry of Agriculture for Northern Ireland for the benefit of producers in that country. Under the new scheme, therefore, each producer has an incentive to adapt his production to the needs of consumers and to find an outlet for the surplus potatoes, often by using them for feeding to livestock on the farm.

The scheme is supplemented by special arrangements to ensure that it does not bear harshly on producers in Northern Ireland compared with producers in remote parts of Great Britain. An Exchequer subvention is given when necessary towards the cost of shipping ware potatoes through commercial channels from Northern Ireland for sale in Great Britain. In addition arrangements may be made in years of heavy surplus for potatoes to be manufactured in government-owned factories in Northern Ireland into potato products for animal feeding.

Just as the riddle regulates the volume of domestic supplies to the ware market, so import licensing regulates imported supplies of main crop potatoes, which are only permitted in years of shortage to such extent as may be necessary to supplement the home crop.

For the first two crops to be covered by the new guarantee arrangements namely those of 1959 and 1960 yields were abnormally heavy and the Potato Board's regulatory powers proved insufficient to maintain prices to growers at a reasonable level. The Government accordingly agreed to contribute two-thirds of the cost of an approved programme of purchase of potatoes by the board to strengthen the market. This strengthened the market sufficiently to avoid the need for any deficiency payment for the 1959 crop and to reduce appreciably that needed for the 1960 crop.

SUGAR

The *modus operandi* of the sugar-beet guarantee is unique. It is the only one financed wholly by the consumer and not the Exchequer. It is the only one (apart from wool) to give the farmer a predetermined fixed price. We shall need to go briefly into past history (and also say something about the Commonwealth Sugar Agreement) to show how this has come about.

Sugar-beet has proved a valuable cash crop to the arable farmers of this country. The acreage of fodder roots, such as mangolds, swedes and turnips has fallen very considerably in the last forty years and the substitution of sugar-beet has helped to maintain a balanced arable rotation.

A farmer, of course, will only grow sugar-beet if there is a sugar factory to purchase it. There are in fact in Great Britain eighteen sugar-beet factories (mostly in East Anglia, with a few in other parts such as Yorkshire and one in Scotland). These were all built before 1929, most of them as a sequel to a government decision in 1924 to pay a subsidy on home grown sugar on a diminishing scale over a period of ten years. When the period covered by the original subsidy legislation came to an end it was clear that as a consequence of the very considerable fall in the world price of sugar the home industry could not hope to continue without further government assistance. Following an inquiry by a committee under the chairmanship of Mr Wilfred Greene, KC (later Lord Greene, Master of the Rolls),[1] the Government decided to continue assistance to the industry on condition that the existing beet-sugar companies were amalgamated into

[1] Cmd. 4871, 1935.

one State-aided corporation with appropriate public control. Such an amalgamation would improve the general standard of efficiency of the factories and, in particular, through the pooling of government assistance, would remove the difficulty that a rate of subsidy necessary to ensure the operation of factories where costs were high (perhaps because of small throughput) would yield unduly high profit to the larger and more efficient factories.

The British Sugar Corporation was accordingly established under the Sugar Industry (Reorganization) Act, 1936 to take over the beet-sugar factories. To the student of public administration it is a curious and interesting hybrid—'neither flesh nor fowl nor good red nationalization', as someone in the Ministry remarked at the time of its birth.

The Corporation is a public company with a share capital of £5 million, originally issued to the old beet-sugar manufacturing companies in payment for the factories and other fixed assets which the Corporation took over from them. It is however in effect a public utility for the processing of sugar-beet, and as such the Corporation is subject to a measure of public control approximating to that applied to nationalized industries such as coal, electricity, gas or the railways. The Chairman and two other members of the board are appointed by the Minister and the Secretary of State for Scotland, and the Chairman has a right of suspensive veto (which has in fact never been used) pending reference to the Government on any proposals coming before the board which, in his opinion, involves questions of public interest; the veto to become absolute if Ministers should so decide. Its Memorandum and Articles of Association were agreed with the Department, and cannot be altered without the approval of the Agricultural Ministers. It cannot without the consent of Ministers pay a dividend exceeding 7 per cent on its share capital.

The Corporation is required to enter into contracts with farmers to purchase sugar-beet up to an acreage limit laid down by Ministers, determined mainly by the amount of sugar-beet which the Corporation's factories can process economically in any year. The Corporation has to buy its sugar-beet at prices laid down by Ministers at the annual farm price review, whilst the price which it gets for its sugar is determined by the world free market price, and that is why the Corporation normally requires special financial assistance. It is only fair to note, however, that the world price of sugar is essentially a 'surplus' price relating only to some 10 per cent of world production, and that the level of the guaranteed price for sugar-beet in this country (when expressed in terms of sugar) is broadly of the same order as that obtaining in other European and Commonwealth countries.

This assistance is in effect a deficiency payment to the Corporation to cover any deficit on trading and in addition to provide for a reasonable rate of interest (as determined by Ministers and the Treasury) on the Corporation's share capital together with an allowance for interest on the Corporation's reserves employed in the business.

In order that the Corporation may have an adequate incentive to keep down costs and improve efficiency, a further payment is made based on the value of economies which the Corporation has been able to achieve by improving its performance on a number of points (such as the amount of fuel consumed per ton of beet processed or the percentage of the total sugar extracted from the beet) by comparison with the standards of previous years. Part of this 'incentive payment' is applied for the benefit of the Corporation's employees and nowadays under statute the Corporation is required to use the remainder primarily for the modernization and replacement of its plant.

This assistance to the Corporation is now provided not by the Exchequer but by the Sugar Board. This Board was established because of the Commonwealth Sugar Agreement and it is accordingly necessary to digress and say a little about that agreement as well as the Sugar Board; a fuller account is given in the article by the Chairman of the Sugar Board, Sir George Dunnett, published in the summer 1960 issue of *Public Administration*, the Journal of the Royal Institute of Public Administration, Volume XXXVIII, page 99.

Under the Commonwealth Sugar Agreement the United Kingdom government has undertaken to purchase each year from various parts of the Commonwealth, such as the West Indies, Fiji, Mauritius and Australia about $1\frac{1}{2}$ million tons of sugar at a guaranteed price which normally is in excess of the free market price.[1] When the Agreement was originally concluded in 1951 this obligation was honoured by Ministry of Food purchase of this sugar at the guaranteed price. When government trading in sugar came to an end this was replaced by the plan set out in a white paper on *Future Arrangements for the Marketing of Sugar*[2] and subsequently embodied in the Sugar Act, 1956.

Under this plan a Sugar Board has been established with a statutory duty to buy at the guaranteed price the sugar which the government has contracted to purchase under the Commonwealth

---

[1] The Commonwealth countries are not by any means unique in being granted special prices for sugar exported to particular countries. The United States, for example, regulate the supply of sugar to their domestic market by quotas which enable certain countries such as the Philippines and Puerto Rico to obtain there perhaps as much at nearly twice the world prices.

[2] Cmd. 9519, July, 1955.

Agreement. The Board do not themselves handle the sugar but resell it in the country of origin at the current world price to refiners and other traders who become responsible for shipment (in practice to the United Kingdom or Canada, to get the benefit of the duty preference). The Sugar Board has also taken over the Ministry's responsibility for the deficiency payments to the British Sugar Corporation.

The Sugar Board gets its revenue for these purposes from the proceeds of a levy (called a 'surcharge') on all sugar and molasses on which customs or excise duty is paid, including the sugar in imported articles such as confectionery and jam. This surcharge is payable to the Customs and Excise at the same time as the duty and is passed on to the Board. Thus the cost both of maintaining the home beet-sugar industry and of implementing the Commonwealth Sugar Agreement falls on the sugar consumer and not the taxpayer.

The distribution of sugar in the United Kingdom is as far as possible left in the hands of the trade. But the complex arrangements described above, combined with the concentration of 95 per cent of production in the hands of the British Sugar Corporation and of Tate and Lyle, has led to certain arrangements approved by the Minister.

Firstly, the British Sugar Corporation has made an agreement with other refiners for the division between them of the United Kingdom market for granulated sugar in terms of geographical areas. Secondly, the Sugar Act gave the Minister power to control the refining margin, i.e. the difference between the price of white sugar and of raw sugar, unless the refiners undertook to do this themselves. In fact Tate and Lyle have given an undertaking to the Chancellor of the Exchequer that the refining margin on granulated sugar will not be increased by more than is necessary to meet increases in the costs of labour and materials. The British Sugar Corporation follows the Tate and Lyle prices. The Ministry makes such periodic checks as are needed to satisfy the Government that the undertaking adequately protects consumers and is being properly observed.

The arrangements which have been described in this section are unusual and artificial. They are, however, determined by the world sugar market. About 90 per cent of the world's sugar is produced and sold under artificial arrangements—subsidies, tariffs, quotas, price controls, etc.—so that the price realized by the remaining 10 per cent, sold on the free market, is affected by the fluctuations in the supply and demand for the whole world. Consequently the free market price may be below the cost of production (as in 1960) or far above it (as in 1956/57). Under the arrangements described some 90 per cent of Britain's sugar consumption is assured by purchase at a price which gives home and Commonwealth producers an economic return for their product and the consumer an assurance of supply.

SPECIAL GRANTS FOR NORTHERN IRELAND AGRICULTURE

When the guaranteed price for farm produce was provided by Ministry of Food purchase the Ministry's buying price was in general a uniform one for the whole of the United Kingdom, so that other things being equal the same price per cwt. would be paid for fat cattle at a remote market in Londonderry in Northern Ireland as, say, at Reading market.

Nowadays the farmer in general gets the market price for his produce, plus, for fatstock and cereals at any rate, a uniform rate of guarantee payment. In Northern Ireland market prices, particularly for fatstock, are generally lower than the average for Great Britain, because much of the fatstock comes over to Great Britain to be slaughtered and eaten, and therefore the price paid to the Northern Ireland producer reflects the higher transport charges which the purchaser will generally have to incur before he can sell the meat.

As some compensation to the Northern Ireland farmers for the lower prices that they are accordingly getting compared with the generality of their fellows in Great Britain Section 32 of the Agriculture Act, 1957, provided for the payment to the Exchequer of Northern Ireland of sums not exceeding £1 million a year to cover the cost of approved schemes administered by the Ministry of Agriculture for Northern Ireland for the benefit of Northern Ireland farmers. Any balance remaining unspent at the end of a year may be carried forward to the following year. These sums are not necessarily used for payments on Northern Irish fatstock. The schemes for the current year (1961/62) provide for payment of subsidies on silage, on fat cattle, and on cows and heifers kept for the breeding and rearing of calves on lowland farms which do not sell milk.

SUBSIDY FRAUDS

The existence of such a wide variety of grants and subsidies schemes presents opportunities for fraudulent claims against which the Department has to be on its guard. This does not mean that farmers (or the middlemen who handle their produce) are less honest than other folk, but there are rogues in all walks of life, to say nothing of a number of otherwise tolerably honest people who tend to regard government departments (like the railways) as fair game.

The primary responsibility for preventing fraud must rest with those administering the various grant and subsidy schemes. It is up to the administrative division to see that the scheme itself is proof against fraud as far as reasonably possible; one of the reasons for the change in the form of the potato guarantee in 1959 was the difficulty of ensuring that potatoes sold at a low price for stockfeed were not subsequently resold for human consumption or even sold back to the Ministry or the Potato Marketing Board. Again, the administration of the scheme itself must provide for a proper check on claims, such as the field inspection of a sample of claims for oats and barley deficiency payments to verify the acreage and other details of the claim. To facilitate such checks Section 5 of the Agriculture Act, 1957, enables orders to be made to require merchants and others to keep specified records, and to enable authorized officers of the Ministry to enter upon land used for the production, storage, grading, packing, slaughter or sale of price guaranteed produce. However, the administration of such a variety of schemes involving the payment of large sums of public money requires not only that the staff responsible for preparing and administering the schemes should act as watchdogs but also that there should be a bloodhound to track down the offenders. The Investigation Division of the Ministry fills this latter role.

The division had its origins in the enforcement organization of the Ministry of Food, whose primary object during the period of food control was to defeat attempts to establish a black market in controlled foods. After the end of food control it soon became apparent that the various price guarantee schemes which the Ministry of Food was having to operate, particularly the fatstock and cereals deficiency payments schemes, would inevitably lead to attempts at fraud. Although the police were willing to undertake local investigations where clear-cut evidence of fraud existed, to produce such evidence was often a long and involved business and the investigating officers needed to have a thorough knowledge of the detailed operation of the various subsidy schemes. The original enforcement organization was therefore retained in being, though considerably reduced in size, for the purpose of conducting such investigations and also to act as liaison between the Department and the police whenever a case initiated by the Ministry was passed to the police for a full investigation which might lead to prosecution for fraud.

After the amalgamation the division was able to offer a service to any department or division of the Ministry to investigate suspected cases of fraud or malpractice in connection with any of the Ministry's subsidy or grant schemes. The division is in fact available to look into any suspected infringement of a Ministry order or scheme; one recent investigation, for example, led to the successful prosecution of a merchant for selling imported potatoes as seed in contravention of the Wart Disease of Potatoes Order. The greater part of the work of the division arises, however, from fraudulent subsidy claims, and it is, therefore, appropriate to describe its activities in the present chapter.

The division has a staff of investigation officers all fully versed in police procedure and most of them men with long experience in the police forces. It has also a small staff of accountants to assist in cases requiring examination of traders' books. If the division's enquiries into any case submitted to it by an administrative division or regional controller discloses evidence of fraud then the further local enquiries are made by the police, who are given a copy of the division's preliminary report; the investigation officer who made the report acts as liaison with the police in their subsequent enquiries. The final police report is submitted to the Ministry's Legal Department who, if the report is thought to justify it, conduct the prosecution, save of course where the police themselves or the Director of Public Prosecutions decide to prosecute.

Where there is sufficient evidence of other offences in connection with subsidy or grant schemes not amounting to fraud, such as breeding from animals on which subsidy has been paid, failure to keep records, or making false or reckless statements on claim forms, the division refers the case to Legal Department for consideration whether it should be brought to court. When Legal Department advise that the evidence is not such as to justify a prosecution the report is turned over to the division (or regional controller) which has brought the matter up, for them to take such action as they consider suitable to recover monies improperly obtained and admonish those who appear to have contravened the conditions of the scheme.

The division has been instrumental in bringing before the courts an impressive number of offenders, some of whom have received long terms of imprisonment or have been heavily fined. The value of the division's work, however, is to be measured not by the number of convictions nor the amount of money recovered so much as by the effect which a successful prosecution has as a deterrent to others who might be tempted to defraud the Ministry.

HORTICULTURE

The price guarantees under the Agriculture Acts, 1947 and 1957 do not extend to horticultural produce—tomatoes, lettuces, strawberries, apples, nursery stock, cut flowers and the like. This is generally accepted as inevitable, since horticultural produce as a whole is so much more perishable and variable in quality and subject to much greater fluctuations in supply and demand compared with the farm produce covered by the price guarantees. Instead, successive Governments have assisted horticulture by means of protective tariffs.

Generally speaking, the object is to give protection to the home producer during his main marketing season without impeding imports when they are needed. Outside the home season the general 10 per cent *ad valorem* duty usually applies. The kind of tariff is adapted to suit the particular crop, the import situation peculiar to that crop and the length of its marketing season. Some tariffs above the 10 per cent *ad valorem* level apply throughout the year; others for a shorter or longer part of the year. Some of these tariffs are at fixed rates throughout their period of operation: others change during the season. If the marketing season is a short one, the tariff remains unchanged. If the season is long, with a build up of home supplies followed by a decline, the tariff may be at different levels according to the stage of the season. Although there are still some tariffs fixed on an *ad valorem* basis, the most common form is a seasonal tariff at specific rates—e.g. so many pence per pound. The *ad valorem* incidence of specific duties is relatively low at times when supplies are scarce and prices high and it is relatively high when prices are low and supplies over-plentiful. In short a specific tariff tends to put a bottom in the market and thus avoid the worst effects of gluts, without unduly raising prices at other times. For example, if, with a duty of 4d a lb., imported tomatoes are selling at 8d wholesale a lb., the *ad valorem* incidence of the duty is about 100 per cent. But if the wholesale price is 1s 4d, with the same duty, that incidence is only about 33 per cent.

Changes in the rates of tariff are constitutionally a matter for the President of the Board of Trade, who presents to Parliament for approval the necessary resolutions under the Import Duties Act, but the Ministry naturally has a very considerable interest in any proposals for amending tariff rates on horticultural produce, and maintains very close contact with the divisions of the Board of Trade responsible for considering applications on proposals put forward by the NFU for increasing the rates of tariff on horticultural produce.

Note (p. 68). Since this book went to press the Minister has announced (March 15th, 1962) that for the future the retail price of liquid milk will cover the full cost of the guarantee.

CHAPTER V

Farming

THE last two chapters dealt with the financial assistance which the State has been giving to agriculture in recent years, more particularly through the system of price guarantees for the principal farm products.

But the Ministry's activities impinge on agriculture in other ways. In the technical revolution in agricultural practices in recent years there has been no branch of pure or applied science—physics, chemistry, engineering, plant and animal genetics, veterinary science, entomology, mycology—which has not had important applications in farming practice. If the fullest advantage is to be taken of all the help that science can give to farmers to secure a greater return from their enterprise with smaller calls on labour, land, equipment and raw materials then three things are needed. The first need is scientific research ranging from pure and fundamental research on such matters as animal and plant physiology to the most practical and empirical investigations, such as determining the optimum amounts of different kinds of fertilizers for growing a particular crop in different conditions of soil and climate. A second need is suitable education for those who are starting on a career in agriculture whether as landowner, farmer, salaried farm manager, or worker, or any combination of these roles. Thirdly, advice and guidance is needed to bring to farmers the discoveries of agricultural science as they continue to be made.

This chapter deals with the Ministry's role in relation to those needs of research, education and advice. The Ministry's responsibilities for the first two of these have in recent years been largely transferred to other departments, but at the same time the scope of the Ministry's activities in the third field of advice, especially in such directions as farm management, have been extended. Schemes recently introduced for improving the efficiency and profitability of small farms have also enlarged the scope of the Department's advisory work and are therefore also dealt with in this chapter.

AGRICULTURAL RESEARCH

Organized agricultural research in this country dates from the days before there was a Ministry. The oldest and most famous agricultural research station in this country, if not indeed in the world, is that at Rothamsted which was established by Sir John Bennet Lawes in 1843 and financed by him out of the profits of his business in the manufacture of agricultural fertilizers. After selling his fertilizer business he established in 1889 the Lawes Agricultural Trust with an endowment of £100,000 to finance the continuation of the work at Rothamsted. Lawes's example was followed by other public spirited individuals and by various associations of farmers and growers.

Agricultural research these days is much more costly than in the time of Lawes, and nowadays, apart from stations maintained by commercial undertakings it is almost entirely financed by the State. State assistance started, virtually, with the passing of the Development and Road Improvement Funds Act, 1909, and for many years grants for agricultural research were made by the Development Commission on the advice of the Ministry. Subsequently the grants were made by the Ministry itself. State assisted agricultural research in Great Britain is now, however, primarily the responsibility of the Agricultural Research Council. This body was established by Royal Charter in 1931 and it is now appointed by and responsible to the Committee of Privy Council for Agricultural Research consisting of the Minister for Science as Chairman, the Minister of Agriculture, Fisheries and Food and the Secretary of State for Scotland.

The Agricultural Research Council is responsible for the organization and development of agricultural research. It reviews and co-ordinates research in progress, promotes new research and sets out to ensure that scientific manpower and resources are used to the best advantage. The Council today has eighteen members. These include the Ministry's Chief Scientific Adviser (Agriculture) and Chief Veterinary Officer as well as two other Officers of the Ministry and of the Department of Agriculture and Fisheries for Scotland respectively. The remaining fourteen members are either distinguished scientists or practical farmers or landowners. Each year it publishes a report on its work.

When the Council came into being its main function was to advise the two Agricultural Departments on the programmes of the research institutes to which they were making grants. The Agricultural Research Act, 1956, transferred to the Council responsibility for all the State-aided institutes in England and Wales. In Scotland, however, the situation is unchanged and the Department of Agriculture and Fisheries continues to pay grants to institutes in that country, although it acts on the Council's advice on research programmes, appointment and promotion of scientific staff and the provision of scientific equipment and facilities.

Most of the older research institutes, like Rothamsted, have their own governing bodies. Some of those founded more recently by the State (such as the National Institute of Agricultural Engineering, the Grassland Research Institute and the Vegetable Research Station) are also administered by Boards of Governors; others (such as the Institute of Animal Physiology, the Animal Breeding Research Organization and the Poultry Research Centre) are directly controlled by the Council. The cost of research at all these institutes is met almost entirely by the Council, either directly or by means of annual grants.

Apart from the institutes, the Council has originated a system of units in the universities. These enable the Council to assist in developing a field of research in a university under a recognized leader. Unlike institutes the units are not permanent. They are created around a Professor or Reader of distinction in a particular field and are usually disbanded on his retirement.

The Council also finances research in the universities through special research grants, usually of short duration, as a means of promoting new and promising lines of work some of which may subsequently be taken over by the universities themselves.

A rough indication of the relative volume of work at various categories of research institutes is given in the Parliamentary Estimates for 1961/62 which provided in round figures £1,900,000 for current expenditure on the ARC's own research institutes and units and £3,270,000 for the current expenditure of grant-aided institutes, together with a further £1,070,000 for the Scottish institutes grant-aided by the Department of Agriculture and Fisheries, and £200,000 for special research grants to universities—a total outlay of £6,440,000 a year.

The Agricultural Research Council is also now responsible for research into the design, construction and layout of farm buildings. The Land Improvement Division of the Ministry arranges for research into other questions connected with the management of land. For example, grants have been made to various research institutes and universities for studies of the effect on animals, soil fertility and local climate of the planting of different types of trees in belts of various shapes and sizes.

The whole of this programme can broadly be described as fundamental as contrasted with applied research—in which the Ministry still engages. For example the Ministry still runs its Veterinary Laboratories at Weybridge and Lasswade, the Plant Pathology Laboratory at Harpenden and the Infestation Control Laboratory at Tolworth. The research work of these laboratories is for the most part essentially applied research directed to the solution of specific problems; it is so intimately connected with the Ministry's statutory

F

and other responsibilities that it is accepted that the work must be under the direct control of the Department.

AGRICULTURAL EDUCATION

This is another of the Ministry's former responsibilities the greater part of which has now been transferred elsewhere.

Broadly speaking there are three classes of institution providing full-time courses of education and training for students in agriculture and horticulture. Firstly, there are the universities, which provide three- or four-year degree courses, secondly, the agricultural colleges which provide mainly two-year diploma courses, and thirdly, county agricultural and horticultural institutes, run by the local education authorities, which provide one-year courses. The distinction is not a rigid one; for example, two of the county agricultural institutes provide diploma courses, and several run a supplementary second-year course.

Originally the Ministry was the instrument for State assistance to all these institutions. Since 1947, however, assistance for the agricultural departments of the universities has been covered by the general grants for university expenditure made by the Treasury on the advice of the University Grants Committee. Agricultural economics work is an exception to this, for reasons explained in Chapter XIV.

At the other extreme, in accordance with a recommendation of the report of the De La Warr Committee on *Further Education for Agriculture provided by Local Education Authorities*[1] the Ministry of Education has now become responsible for the farm institutes and other agricultural education activities of local authorities in the same way as for other grant-aided educational activities.

With the agricultural departments of universities now under the aegis of the University Grants Committee and the education provided by local education authorities now the responsibility of the Ministry of Education, the Ministry is left with responsibility for the five independent agricultural colleges—Harper Adams in Shropshire; the Royal at Cirencester; Seale Hayne in Devon; Shuttleworth in Bedfordshire; and Studley in Warwickshire. In considering college questions the Ministry is advised by a committee. Where grants are made, they are reviewed every five years.

Another remaining responsibility of the Ministry in the field of agricultural education is the awarding of grants for post-graduate work in husbandry and agricultural science which fall outside the purview of the Agricultural Research Council (which makes awards to those who are contemplating a career in agricultural research).

[1] Cmnd. 614 of December, 1958.

The Ministry's grants, which are parallel to the awards made by DSIR and the Ministry of Education in other post-graduate fields, are made on the advice of small selection boards under the chairmanship of the Ministry's Chief Scientific Adviser (Agriculture).

The objects of the National Federation of Young Farmers' Clubs which the Ministry helped to form in the years before the war are educational as well as social. An annual grant is paid to this Federation in equal shares by the Ministry and by the Ministry of Education. The Ministry does not seek to exercise any detailed control over the Federation's activities but is consulted on its general plans in connection with the grant applications. The individual Young Farmers' Clubs in addition to their social activities also encourage their members to become technically more proficient, more particularly through its scheme of proficiency tests and badges.

The Ministry also advises the Development Commission on their grants to various organizations concerned with promoting rural industries and social and cultural activities. These include the Rural Industries Bureau, which provides a service of technical advice and instruction to rural craftsmen, the National Federation of Women's Institutes and the National Council of Social Service. This last body, in addition to promoting and fostering the establishment of Rural Community Councils, provides the secretariat for the Village Halls Loan Fund, from which assistance is available for the building and equipment of village halls, and for the Rural Industries Loan Fund from which craftsmen can obtain advances for erecting or improving workshops and for buying equipment.

NATIONAL AGRICULTURAL ADVISORY SERVICE

If the Ministry in recent years has become less directly concerned with the conduct of agricultural research and the provision of agricultural education, it has on the other hand taken a much more direct responsibility for the provision of advice to farmers.

Before the war responsibility for the provision of advice to farmers was divided between the staffs of the county councils and of the university departments of agriculture and agricultural colleges that participated in a Provincial Advisory Service. These services were disrupted by the war and the staffs for the greater part were taken over by the war agricultural executive committees, and in 1944 the Government announced its decision to establish one comprehensive National Agricultural Advisory Service for England and Wales (NAAS) directly administered by the Ministry.

With the setting-up of this Service in 1946 the Government took on direct responsibility for providing technical advice to farmers.

There was no question of setting up a monopoly of advice; anyone can enter this field and many commercial bodies such as the manufacturers of animal feedingstuffs and fertilizers have done so. The State has, however, undertaken to provide free of charge, as required by the Agriculture (Miscellaneous Provisions) Act, 1944, a service of qualified and accessible advisers for the farmers. The establishment of the service recognizes the importance for present day agriculture of scientific development and of getting it over to the farmer. It also meets the need to have a unified system bringing together the specialist scientific adviser and the general adviser who is locally available to the farmer.

The general structure of the NAAS follows from the functions which the service has to perform. The general aim is that every farmer should have a local advisory point to which he can apply and this means, in practice, that the average county must be divided into several districts, each with its own adviser, if the service is to be at all effective. But the district adviser is not qualified in specialist branches of production and therefore county advisers have to be provided in such fields as horticulture and poultry. More than this, however, the local adviser cannot himself be expected to answer all the farmer's problems. Many of these require the assistance of the specialist scientific adviser who has the facilities for the analysis of soils and feedingstuffs, and the scientific knowledge to enable him to advise on the more specialized problems which confront the adviser. Behind the local adviser, therefore, stand the regional teams of specialists whose duty it is to keep abreast of developments in research so as to be able to bring the latest knowledge to bear on the problems coming in from the field. In all there are now in round figures some 1,350 officers in the NAAS of whom nearly 500 are on general agricultural advisory work, 300 on specialist branches of husbandry and 150 on horticulture. Over 300 are regional science specialists, with supporting laboratory staff and fieldsmen and nearly 100 are at the experimental centres mentioned below.

The NAAS can advise the farmer not only on technical questions of husbandry but also on the management of his farm. Success in farming requires not only a mastery of the techniques of growing crops and raising stock but also the ability to allocate and use the resources available on the farm so as to give the maximum continuous net return.

Advice on this subject has been given for many years by agricultural economists and the more experienced advisory officers, but it is an aspect of advisory work that has become increasingly important in recent years. District Advisory Officers and other NAAS officers are now given special training in farm management techniques, and each of the University Provincial Agricultural Economists (see Chapter XIV) has on his staff a Senior Agricultural Economist fully engaged on farm management work who acts as liaison officer between the economists and the NAAS officers in the province.

In addition to its main business of giving advice to the individual farmer, the NAAS arranges a whole series of group activities such as farm walks, lectures and demonstrations by which new technical developments are publicized and kept before the local farmers generally.

Another important activity of the service is experimental work. It is found in practice that the results obtained by the research stations need a good deal of local interpretation under the very varied conditions obtaining in this country before they can be satisfactorily applied. This means in practice much investigation has to be done to get the best out of the findings of the research worker. Accordingly the NAAS has set up a number of experimental centres both for agriculture and horticulture. This has been a major development since the war. The centres are being set up under a general plan designed to ensure that they cover all the major types of soil and climate met with in this country. The NAAS also conducts a wide range of regional and county experiments on private farms, many of them inspired by the regional scientists of the service. In short the aim is to conduct a series of field experiments, so that the practical value of discoveries in fundamental research can be demonstrated and made available to individual farmers.

While the main work of the service is advisory, quite an appreciable amount of its work nowadays arises from the fact that it is part of a Ministry which has introduced a number of improvement schemes which involve grants to the farmer. Administration is not the function of the service, but a number of these schemes call for the provision of technical advice when applications for grant are being considered, and a great deal of assistance is given by the NAAS in this way. The new Small Farmer and Horticultural Improvement Schemes depend heavily on the NAAS and these schemes moreover provide opportunities for getting in touch with farmers who could benefit most from the advice and assistance of the NAAS.

THE AGRICULTURAL IMPROVEMENT COUNCIL

In its technical development work the Ministry relies not only on the NAAS and the other scientific and technical services. The Agricultural Improvement Council, under the chairmanship of the Permanent Secretary of the Ministry, enables the Ministry to get the best available information on technical matters from leading farmers and agricultural scientists. The main tasks of the Council are, on the one hand, to see how the results of research can best be incorporated in commercial farming practice and on the other to formulate the technical problems of the industry which need research. The Council was set up in 1941 when there were many pressing technical problems to be considered arising out of the war-time food production campaign. The need for advice from the Council has continued and in general the AIC has extended its activities as the years have passed to cover more and more of the technical matters arising in different aspects of the Ministry's work. In particular the Council has been entrusted with making detailed recommendations about the experimental centres of the NAAS. The Council has advised on the general programme for these stations and through its various committees works out proposals for the actual programmes of experiments to be undertaken. The Council maintains the closest contact with the Agricultural Research Council and there is a good deal of common membership between the two bodies and their subcommittees. The Council publishes every five years or so an account of its activities; its fourth report, published by HMSO, covers the years 1956 to 1959.

THE SMALL FARMER SCHEME

Under the Agriculture (Small Farmers) Act, 1959, the Government has introduced a scheme designed to improve, both by grants and by advice, the standards of management and of husbandry on a particular type of farm.

There are in all parts of the country, but more particularly in the grassland areas of Wales and the West, a large number of farms that are small in the sense that the scope for developing the farm business is limited in various ways, for instance by acreage, soil, climate, remoteness and lack of capital resources. They are mainly worked by the farmer himself and his family with little or no hired labour. Many such farmers have been handicapped in recent years by lack of financial and other resources in adapting their farming methods in the way they must if they are to earn a satisfactory living from their farms in conditions of increasing competition. They produce mainly milk, pigs and eggs but they have been unable to benefit in the same way as larger farmers from recent developments in arable and animal husbandry. Generally they have been less ready than the occupiers of larger farms to seek assistance from the NAAS and other qualified advisers even though they were amongst those most in need of it. They have also been more dependent on bought-in feedingstuffs than larger farmers and have suffered in various ways from lack of capital resources.

There are tests to ensure that the farm is sufficiently large to be capable of providing full-time employment for the farmer and of yielding him a living broadly equivalent to the wages earned by the skilled agricultural worker; on the other hand, there is an upper limit to ensure that assistance is concentrated where it is most needed.

The first test is that the area of the farm, excluding rough grazing, shall be between 20 and 100 acres. Farm land, however, can vary considerably in its quality and the labour needed to work it. There is therefore a further test of the 'standard labour requirements' of the farm, that is to say, the amount of manual labour required *on average* for the production of the crops and livestock with an allowance for essential farm maintenance and other necessary tasks. Standard figures are available, based on wide sampling by agricultural economists, expressed in terms of so many 'standard man days' a year per acre of crops or per head of livestock that the farm could be expected to carry; each 'man day' represents eight hours manual work for an adult male worker under average conditions. For example, an acre of wheat represents $3\frac{1}{2}$ standard man days and an acre of oats $4\frac{1}{2}$, a dairy cow in milk represents 15 standard man days, but a beef cow only $4\frac{1}{2}$. The lower limit is 275 standard man days (after the plan for improving the farm has been completed), and the upper limit 450 (under current conditions). Both figures are subject to review in the light of experience.

The basis of the scheme is that the farmer himself, with any necessary assistance from the Department's advisory officers, must put forward a plan covering a period of three to five years for improving the efficiency and profitability of his farm business.

The farm business plan must cover such details as changes in the cropping of the farm, what stock is to be kept and what new equipment bought. It is normally drawn up in consultation with the District Advisory Officer of the NAAS, which provides an opportunity for the NAAS to give advice to those most needing it. In fact one of the attractions of the plan is that it gives the NAAS officer an entrée on farms where hitherto there might have been a reluctance to seek advice from outside. Opportunities for continuing advice is provided by the requirement that the NAAS must satisfy themselves by periodic visits that the plan is being properly implemented.

The plans are drawn up to suit the individual needs of each farm. A typical plan for a small dairy farm where pigs were also kept might be to improve or expand the dairy herd and to keep some sheep in place of the pigs and to improve the grassland so that it may play a greater part in the feeding of both the cattle and the sheep. On a small arable farm the plan might be to increase the output by putting a greater acreage under crops such as potatoes and wheat that can be sold for cash, and fattening some beef cattle.

If this farm business plan is approved by the Department then the farmer is eligible for two kinds of special grant which together cannot exceed £1,000. First there is a farm business grant payable in instalments over a period of three years, subject to the Department being satisfied that the farmer is making satisfactory progress with the implementation of his approved farm business plan. The grant is at a flat rate of £6 per acre of the farmer's holding (excluding rough grazings) with a maximum of £360, payable by instalments over a period of three years.

In addition to the farm business grant, field husbandry grants are payable in respect of various operations approved by the Department, namely, renovation and ploughing up of grassland (as an addition to the normal ploughing grant), ditching work to make the foregoing operations effective, and any minor land reclamation work essential for the fulfilment of the farm business plan.

In addition to the main scheme there is a Supplementary Scheme intended for small farmers for whom approved farm business plans are not immediately practicable, because for example they were not themselves ready to embark on such plans or because the Ministry is not in a position to handle their applications straight away. Grants under the Supplementary Scheme take the form of additions to the standard rate of grants payable to all farmers for ploughing of grassland, liming, ditching and the supply of fertilizers.

The Small Farmer Schemes have now replaced the Marginal Production Scheme under which grants were made towards the cost of various goods and services 'for the purpose of promoting efficiency in agriculture or facilitating food production' supplied to the type of producer who rarely had any margin of profit to plough back in improvement because his farm was handicapped by such factors beyond his control as poor soil or remoteness.

CHAPTER VI

Farming (continued)

THIS chapter describes a number of the grants and subsidies made by the Department to promote the efficiency and productivity of farming, as well as measures for the control of diseases and pests and a variety of other 'farm efficiency' measures.

PLOUGHING GRANTS

Grants for the ploughing up of grassland were introduced in the spring of 1939 as a peace-time defence measure for increasing the food producing potentiality of our land, and with a brief interval they have been continued ever since. Statutory authority for the grants is now provided by the Agriculture (Ploughing Grants) Act, 1952, under which there is presented to Parliament each year for approval by affirmative resolution a scheme specifying the conditions governing grants for land ploughed in the ensuing twelve months (June–May).

There are at present[1] two rates of grant; a lower rate of £7 per acre for grassland that has not been ploughed for at least three years and a higher rate of £12 per acre for land that has been continuously under grass since June, 1946, the ploughing of which presents special difficulties.

To qualify for the £7 an acre grant the farmer must notify the local divisional office of the Ministry within twenty-one days after he has ploughed the land. This notification is made to enable a field officer to make sample inspections to satisfy himself not only that the acreage claimed has been ploughed but also, from the appearance of the land (in conjunction where necessary with records of previous ploughing grant claims), that at least three years have elapsed since any previous ploughing. The grant is also conditional on the land being cultivated and sown to produce a crop (which may include grass). Accordingly the farmer can only apply for the grant after he has sown the crop, when again a sample of the claims is checked by an inspection by a field officer.

The prior approval by the Ministry's divisional office is required before ploughing if the higher rate of £12 an acre is to be claimed, and such approval is only given after the land has been inspected by a

[1] At the time of writing the rates and conditions of grant are under consideration.

field officer to confirm that the land is 'difficult' land and that the cost of ploughing it and bringing it into a state of cleanliness, fertility and fitness for cropping would be substantially heavier than normal. The land is inspected again after the land has been ploughed and cultivated and the crop grown so that the field officer can satisfy himself that these operations have been performed in accordance with the conditions laid down by the Ministry when approving the original application.

The primary object of the grants nowadays can be regarded as the encouragement of ley farming, i.e. the ploughing up of grass after it has been down for three or four years (or possibly longer). Normally the land would be cropped with cereals and perhaps roots for several years before going down again to grass, but 'direct reseeding', i.e. sowing down to grass again immediately after ploughing is now permitted. In this way the grants also serve as a means of encouraging the improvement of permanent pasture and the regeneration of old leys. The theory has been that to 'take the plough right round the farm' with each field switching from grass to arable crops or vice versa every few years generally enables a farm to produce more than if part of it were permanently under grass and the remainder permanently under arable crops. In particular, grass leys in the first four or five years of their existence generally provide better grazing than permanent pasture save perhaps in some of the finest permanent grass to be found in the Midlands and in places such as Romney Marsh. Many farmers, of course, would continue to plough up their grassland even if there were no grants, but there seems little doubt that without the grants it would be done by fewer farmers and less often.

SILO SUBSIDY

Grass is this country's most important farm crop. Most of the growth occurs in the summer months, and although it is now possible to extend the grazing season quite appreciably at both ends by sowing the right varieties and strains of grass and applying suitable fertilizers, by and large, if the farmer is to use his grass for the feeding of his cattle in winter he must conserve it by one of the three established techniques, namely, haymaking, grass drying and ensiling.

Each has a place in the farming economy of the country. Silage making, however, is not nearly so dependent on the weather as haymaking and does not require the relatively expensive apparatus needed for grass drying. It can be used for preserving not only grass but arable forage crops cut green such as a mixture of oats, beans and vetches. The process consists of cutting the crop at an early stage (grass when it is about six to ten inches high is much more nutritious than if left to grow for hay) and placing it, generally after adding some material such as molasses, in a silo, which may be either a tower silo, a suitably drained pit, or a clamp (that is to say a building with walls on one, two or three sides but open on one side at least to permit filling with the grass or other crop). When the silo is full it should be covered with an airtight seal; for the pit or clamp silo this may be no more than a layer of earth or chalk. The crop in the silo is preserved by the action of bacteria which convert the plant sugars into various organic acids, of which lactic acid is the most important for good silage; the process is, therefore, essentially similar to that of the pickling of food in vinegar.

For many farmers, more particularly the smaller man in the wetter part of the country, silage making may be the most economical and satisfactory way of conserving grass and other fodder crops for winter feed, though not necessarily to the entire exclusion of haymaking.

Silage making in this country is, however, a comparatively new technique, and has suffered from the prejudice caused by the many failures in its early days. In order therefore to encourage silage making as a means of reducing our dependence on imported feeding-stuffs the Agriculture (Silo Subsidies) Act of 1956 authorized the payment of grants towards the cost of installing silos of a size and design previously agreed by the Department or improving existing silos.

The schemes made under the Act marked an interesting development in subsidy technique. Previously grants for any form of farm building or similar fixed installations, such as farm water supply had been calculated as a percentage of the approved cost. This meant that the applicant's plans had to be examined in detail and possibly modified to cut down the cost, and then the department had to see that competitive tenders were obtained wherever possible and finally the contractors' bills had to be checked. To simplify administration the silo grants are calculated instead in accordance with 'standard costs' representing about 50 per cent of the average cost of construction, e.g. so much per cubic yard capacity for a tower silo, so much per square yard of superficial area for the lining or sides of a pit or clamp silo, subject in any case to an overall maximum of £250 or £125 per farm according to the type of silo.

This principle of 'standard costs' has incidentally now been extended to various other schemes mentioned in later chapters such as those for Farm Improvement, Horticulture Improvement, and Improvement of Livestock Rearing Land. Where it is practicable to calculate satisfactory 'standard costs' for building works, fencing etc. under these schemes, the farmer can elect to have his grant based on such standard costs instead of on actual costs.

The District Advisory Officer of the NAAS discusses each proposal for a grant-aided silo with the applicant before approval is given. In this way not only is the Department able to satisfy itself that the design of the silo is technically sound and of a capacity appropriate to the size of the farm and the amount of stock it is carrying, but also the farmer can be given the necessary technical advice to enable him to produce good quality silage.

CALF REARING SUBSIDY

This subsidy was introduced in 1947 to encourage a general increase in our cattle population. The justification for this form of subsidy was that a payment to the rearer of the calf gave him a more direct and immediate incentive to increase his output than waiting for higher prices for beef and milk to stimulate a stronger demand for calves. When, however, the scheme was renewed under the authority of the Agriculture (Calf Subsidies) Act, 1952, the emphasis was switched to the encouragement of the rearing of calves for beef production. In particular owners of dairy herds were encouraged to use beef bulls on their lower yielding cows to produce cross-bred calves suitable for beef rather than pure bred dairy calves, most of which would normally be slaughtered when only a few days old as not worth rearing. Accordingly a higher rate of subsidy is paid on steer calves than on heifer calves and no subsidy at all is paid on heifer calves of the four purely dairy breeds (Ayrshire, Friesian, Guernsey and Jersey).

The calves are inspected when they are not less than eight months old (six months for spring born calves in hill areas) and before they have cut their first permanent incisor tooth by certifying officers of the Ministry, who need to be satisfied that they are suitable for making good beef animals. Uniformity in the standards applied by the certifying officers is ensured as far as practicable by periodic test inspections by the Livestock Husbandry Officers of the National Agricultural Advisory Service, who also hear appeals against rejection of calves by certifying officers.

HILL SHEEP AND HILL COW SUBSIDIES

The livestock rearing land of this country is defined as 'consisting predominantly of mountains, hills or heath and suitable for rearing sheep or cattle but not to any material extent for dairying, fattening or cash cropping'. Such land is found in Wales, in certain specified counties in the north and south-west of England and in corresponding parts of Scotland and Northern Ireland.

This land is important in the livestock husbandry of this country as a source of store sheep and cattle which are sold for fattening in the lowland areas. Farmers in the hill areas however do not benefit *directly* from the guaranteed prices for fat sheep and fat cattle, and they may suffer severely at times when the demand for store stock falls off. Special assistance is accordingly given under the Hill Farming and Livestock Rearing Acts, 1946 to 1956, to encourage the rearing of hardy sheep and cattle in these areas.

Hill sheep subsidy is only payable in any year if a review of the available evidence, including data collected by university agricultural economists, shows that the income of hill sheep farmers as a whole has fallen below a reasonable level. The subsidy, if payable, is at a uniform rate per head on breeding ewes in self-contained flocks of hardy mountain breeds, with a half rate of subsidy for flocks kept for producing cross-bred lambs or for flocks which are maintained wholly or partly by the purchase of ewes or ewe lambs. The scheme is not an easy one to supervise as the ewes are widely dispersed over wild and rough country and can usually only be conveniently inspected at the times when the ewes are gathered for such purposes as dipping and shearing. As large a sample as possible, about one-third of the flocks, is however inspected by the Ministry's field officers at suitable times during the year.

A subsidy at present at a rate of £12 per head is paid on beef cows kept in regular breeding herds on livestock rearing land. The applicant may be required to devote up to 40 per cent of the subsidy to specified improvements of the grazing land, such as liming, surface drainage and bracken cutting. One additional reason for the hill cow subsidy is that the sheep are much more selective and fussy grazers than cattle. Unless, therefore, the coarser grasses left untouched by the sheep are grazed by the cattle they will eventually smother the finer grasses favoured by the sheep.

The special grants payable for the comprehensive improvement of farms in the hill areas are described in the next chapter.

ANIMAL HEALTH

It is difficult to estimate with any accuracy the losses which disease causes to our livestock population. In Great Britain alone, despite widespread control measures, the losses have been estimated to be in the region of £80 million per annum. The Food and Agriculture Organization of the United Nations have calculated that the direct loss of livestock arising from one widespread epidemic of foot-and-mouth on the continent of Europe in 1951/52 amounted to £143 million, and the indirect losses were probably even greater.

As mentioned in Chapter II, one of the forerunners of the Department was the Cattle Plague Department of the Home Office, established in 1865 to deal with serious outbreaks of cattle plague or rinderpest introduced by imported cattle, and the control of animal diseases has been one of the most important functions of the Ministry throughout its history. Animal disease, incidentally, is one of the few matters for which the Minister still has responsibilities north of the Border. On many animal health matters the Minister has a joint responsibility with the Secretary of State for Scotland and local executive action in Scotland is taken by the Department of Agriculture and Fisheries for Scotland. That Department, for example, would be responsible for granting licences for the importation of cattle into Scotland from abroad in accordance with policy jointly agreed between the two departments. When, however, it is a question of speedy action to control outbreaks of epidemic diseases which are no respecter of national boundaries, such as foot-and-mouth disease, then the Minister has sole administrative responsibility for the whole of Great Britain.

The veterinary profession in this country consists in the main of fully qualified veterinary surgeons in private practice and those in the Ministry's service. In general, it is the responsibility of the Government to take all practicable steps to check the spread of animal diseases, more particularly those for which the Minister and the Secretary of State have a specific responsibility laid upon them by Parliament. Treatment of most other cases of disease is a matter for the private practitioner.

For the discharge of its responsibilities in this field the Ministry maintains a large staff of veterinary surgeons under its Chief Veterinary Officer, some stationed at headquarters, some at the ports, and the rest as field staff situated at local offices; two or three are stationed permanently in South America to assist and advise the authorities there on precautions against the spread of animal disease through meat exported to this country. In addition to the permanent whole-time staff a large number of veterinary surgeons in private practice are employed part-time as the Department's local veterinary inspectors.

The greater part of the Ministry's activities to safeguard the health of our livestock, under legislative powers now consolidated in the Diseases of Animals Act, 1950, fall under three headings. Firstly, control over the importation of animals or materials that may introduce disease into this country. Secondly, eradication through slaughter of sporadic outbreaks of disease that despite the Ministry's precautions may be introduced from time to time from abroad, and, thirdly, dealing with diseases which are endemic in this country, by a combination of slaughter, movement restrictions, voluntary vaccination, and advice to veterinary surgeons in private practice, according to circumstances. In recent years there has been an outstanding example of a successful campaign for not merely keeping in check but eliminating an endemic disease, namely, bovine tuberculosis.

In the last war the English Channel was described as a very effective tank trap; it has certainly saved us from the spread of various animal diseases, such as foot-and-mouth, which are endemic over much of the continent of Europe. Our freedom from such diseases, as well as others like rabies which are prevalent in other parts of the world, has, however, only been achieved and maintained through a strict control over the importation of animals and of materials that might carry infection, coupled with determined and drastic action to stamp out any diseases that may slip through the barrier.

Under the Diseases of Animals legislation the importation of live cattle, sheep and other ruminants, and pigs, is in general prohibited save as allowed by order of the Minister. The practice varies according to the animal and country of origin. Thus cattle, sheep and pigs from other parts of the British Isles (e.g. the Irish Republic) and cattle from Canada are normally admitted without restrictions, but similar livestock from other countries must be slaughtered at the port of entry unless covered by a special order made by the Minister and the Secretary of State for Scotland which needs to be laid before Parliament. Such orders may be made for example for the importation of exotic species for zoos, or special importations to improve the quality of our native livestock, e.g. Friesian bulls from Holland.

Dogs and cats from countries outside the British Isles need to go into quarantine for rabies immediately on landing for not less than six months. This rule has never been relaxed, even in the most exceptional circumstances, despite the heart-burnings that occur, say, when a blind student has to be parted temporarily from his own guide dog. Only those who have seen rabies—and humans as well as dogs and cats can get it as a result of coming in contact with a rabid animal—can fully understand why it is so very necessary to avoid the slightest risk of the reintroduction of this dreaded disease. Rabies, incidentally, was only eradicated as a result of orders made by the Department which required all dogs in this country to be muzzled.

Carcase meat can be, and indeed is, a source of danger to the country's livestock because the virus of disease may be present in the meat itself, perhaps in the marrow bones or in the wrappings. Much the same is true of a wide range of animal products, for example, blood, bones, bone meal, horn meal and so on. Importation of such goods is therefore also controlled by orders under the Diseases of Animals Act.

In deciding on such controls a balance has to be struck between our needs for imports of meat and livestock on the one hand and the degree of disease risk on the other. From the point of view of veterinary control, for example, the ideal would be to prohibit altogether imports from any country in which foot-and-mouth disease was present, but this would mean denying ourselves supplies from Argentina and other South American countries. In practice a sensible balance has to be struck and countries and products are grouped according to the assessed disease risk and safeguards applied, ranging from absolute prohibition to allowing imports covered by a certificate from the Government of the country of origin that certain requirements have been fulfilled. It is the responsibility of the Ministry's Animal Health Division to keep abreast of changes in the animal disease field all over the world so that adjustments may be made from time to time in the statutory control of imports. Disease statistics are received regularly from very many countries; and there is a constant interchange of information between State veterinary surgeons over the greater part of the world. There is also an international organization based on Paris (the *Office Internationale des Epizooties*); and the Food and Agriculture Organization of the United Nations and the European Commission for the control of Foot-and-Mouth disease (both at Rome) play an important part in securing collaboration between the different countries.

As an additional precaution against the introduction of disease, meat, bones, offal and other waste foodstuff has to be boiled for at least an hour before being fed to animals or poultry. In their own interests it is very important that farmers should observe these precautions strictly.

In addition to its control over the importation of animals the Department administers measures to protect animals during transit, including veterinary examination before export. The Department is also responsible for giving the certificates required by various overseas governments in respect of livestock and animal products exported from this country. To enable exporters of livestock to comply with the regulations of various overseas governments the Ministry maintains two quarantine stations at Liverpool and London respectively; the Department of Agriculture and Fisheries for Scotland is responsible for a third at Glasgow.

Foot-and-Mouth Disease

Complementary to the measures to prevent the introduction of disease from overseas is the action which the Ministry takes to stamp out any outbreaks which, despite these precautions, may occur in this country from time to time.

The best known and most spectacular are the measures necessary to deal with foot-and-mouth disease whenever it occurs. This disease is in a class by itself because of the astonishing speed at which it can spread and the multiplicity of agents that can be responsible for its dissemination. The control measures have to be exceptionally severe. The diseased or incubating animal must necessarily be the most serious menace in its passage through markets, on the roads and in railway trucks. The virus may be conveyed indirectly by humans, or on the wheels of cars, lorries and tradesmen's vans, or by birds and vermin. Indeed, there is practically no limit to the media through which infection can be carried over great distances in a matter of hours.

A brief description of what happens when an outbreak of foot-and-mouth disease occurs may help to explain how the machinery of disease control works.

A farmer in a remote part of, say, the north of England notices that one of his cows is salivating, and that some lameness is apparent; perhaps he detects blisters on its tongue and inside its mouth and on its feet. He suspects foot-and-mouth disease and straight away reports his suspicions (as he is required by law to do) to the police, who immediately send a priority telegram to the Ministry and telephone the Department's Divisional Veterinary Officer and the inspector of the Local Authority. The Local Authority inspector (usually, in country districts, a police officer) thereupon serves on the owner of the stock under suspicion a notice controlling the movement of persons and stock in and out of the farm, which at that stage is declared to be an infected place. The inspector also warns his Local Authority. The Divisional Veterinary Officer, for his part, sends one of his veterinary staff to examine the suspected animal immediately.

At the Ministry the necessary staff is detached from other duties to determine a precise Infected Area for the purpose of an Order under the Diseases of Animals Act, 1950, which is got out with all possible speed. No animals are allowed to be moved out of an Infected Area, movements within and into it are restricted, and markets within the area are controlled. The farm where the outbreak is suspected is plotted, and a circle of about ten miles radius drawn around it, following the line of parish boundaries where possible. The location of bacon factories and slaughter-houses are carefully considered so that the Infected Area as finally determined may include essential facilities for dealing with stock inside the area as they become ready for slaughter (they are not allowed to be moved outside). Most of this work is done before the presence of disease is confirmed, since time is vital in checking its spread. It is far better to have everything ready, even if the preparations have to be scrapped if

G

disease is not confirmed, than to wait for confirmation before getting all the details worked out. While the Infected Area is being defined telegrams are got ready, to be sent, if the outbreak is confirmed, to the many interests likely to be affected by an order; they include other government departments, representatives of Commonwealth and foreign countries, port authorities, local authorities, police and British Railways.

Within a very short time after his arrival at the farm the veterinary officer will have completed his examination of the suspected animals. He immediately telephones his diagnosis to the Ministry, and discusses his findings, the symptoms and the history of the case with senior veterinary officers. Disease is either confirmed or not confirmed as the case may be (in some instances material from the suspected animal has to be examined by laboratory methods before a diagnosis can be confirmed; in such cases restrictions remain on the farm pending final diagnosis). If disease is confirmed, the veterinary officer is authorized to slaughter the affected stock and all other cloven-hoofed animals on the farm which in his opinion have been exposed to infection. At the same time the order is made and the notifications (some 200 of them) are sent out over the teleprinter network. The Press and the BBC are told; the making of an Infected Area Order is usually broadcast in the earliest news bulletin put out after the receipt of the message. Restrictions are maintained within the ten-mile Infected Area for fourteen days after the outbreak, reduced to a radius of about five miles for a further seven days and then generally withdrawn unless further outbreaks occur in the neighbourhood.

As soon as an outbreak of foot-and-mouth disease is confirmed the Divisional Veterinary Officer establishes what is in effect an advance operational centre in a conveniently situated town. It is to this centre that veterinary officers from other areas are instructed to report with all speed to reinforce the local staff.

Back at the farm the animals are slaughtered after being valued by a professionally qualified valuer acceptable to the farmer. If the owner does not agree the valuation it can be referred to arbitration subsequently. The carcases are disposed of by cremation or burial, whichever is the more expedient and efficient. Burial pits are generally dug with the aid of mechanical shovels. The premises are thoroughly disinfected, supplies of disinfectant are made available for the disinfection of all leaving the farm, and a constable or some other responsible officer is posted at the gate to see that only those with business there enter.

Among the other innumerable details that must be attended to are protective clothing for the veterinary officers at the farm, spraying of clamps of harvested roots and potatoes and other animal feeding-stuffs, and the disinfection of utensils, troughs and milk churns. All poultry, dogs and cats on the infected premises have to be 'confined to barracks' and neighbouring residents warned to prevent their animals (including pets) from wandering. Footpaths may be closed and notices forbidding admission are then affixed at strategic points. All susceptible animals within two miles of the infected farm are examined by veterinary officers and kept under close observation.

When an outbreak seems to have no connection with any other outbreak, material from the diseased animals is sent to the Foot-and-Mouth Disease Research Institute at Pirbright for expert examination to determine precisely what type of virus caused the outbreak.

Three quite separate types of foot-and-mouth disease virus have been encountered in this country. All are found in Europe and South America, and there are many different strains and variants of each. All the viruses are capable of multiplying or reproducing themselves extensively in certain tissues of susceptible animals. Imported meat, scraps and bones which may be thrown to domestic animals are one possible source of infection, and if raw bones are under suspicion, samples containing unexposed marrow go to the Foot and Mouth Research Institute at Pirbright, as do the carcases of rats destroyed on the infected premises and of hedgehogs found near an outbreak if they show any clinical evidence of disease. In this way it is possible to determine what if any of the suspected material is in fact infected with virus of the same type that has caused the disease, and so provide a valuable clue as to how the infection may have arrived at the farm.

The most exhausting and tedious part of the whole operation for the veterinary staff is tracing every animal that entered or left the infected premises shortly before the outbreak, as well as any contacts made by the infected animals themselves. This may involve tracking down all the stock that have passed through a market before the confirmation of disease, and beyond that, other animals with which they may have come into contact if there is reason to think that they had been exposed to the risk of infection. (The incubation period of foot-and-mouth disease is usually three to six days, but it may be as short as twenty-four hours or exceptionally as long as three weeks.) Thus the area of search may get wider and wider until in the end it may cover the greater part of the country. It is not difficult to visualize how far afield from the initial outbreak enquiries and examinations may have to be made by the Ministry's veterinary officers if the infected cattle had been at an important market a few days before the disease was diagnosed.

The results of all these inquiries are analysed and studied so that headquarters may know and keep track of the likelihood of spread. Very often preliminary restrictions on the further movement of some animals have to be imposed. If foot-and-mouth disease is found to exist in any of them the whole business begins all over again with one or more new areas of infection. Time is the most vital factor in waging war on the disease. If a farmer neglects to warn the police of his suspicions for only a few hours what might otherwise have been an isolated case may end in a widespread outbreak.

Staff of the Ministry's Animal Health Division are always available, day or night, at their office or their homes. A special duty rota is rigidly observed and details of it are regularly circulated to the veterinary officers in the field. Whenever the call comes, there is someone whose job it is to take all the essential steps. So far as human ingenuity can devise the system is fool-proof; and it has stood the test of time. To what extent the machinery will need to be kept going following a single initial outbreak can never be determined in advance. There may be but that one outbreak. There may be many others arising directly from it or at much the same time from some other source of infection. In November, 1951, an outbreak was confirmed. There was no reason to suspect anything unusual. But before the disease was finally brought to a halt toward the end of 1952, some 600 separate outbreaks had occurred covering the greater part of the country and involving the slaughter of over 85,000 animals. Almost a year was to elapse from the first of this series of outbreaks before the staff of Animal Health Division could relax from foot-and-mouth disease duties and once more concentrate on other matters. Similarly after a relatively quiet period for three years, in September, 1957, a series of outbreaks spread over the country and it was not until May, 1958 after 223 outbreaks had been confirmed, that the country was once more free of the disease. In the winter of 1960 there was another very serious series of outbreaks.

Bovine Tuberculosis

In contrast with the action to eliminate sporadic outbreaks of disease introduced from abroad is the control, and where practicable elimination, of diseases endemic in the country.

The latest disease to be eliminated in this way has been bovine tuberculosis, with which at least 40 per cent of all cows in dairy herds alone were estimated to have been infected in 1934. The first step in the elimination of the disease was the establishment in 1935 of a voluntary Attested Herds Scheme under which farmers who undertook to observe prescribed rules thereby qualified for an incentive payment. The scheme was subsequently amended in detail, and finally emerged as an arrangement to pay bonuses for a maximum period of six years on cattle passing the tuberculin test.

A plan for the progressive compulsory eradication of tuberculosis was started in 1951 and proceeded in three stages. The first was the announcement of the Minister's intention in about two years' time to declare an eradication area, generally a group of counties. Owners of herds in the area were offered free testing of their animals with tuberculin to encourage voluntary entry into the Attested Herds Scheme.

The second stage was when the eradication area was actually declared. All herds in the area which were not already attested or well on their way to becoming so were compulsorily tested with tuberculin and all beasts reacting to the test were slaughtered. The owners of such herds did not get the bonus payments of the Attested Herds Scheme. Declaration of the eradication stage did mean, however, that compensation became payable for all reactor cattle disclosed whether or not they were in an attested herd.

Finally the area was declared an Attested Area, when bovine tuberculosis had for practical purposes ceased to exist in it.

By the end of 1960, bovine tuberculosis as a national problem had been eliminated and the plan was completed, apart from routine check testing of herds with tuberculin and immediate removal of reactors which will have to continue for some considerable time.

There is not space in a volume such as this to deal at any length with the Department's activities in the control of other diseases such as compulsory slaughter in cases of fowl pest and swine fever and the encouragement of vaccination of calves against contagious abortion.

Facilities for diagnosis, investigation and research are essential parts of the Department's machinery for the control of disease. The Department maintains a central veterinary laboratory at Weybridge, Surrey, and a smaller one at Lasswade, just outside Edinburgh. These two laboratories cover the entire field of animal disease except foot-and-mouth disease, for which there is a separate research institute at Pirbright, Surrey, under the aegis of the Agricultural Research Council. Additionally, there are veterinary investigation officers at centres located at strategic points up and down the country, each one equipped with a laboratory and staffed by technicians. The purpose of these centres is to assist private veterinary surgeons in the diagnosis of disease, to bring to their notice the results of research into and methods of control of animal disease, to investigate local problems and to carry the results of the work done at the central laboratories a stage further by trials on a field scale. Any major problems that might be encountered are referred to the central laboratory for further study.

BEES

The Ministry is also concerned under the Agriculture (Miscellaneous Provisions) Act, 1941, with measures to prevent the spread of disease among bees. Bees are important not only as producers of honey but also in some districts as pollinators of fruit trees. One order prohibits the importation of bees without a certificate of health issued by the responsible Department of the exporting country. The other orders under the Act are designed to check the spread of the highly infectious foul brood diseases of bees. Where the existence of such disease in any apiary is confirmed the Minister can order the destruction of the infected colony and the disinfection of the hive and equipment and also serve a standstill notice prohibiting the removal of bees, honey and equipment from the premises.

PESTS AND CROP DISEASES

The Ministry and its predecessors have been concerned with the pests and diseases which affect farm and horticultural crops for almost as long as they have been with diseases of animals. It was in 1877 that an Act was hurriedly passed by Parliament to give the Privy Council powers to prevent the introduction into this country of the Colorado beetle, which was doing great damage to the potato crop in America. In 1907 the spread of American gooseberry mildew, a fungus disease introduced by imported stocks, led to the extension of the Act to cover any insect, fungus or other pest that was destructive to agricultural or horticultural crops or to trees or to bushes, and the Act was further amended in 1927.

The Plant Health Branch of Horticulture Division deals with the fungus, bacterial and virus diseases and the pests of agricultural and horticultural crops, whilst there is an Infestation Control Branch in another division which deals with animals and birds such as rabbits, wood pigeons, rats and mice which prey on farm crops, as well as with the insect and other pests of stored foodstuffs.

Plant Health

The Ministry's responsibilities for plant health are broadly similar in purpose and in scope to those for animal health described above, though naturally details vary considerably. Thus they include control of the importation of material that may introduce and spread disease, domestic controls designed to limit the spread of the more important pests and diseases already present in this country and where possible to eradicate them, and inspections necessary for giving the certificates required by various overseas governments as to the health of exported material. The Department also administers various schemes for the inspection and certification of various growing crops to provide growers with an assured source of disease-free material.

The organization for the discharge of these responsibilities is again broadly similar to that of the Animal Health Division. Thus the Ministry's Plant Pathology Laboratory at Harpenden has a role corresponding to that of the Ministry's veterinary laboratories for diagnosis and research and for acting as a general clearing house of technical information. The work in the field is done by the Plant Health Inspectorate whose duties are analogous to those of the Veterinary Officers of the Animal Health Division.

As with animal diseases the range of plant pests and diseases with which the Ministry has dealt is so vast that it is impossible to provide anything like a complete catalogue, and only a relatively few illustrative examples can be given.

The best known, as well as the oldest, of the import controls is that to guard against the introduction of the Colorado beetle, a pest now present in many European countries. The beetle feeds on the leaves of potatoes and if allowed to spread reduces yields considerably.

Imports of potatoes and all leafy vegetable which might harbour the beetle are, as far as practicable, allowed only from countries and districts known to be free from the beetle. Such imports are, however, allowed from certain countries which are not entirely free of the beetle, but only during the period of the year when the beetle is normally still in the larva stage, so as to minimize the risk of its presence on the produce. Check inspections of all produce are made at the ports and rail head depots by the Plant Health Inspectors and any consignments in which the beetle is found may be denied admission to this country.

Holidaymakers returning from abroad may encounter another of the Ministry's import controls when they have to complete a Customs form for the plants they have brought home to plant in their garden, and subsequently receive a visit from one of the Ministry's Plant Health Inspectors to see that the plants are free from pests and diseases. The importation of some plants is prohibited entirely, and these will be confiscated by the Customs. Travellers who want to bring back small quantities of wild plants which they have collected on their travels for planting in their own private gardens can apply to the Plant Health Branch of the Ministry at Whitehall Place, London, sw1, for a licence before leaving this country. These wild plants may also be examined by a Ministry inspector in due course.

The Colorado Beetle Orders, as the details given above have indicated, are an example of a domestic control designed to prevent a pest becoming established here. There are other pests which we cannot hope to eradicate but whose growth and spread we can hope to contain by domestic control measures. One example is the sugar-beet eelworm, which has become prevalent in certain districts, particularly in East Anglia, as a result of sugar-beet being grown too frequently on the same land. The Beet Eelworm Order, 1960, administered by the county agricultural executive committees under powers delegated to them by the Minister, controls the growing of sugar-beet and other host crops in infested fields so as to ensure that a sufficient number of years is allowed to elapse between one crop and the next to keep the eelworm population down to a tolerable level.

Some pests and diseases are so widespread that statutory controls would be quite impracticable and ineffective and we can only rely on education and advice to reduce the damage they cause. One example is potato blight, the cause of the famous Irish potato famine of 1845–49. This is caused by a fungus whose spores are present in all the main potato growing areas, but which can multiply only during a period of moist warm weather. The critical temperature and degree of humidity are now known, and the Ministry's Plant Pathology Laboratory in collaboration with the Meteorological Office is able to predict with a considerable degree of accuracy when serious outbreaks are imminent in any part of the country. The news is then immediately publicized in the farming Press and elsewhere so that growers can spray their crops with an appropriate fungicide (or, alternatively, with an acid to burn off the leaves of the plant so as to deny the fungus space to multiply) at the time when it will be most effective; they are thus saved the expense of unnecessary spraying.

Under the International Plant Protection Convention of 1951 this country has undertaken to maintain a Plant Protection Organiza-tion under which technically qualified and duly authorized officers are available to give the certificates required by various overseas governments as to the health of exported plants. This service is provided by the Plant Health Inspectorate in collaboration with the Horticultural Officers of the NAAS who visit growers' nurseries and farms to satisfy themselves as necessary that specified diseases and pests are absent and also that any other condition that may be laid down by the importing country, such as the fumigation of material before it leaves the holding, are being observed.

Growing crops are also inspected under various voluntary certifica-tion schemes designed to give purchasers an assurance, so far as is practicable, that the seed potatoes or plants which they purchase are healthy and true to type. The schemes cover seed potatoes, blackcurrant bushes, fruit tree rootstocks, raspberry and loganberry canes, strawberry runners and hop plants. The Ministry issues each year registers of growers of certified stocks and copies may be obtained free of charge from the Ministry's Plant Health Branch, Whitehall Place, London, sw1.

Weeds

Weeds, as well as pests, are the subject of statutory control, administered this time by the Land Improvement Division. Under the Weeds Act, 1959 (which consolidates legislation dating from 1917), the Minister can require certain weeds whose seeds are particularly liable to harm neighbouring agricultural land, namely ragwort, thistles and docks, to be cut or destroyed. The Minister has delegated these powers to county agricultural executive committees (and to county borough councils). In practice statutory powers are only invoked as a last resort when advice and persuasion have failed.

Infestation Control

The work of the Infestation Control Branch falls under four headings —scientific research and investigation, statutory controls, grants for the destruction of farm pests, and general encouragement and advice in the control of such pests.

Control of any pest needs to be based on extensive and detailed scientific knowledge of its life cycle, habits and physiology in order to find out how best to attack it at its weakest spot.

The Pests Infestation Laboratory at Slough, now under the control of the Agricultural Research Council, undertakes fundamental research into the infestation of stored foods by insects and mites. The Ministry's Infestation Control Laboratory at Tolworth uses the results in developing chemical and other methods for controlling these pests, and also methods for detecting and assessing the degree of infestation. The Infestation Control Laboratory also carries on research on rats and mice and (at a branch situated at Worplesdon) other animals harmful to agriculture and forestry such as the rabbit, squirrel and wood pigeon. For a number of these pests we have not yet got the knowledge necessary for devising fully effective methods of control, but work is proceeding all the time.

Pests-control work in each region is supervised by a Regional Pests Officer, who keeps closely in touch with the Infestation Control Laboratory. He has under him two groups of staff. First of all the Divisional Pests Officers and their assistants, who deal with animal and bird pests, and secondly the inspectors, stationed mainly at the big ports, who deal with the insect pests of stored foodstuffs and other produce.

The rabbit is one of the most important pests with which the Ministry has to deal. At one time this animal was valued as a source of meat and closely preserved, but as agriculture became more intensive and more mechanized the damage caused by rabbits became more important and more obvious. Rabbits can do an immense amount of damage to arable crops, and even on grassland, grazing by rabbits can well lead to weeds replacing grasses useful for farm stock.

Many farmers only realized to the full the extent of damage caused by wild rabbits when the disease myxomatosis first appeared in this country in 1954, and in the following year almost eliminated the rabbits in many parts of the country. Some rabbits, however, escaped infection; milder forms of the disease appeared in various areas, and in many parts of the country the rabbit began to reappear and multiply. Divisional Pests Officers accordingly have encouraged farmers in any area in which rabbits were reappearing to join together in a rabbit clearance society to take co-operative action to destroy any rabbits before they became re-established. The Ministry makes a grant of 50 per cent of the approved expenses of these rabbit clearance societies. Some of the societies also undertake measures for the destruction of the coypu (a beaver-like animal, originally imported from South America for its fur, which is now becoming a nuisance in parts of East Anglia) and also, as explained below, for the control of wood pigeons and other bird pests.

The Ministry also makes grants at the rate of 50 per cent (75 per cent in some cases) to landowners and farmers towards the cost of clearing or fencing scrubland and similar areas which provide harbourage for rabbits. Divisional pests staff also destroy rabbits on common or derelict land where no owner can be found who could be made responsible for doing the job. In the last resort if persuasion fails county agricultural executive committees under powers delegated to them by the Minister can make an order under the Pests Act, 1954, to designate an area a rabbit clearance area, and then all occupiers of agricultural land in the area are required to take the necessary steps to destroy the rabbits on their land.

In recent years the wood pigeon has become a serious pest in various parts of the country, more particularly in parts of eastern England where there is cover for it to nest in and grain for it to feed on.

The Infestation Control Laboratory has done considerable work on means for controlling this pest. At the moment the most promising line of attack seems to be the destruction of the eggs and young birds by the poking out of nests from the trees by means of long telescopic poles. An extensive survey in East Anglia showed that, although wood pigeons nest throughout the summer, 70 per cent of the young birds that are successfully reared leave their nests during the months of August and September, and that if nests are systematically destroyed late in July or early August and again six weeks later then the number of young that are reared can be reduced by nearly two-thirds.

There are already rabbit clearance societies in most areas where the wood pigeon is a serious nuisance, and Divisional Pests Officers have encouraged them to take on the task of nest destruction.

For effective control, however, nest destruction needs to be supplemented by organized shooting. At one time the Ministry made a grant of up to 50 per cent of the cost of cartridges for organized shoots. This has now, however, been replaced by a grant of 50 per cent towards expenses incurred by rabbit clearance societies in shooting not only wood pigeons but also members of the crow family such as rooks and jackdaws.

Research is being continually conducted into methods of control of other bird pests. Bullfinches, for example, can cause severe damage during the winter to the buds of gooseberries, apples, gages and plums and tests have been made of the efficiency of various repellents that can be sprayed on to the tree; scaring devices and trappings have also been investigated.

Local authorities (borough and district councils) are now under Part I of the Prevention of Damage by Pests Act, 1949, responsible for control of rats and mice. It is their duty to inspect premises (including farms) and investigate any complaints of the presence of these animals, and they may serve on owners and occupiers notices requiring them to destroy rats and mice on their premises and in default can enter and do the work themselves. The Ministry used to make a 50 per cent grant to the expenditure of local authorities on this service but this has now been absorbed into the general Exchequer grant to local authorities. The Ministry's only responsibilities now are to provide technical advice to local authorities and to protect government premises against rats and mice.

Under Part II of the Prevention of Damage by Pests Act, 1949, the Ministry is responsible for the control of insect and other pests of stored foodstuffs. All who manufacture, store, transport or sell food are required to report to the Ministry any signs of infestation by such pests, and the Department can then serve a notice requiring steps to be taken for the destruction of the pests by fumigation or otherwise and for precautions against reinfestation. In practice the Ministry relies on consultation and advice rather than statutory action to ensure that adequate precautions are taken against these pests.

The Department has a particular responsibility, however, for seeing that pests are not introduced in imported produce, and inspectors stationed at the main ports have a right of entry on ships to examine cargoes and holds. When they discover signs of infestation they may require the cargo to be treated to prevent further damage and spread of infestation, and they can also require empty ships' holds to be treated to prevent the infestation of new cargoes.

LIVESTOCK IMPROVEMENT

It is often claimed that Britain is the stud farm of the world, and certainly the best of our pedigree stock, cattle, sheep and pigs are the equal of those anywhere. On the other hand in the past a lot of our commercial stock has left much to be desired, and the Ministry is responsible for a number of measures for improving the standard of our livestock.

The quality of livestock can be most easily improved through the male animal, since each of these can produce many hundreds of offspring in the course of its life, or thousands with the assistance of artificial insemination. In the past there were complaints about the prevalence of the 'scrub' bull which a farmer might keep for getting his cows in calf, and therefore in milk, without regard to the quality of the progeny. In order to raise the general standards not only bulls but boars and stallions (with some exceptions) may now only be kept for breeding if they have been licensed after inspection by one of the Ministry's Livestock Husbandry Officers; stallions also have to pass a veterinary inspection. Appeals against the refusal of a licence are heard by independent referees chosen from panels nominated by the Breed Societies, the National Farmers' Union and the British Veterinary Association. Animals that fail to get a licence must be castrated or slaughtered. There is no similar licensing of rams, but in hill areas the Control of Rams Regulations, administered on the Minister's behalf by the county agricultural executive committees, ensure that only suitable rams are allowed, and at the right time of the year, on unfenced hill grazing land where more than one flock of ewes is running.

Nowadays nearly two-thirds of the calves born in England and Wales are conceived through artificial insemination. Bulls for this purpose are kept at thirty centres which between them now cover the whole of the country. After the semen has been collected it is diluted and either used fresh within two days or frozen and kept at a very low temperature, which enables it to be kept indefinitely. The staff based on the centres and associated sub-centres travel round in vans to inseminate the cows on the farm. The number of progeny that a bull can sire in this way is much greater than by natural mating. The general standard of the bulls standing at the centres is well above that of the animals available at a similar fee for natural mating and the system is therefore well adapted to raising the general standard of breeding of our cattle. Most of the centres are run by the Milk Marketing Board, but a number are run by farmers' co-operative societies and other organizations, and the Ministry itself runs a centre at Reading, primarily for purposes of research. All the centres are licensed and inspected by the Ministry, and no bull is allowed to be kept at a centre until after a special veterinary examination and unless it reaches a very much higher standard than required for an ordinary bull licence.

For various reasons artificial insemination is not very suitable for small beef herds in some parts of the country, more particularly the hill areas on the borders of England and Wales, and to ensure that superior sires are available for these herds, 'premium' grants are made to owners of suitable bulls who agree to make them available for the service of their neighbours' cows.

Many of the measures, apart from boar licensing, which the Ministry used to administer for the improvement of pigs, have now been taken over by the Pig Industry Development Authority (see Chapter X). For example, the Ministry has for over forty years been paying 'premiums' to owners of suitable boars, as with the similar scheme for bulls, to ensure that suitable sires were available for small pig breeders. The PIDA has now taken this scheme over and in fact increased the size of the grant. There is a demand for premium boars all over the country, since the artificial insemination of pigs has not yet been developed to a stage where it is as reliable and satisfactory as it is for cattle. The PIDA, however, as well as making grants to those cattle artificial insemination centres which also provide a service for pigs in financing further research in this subject.

In recent years the Department has established a series of stations for boar progeny testing, the capital cost of the stations being recovered from pig producers by a deduction from the guarantee payments for fat pigs. The principle of the scheme is that to assess the potentialities of a boar as a producer of good stock a number of his progeny by different sows are kept at the testing stations under standard conditions, and careful measurements are made of their rate of growth, food consumption and finally carcase quality. In this way genetic differences are revealed, and boars whose progeny show above average results on test can be retained for breeding. The scheme is operated by a National Pig Progeny Testing Board on which the PIDA is represented. The PIDA has now assumed financial responsibility for the scheme and is taking over the stations from the Government.

The PIDA has also taken over from the Department the national scheme of pig recording; members of the scheme are able to assess the standards of breeding and also of management in their herds by keeping suitable records of the sizes of litters, the weight of the pigs at different ages from birth onwards, mortality, and so on.

THE POULTRY STOCK IMPROVEMENT PLAN AND POULTRY PROGENY TESTING SCHEME

The successful poultry keeper today needs healthy stock which will convert feed into eggs or meat efficiently and economically. Some idea of the importance of this is given by the fact that whilst in 1949 about 100 eggs covered the cost of carrying a laying bird over its eighteen-month life cycle, today the number is about 165 eggs. Again, in the rapidly expanding industry of producing the young table birds known as 'broilers' a death rate of anything appreciably above 5 per cent in the short ten weeks' period of rearing can convert a profit into a loss.

The Poultry Stock Improvement Plan in England and Wales is run by the Ministry, with the assistance of an advisory committee, with the object of providing an assured source of good healthy stock. There are now over 3,750 hatcheries and other breeding establishments which belong to this voluntary plan and they provide about four-fifths of the birds raised both for egg production and for table poultry. To enable poultry farmers to know where they can obtain suitable stock the Ministry publishes each year a Register and County Lists of members of the plan, who are also entitled to use certification trade marks.

Before being admitted to the plan a member must comply with prescribed conditions as to husbandry standards, achievements of the breeding stock (in terms of production of eggs or of table birds as the case may be), and hygienic state of premises. The stock and premises are inspected by Poultry Advisory Officers of the National Agricultural Advisory Service. The stock must also pass blood tests for freedom from pullorum (b.w.d.) infection, and free veterinary advice is given by the Ministry's Veterinary Officers. Once a member is accepted into the plan his stock is blood tested by the Ministry regularly and if any disease is detected among his flock he may be required to suspend sales until it has been eliminated.

Members of the breeders' grade (egg production) are required to participate in the progeny tests for pure breeds conducted at the Ministry's three Progeny Testing Stations. Random samples of hatching eggs are taken from each member in this grade and sent to one of the testing stations where the birds, when hatched, are recorded for various traits such as egg production and mortality and their ability to transmit these characteristics to their offspring. The test covering the two generations takes nearly two and a half years.

The improvement in the standard of our poultry stocks which the plan has helped to bring about has been one of the important factors which have resulted in the increase in the figure of annual average egg production per bird from 154 for 1938 to about 184 today.

At the time of writing discussions are taking place with the industry with a view to revising the plan in the light of current conditions and transfering to the industry the responsibility for its running.

THE NATIONAL STUD

One rather unusual activity of the Ministry is the running of a stud farm of racehorses. This started in 1916 when the late Lord Wavertree offered to the nation his entire stud of thoroughbred horses at Tully in County Kildare. The Government accepted the gift and established the National Stud in order to encourage the breeding of the highest class of thoroughbred as foundation stock for the cavalry and other riding horses required at that time by the Army.

The Army of course no longer needs such horses except on ceremonial occasions. The Government, however, has continued to run the Stud for a rather different reason, namely to assist the breeding in this country of thoroughbred horses of the highest class. Exports of thoroughbreds probably amount to between £2 million and £2½ million a year. The industry is thus an important one but has to face keen competition from breeders in the United States and France. The continued success of British breeders depends on our retaining in this country sufficient of the small number of really first class stallions. As a stallion nowadays may cost anything from £100,000 upwards this is something beyond the reach of more than a handful of private breeders.

In 1943 the property at Tully was handed over to the Government of Eire under the Irish Treaty and the National Stud was transferred to Gillingham in Dorset, and additional premises were subsequently leased at West Grinstead in Sussex to provide accommodation for additional stallions and to grow feedingstuffs for both establishments.

The policy of the Stud, which was reviewed in 1954 by a committee under the chairmanship of Sir Percy Loraine, is to have at the Stud stallions of the highest quality available for private breeders and also to maintain there an establishment of breeding mares representative of some of the best blood lines. There are nowadays four stallions and between fifteen and twenty mares at the Stud.

The purchase and sale of the National Stud's bloodstock presents problems that are unusual by normal departmental standards. The market for the very highly priced horses is naturally limited. The top-class stallion provides the extreme illustration of this because the interest in these is international and prices may be determined by their earning capacity in countries where the incidence of taxation, or potential racing rewards, make stallion ownership more attractive than in Britain. The Minister is, therefore, advised by a small expert committee on proposals for the acquisition and disposal of blood-stock by the National Stud, other than sales of yearlings and foals which are normally by auction.

Horses bred at the Stud which are not required as potential breeding stock are sold as yearlings before they start their racing career. Those which are thought to be suitable for breeding have to be given the opportunity to prove themselves on the racecourse. The Ministry does not directly race these horses; they are leased to Her Majesty the Queen who defrays all the expenses of maintaining the horses during their racing life, apart from the cost of training. In return for the lease of the horses the Ministry receives one half of their net winnings.

In the short-run the breeding and racing of horses is clearly an uncertain business and successes are bound to be accompanied by failures. The judgement of those who direct the Stud's affairs can only be decided fairly over a period of years long enough for the results of chance to cancel out to a large extent. The Stud accounts are published, and the balance sheet at December 31, 1960, showed a cumulative profit of over £160,000 since 1917. The Stud also had assets worth about £630,000, and the capital amounts advanced by the Exchequer had been repaid. By the financial test, therefore, the Stud must be accounted a success.

The horses bred at the Stud include Blandford (sire of the four Derby winners, Barham, Blenheim, Trigo and Windsor Lad); Big Game (winner of the 2,000 Guineas and the Champion Stakes) and Sun Chariot (which won the 1,000 Guineas, the Oaks and the St Leger). The Stud has not yet bred a Derby winner, but the Ministry always lives in hopes.

CHAPTER VII

The Land

THE earliest of the direct forerunners of the present Department were bodies of statutory Commissioners established well over a hundred years ago to deal with such legal questions as the commutation of tithe and the inclosure of common land. Nowadays the Ministry is more concerned with measures for the improvement of land and making it more productive.

THE AGRICULTURAL LAND SERVICE

The Agricultural Land Service can be regarded as the counterpart of the National Agricultural Advisory Service in the field of estate management and similar work. It was established in 1948, but a good deal of its work is a continuation of that done previously by the Ministry of Agriculture's Land Commissioners, who were first appointed under the Small Holdings and Allotments Act of 1908 and were in fact the foundation for the new service. The service, like most of the other professional and technical services of the Ministry, is now organized locally in regions and divisions as explained in Chapter XVIII. Under its Director and Deputy Director at headquarters there are Regional and Divisional Land Commissioners supported by Senior Assistant and Assistant Land Commissioners, a total of about 200, all with professional qualifications of the Royal Institute of Chartered Surveyors, the Chartered Land Agents' Society, or the Chartered Auctioneers' and Estate Agents' Institute. There is a Chief Architect and Buildings Officer at headquarters with a staff of nearly 30 Farm Buildings Advisory Officers in the regions who hold professional architectural or surveying qualifications. Finally, the professional officers are assisted by about 120 non-professional Land Service Assistants, Clerks of Works and Draughtsmen.

The primary task of the National Agricultural Advisory Service as its name implies is giving advice to farmers, although its members also play an important part as technical advisers in connection with various grant and subsidy schemes, such as the Small Farmer Scheme, and other measures such as the Poultry Stock Improvement Plan and bull and boar licensing. With the Agricultural Land Service the emphasis is different. The service has to assist in the

H

administration of a wide range of schemes and statutes concerning the improvement, management, tenure and use of agricultural land. They also act for the Ministry in the purchase of any land required by the Department for such purposes as experimental husbandry farms and advice on its equipment. But that does not prevent it from undertaking a considerable amount of advisory work. For example, farm visits in connection with grant-aided schemes provide opportunities for members of the service to give general advice to farmers and landowners on problems of estate management, more particularly on the design, layout and construction of farm buildings and other fixed equipment. The advice given by the service does not include the provision of working drawings or specifications or the supervision of building work; for these the farmer or landowner will need to employ professional men in private practice.

IMPROVEMENT OF HILL FARMS

A large part of Great Britain consists of mountain, hill and heath land. It is poor land agriculturally but none the less important for our home produced supplies of meat, since on it are reared hardy sheep and cattle sold for fattening in the lowland areas.

These areas could not in the nature of things make any contribution to the war-time ploughing up campaign. It was rather a question of making the fullest use of the hill grazings. During the war subsidies were paid on hill sheep and hill cattle as a means of keeping production going in these areas, and these are still continued in a modified form.[1]

It was felt, however, that something more radical was needed if the farms in these areas were not to sink into decay. Two committees were appointed to consider the problems of hill sheep farming in England and Wales and in Scotland respectively. The reports of these committees[2] indicated that what was needed above everything else was the provision of fresh capital for buildings and fixed equipment on such farms on a scale not likely to be available from private sources. The Hill Farming Act of 1946 accordingly provided for grants of up to £4 million to defray one-half of the cost of comprehensive schemes for the improvement of hill farms, whilst the subsequent Livestock Rearing Act of 1951 extended somewhat the definition of land eligible for these improvement grants. It is now called 'livestock rearing land' and is defined as comprising land in an area consisting predominantly of mountains, hills or heath which is suitable for the breeding, rearing and maintenance of sheep or cattle

[1] See Chapter VI.
[2] Cmd. 6498 and 6494, 1944.

but which would not, even after improvement, be suitable to any material extent for dairy farming, the fattening of livestock or the growing of crops for sale. The 1951 Act and subsequent legislation increased the upper limit to the grants to £27 million (for the whole of the United Kingdom) and extended the period for making applications to 1963. It now seems likely that all this money will be needed, and that something like one-third of eligible farms will be improved.

The essence of the schemes is that they shall be sufficiently comprehensive to enable a farm to carry on for the future at a high level of efficiency. They can cover the improvement or even rebuilding of farmhouses and cottages, since people nowadays won't come to farm such land unless they can live in conditions that do not compare too unfavourably with those in urban areas. Schemes may provide for the application of lime and fertilizers to the land to bring it into good heart and also for its drainage. Additional buildings may be needed to house the extra stock which the improved land can carry, and again the land may need fencing. Farm roads and bridges may need to be improved to provide reasonable access to the farm.

The administration of this legislation has raised a variety of problems. First of all there was the question whether land was eligible under the statutory definition, or whether it was perhaps ruled out by the extent to which milk or crops for sale were produced on the farm; the test decided on here was 'what is the predominant use of the land?' Again, the need for a scheme to be comprehensive had to be reconciled with the requirement that its cost was likely to be reasonable in relation to the benefits to be derived from the improvements.

The working out of sensible solutions to these questions imposed a heavy task on the Agricultural Land Service who both advise the Ministry on the eligibility of proposals and frequently help applicants to get them into proper shape. In administering the Acts the Department has also drawn heavily, especially in the early days of the scheme, on the detailed knowledge of local farming conditions possessed by members of the county agricultural executive committees.

There are two other measures which benefit farmers in hill areas.

An improvement scheme can cover the improvement and repair of roads actually on the farm, but not of course any of the public highways which provide access to the farm, and in fact many of the unclassified public roads in upland areas which were not eligible for Ministry of Transport grants had either never been adequate for modern traffic or had been allowed to get into a derelict state through lack of adequate maintenance. Accordingly the Agriculture (Improvement of Roads) Act, 1955, authorized the Minister to make grants to highway authorities (county councils) up to a maximum of £4 million (Great Britain) towards the cost of improving unclassified or un-adopted roads in livestock rearing areas, where this was necessary in the interests of farming in such areas. The rate of grant is 65 per cent for unclassified roads, and 75 per cent for unadopted, and an additional 10 per cent is paid to some of the poorer county councils.

Another scheme which in practice is of benefit mainly to farms in hill areas is that for grants for the eradication of bracken. These grants can cover one-half of the cost of cutting the bracken by hand, of getting contractors to do it, or of the purchase of approved types of machine for this purpose. The scheme operates mainly in Scotland —grants in England and Wales are of the order of £1,500 per annum, or about one-tenth of the Scottish total.

THE FARM IMPROVEMENT SCHEME

As a result of the depressed state of agriculture in the inter-war years and war-time and post-war shortages comparatively little was spent on the maintenance, repair and improvement of the farm buildings and other landlords' equipment on many of our farms. Accordingly many were saddled with buildings that had been put up at a time when labour was much more plentiful and cheaper than it is today and were not at all suited to modern farming practices like the mechanized milking of cows and hygienic milk production and with inadequate facilities for storage of tractors and other machinery and for grain drying. The majority of government grants had been for current farming activities such as ploughing up and application of fertilizers, though there were of course some exceptions such as the grants for field drainage and water supplies and those just mentioned for the improvement of hill farms.

The Farm Improvement Scheme authorized by Part II of the Agriculture Act, 1957, was the first comprehensive measure designed to improve farming efficiency by government grants towards the cost of fresh capital equipment. It departed in a number of ways from that for grant aiding improvements to farms in the hill areas described earlier in this chapter. In the lowlands there is usually no question of completely reconditioning semi-derelict farms, but rather of improving items of equipment within a fairly acceptable existing framework. Accordingly the proposals submitted are not required to be comprehensive, and successive improvement proposals are accepted provided that each in turn meets the statutory require-ments. Also the Government felt that a grant of one-third of the approved cost would be adequate.

Proposals can be submitted for a farm anywhere in the United

Kingdom, provided it is one capable of giving a sufficient livelihood to an occupier reasonably skilled in husbandry. The list of eligible improvements is rather more restricted than under the scheme described in the previous section for the improvement of farms in the hill areas. Improvements to farmhouses and farm cottages for example are excluded from grant as the present scheme is essentially one for improving and cheapening production methods by the use of more modern buildings and equipment and there is not the same element of social need as in the other scheme. Under other legislation, however, the local housing authority can, subject to certain conditions, make grants for the improvement of dwelling-houses.

Eligible improvements must be such that a prudent landlord could be expected either to make himself or be willing to compensate a tenant for making. This condition was dictated mainly by the consideration that whereas generally speaking only one sort of farming is possible on a hill farm, the alternative being to let the land go derelict, in the rest of the country there may be quite a number of alternative methods of farming the land or indeed the land could often be used for some quite different purpose. The effect of the 'prudent landlord' test accordingly is to rule out buildings designed for intensive or factory type production of livestock such as broiler houses or specialist buildings designed for pig rearing and nothing else, since on the long term view such buildings might become useless if a new occupier (or indeed the same occupier, as the result of changes in the profitability of different types of farming) decided to switch to some other sort of enterprise. Again a farm is excluded if it seems unlikely to endure in its present state, e.g. if the farmer is renting separate parcels of land from a number of different owners. The expected life of any improvements, even without maintenance must not be less than fifteen years.

Grants can also be made under the 1957 Act towards the incidental costs of amalgamating two or more units, since there are many holdings which are not economic to run in their present form but which could be made economic if further land were available.

The 1957 Act authorized total grants of £50 million for proposals submitted over a period of ten years; the figures can be increased to £55 million and twelve years respectively with parliamentary approval.

The most important thing about the Farm Improvement Scheme is that it is intended for the long term improvement of our farms. One may reasonably hope that benefits from the current expenditure on capital equipment will be reflected in greater farming efficiency for the rest of this century and beyond.

CREDIT

It is convenient to cover agricultural credit in this chapter, since the aspect of this with which the Ministry is most directly concerned is loans for the purchase and improvement of agricultural land, including buildings and equipment.

The most important source of such loans nowadays is the Agricultural Mortgage Corporation. This body was established under the Agricultural Credits Act, 1928, and as its title suggests nearly all its loans are for the purchase and improvement of agricultural land, secured by a mortgage on such land. The Corporation's equity shareholders are the Bank of England and nine joint stock banks, whose branches act as its agents for obtaining business. The Exchequer is authorized to make interest-free loans to the Corporation's guarantee fund up to a limit now fixed at £5 million. The Corporation, however, gets the bulk of its capital by the issue of debenture stock, the amount of outstanding debentures at any time being limited under the Corporation's Memorandum of Association to ten times the sum of the share capital, guarantee fund and reserves. On March 31, 1961, the Corporation's total loans outstanding amounted to approximately £40¾ million. Total debenture stock outstanding at that date amounted to approximately £41 million, in addition to the interest-free government loans to the guarantee fund of £3,350,000. Two of the Corporation's Directors are appointed by the Ministry and one by the Treasury for so long as any part of the interest-free Exchequer loans is outstanding.

The main object for which the Corporation was established was to assist tenant farmers and others in buying their farms, but owners can also obtain loans for the improvement of their land by, for example, the erection and modernization of farm buildings. As an alternative to a mortgage, loans for such improvement can be obtained under the Improvement of Land Acts, 1864 and 1899. The security for the loan is not a mortgage but a rent charge on the land and the Ministry is required to certify (after inspection by a member of the Agricultural Land Service) that the increase in the rental value of the land arising from the improvement is not less than the annual cost of the service of the loan. Loans under this procedure are available not only from the Agricultural Mortgage Corporation but also from a statutory company, the Lands Improvement Company.

The only other form of agricultural credit with which the Ministry is directly concerned is the scheme for loans to smallholdings' tenants for working capital mentioned later in this chapter (p. 124).

The greater part of credit for farming is, however, provided by the joint stock banks and the agricultural merchants. Bank advances to 'agriculture', including advances to agricultural merchants and forestry, totalled some £357 million at August, 1960 (Great Britain). The amount of credit provided by agricultural merchants is of lesser magnitude but is known to be large.

The whole question of agricultural credit was reviewed by the Radcliffe Committee on *The Working of the Monetary System*[1] who were not able to find any obvious and serious gap in the provision of credit for credit-worthy agricultural borrowers which would justify the establishment of any new institutions in this field. In accordance with a recommendation of the Radcliffe Committee several of the joint stock banks now offer term loans to farmers which in effect guarantee that unlike an ordinary overdraft the loan will not be liable to be called in provided the farmer does not fall into arrears with his repayments and continues to farm efficiently.

The National Farmers' Union have also established an Agricultural Credit Corporation which guarantees bank loans to farmers who satisfy the Corporation that they require money for financing developments under an approved farm management programme and are able to carry it out effectively.

LANDLORD AND TENANT

Although nowadays a larger proportion of farmers than hitherto own their own farms, there are still over half who rent them or rent part of their land from a landlord. It is important for efficient farming of the land that the respective rights and obligations of the two parties should be defined clearly and unambiguously. This is something that should be done in the tenancy agreement, just as it is for the rental of a house or flat. In the past, however, many farms have in fact been held on very sketchy agreements, sometimes purely verbal, and difficulties have arisen in deciding such questions as whether the landlord or the tenant is responsible for the maintenance of particular buildings, and in settling up when the tenant leaves the holding for such things as improvements made by the tenant and the residual value of the manures he has applied to the land. Various Acts dating from 1908 have accordingly attempted to regulate the relationship between landlord and tenant in a satisfactory manner and to lay down what the position is on various points if they have not been explicitly covered in a tenancy agreement; these were consolidated in the Agricultural Holdings Act, 1948 (later amended by the Agriculture Act, 1958).

The same Act (following on war-time legislation and continuing provisions made in the Agriculture Act of 1947) gave the efficient

[1] Cmnd. 827 of 1959.

tenant farmer a considerably greater degree of security of tenure than is enjoyed by the tenant of ordinary dwelling-house or of business premises. This was felt to be necessary to ensure efficient farming of the land, since a farmer may not be willing to spend money on developing the productive capacity of his farm to the full if he knows he will be forced to leave it in a few years' time. Normally the landlord must give a minimum of twelve months' notice to quit and, except in certain circumstances, such as a breach by the tenant of his tenancy agreement, the tenant can object and the notice will not take effect unless the landlord can establish his claim for possession before the Agricultural Land Tribunal, an independent quasi-judicial body appointed by the Lord Chancellor. Accordingly an efficient tenant farmer can now normally plan on the basis that he will be left in undisturbed occupation of his farm provided he pays his rent regularly and observes the other conditions of the tenancy agreement. The Department may, however, in suitable cases sanction short-term tenancies of agricultural land of under a year in duration under which the tenant does not enjoy any special security of tenure. This would enable, for example, a landowner who has land on which he is planning to build in a few years' time to let it temporarily to a neighbouring farmer for grazing without the fear that when he is ready to take the land for building he will find himself saddled with a tenant whom he cannot get rid of.

Disputes between landlord and tenant may be referred to arbitration. Arbitration may take place on a wide range of matters, but the most common matter for dispute is the rent to be paid for the holding. The Minister is not a party to disputes between landlord and tenant and does not intervene in them. He may, however, be called upon to appoint an arbitrator where the parties cannot agree on the choice of one. A panel of arbitrators, from whom the Minister makes his appointment, is maintained by the Lord Chancellor. The panel consists of men of experience and standing in the professions of surveying, land agency and estate management. The Minister appoints on average some 300 arbitrators a year to settle disputes under the Agricultural Holdings Act, and many more are appointed by agreement between the parties.

UNIVERSITIES AND COLLEGE ESTATES ACT, 1925

The Minister as successor in title to the Copyhold Commissioners acts in effect as trustee for much of the land and securities owned by the Universities and Colleges of Oxford and Cambridge as well as the University of Durham and the Colleges of Winchester and Eton. Thus the Minister's consent is needed by these bodies for any sale of land and for the reinvestment of the proceeds, which are held in the Minister's name. The Agricultural Land Service advises on questions such as the proper price for land and the provision to be made by the university or college by way of a sinking fund where a reversionary interest is sold or capital money is invested in a depreciating asset such as a leasehold interest or a building with a short life.

This control has its origin in legislation passed in the last century in order to abate the rigours of certain statutes of Elizabeth I which prevented the colleges from selling land freehold; the numerous Acts were consolidated in 1925. The object of the Minister's control is to ensure that the colleges' investments are effectively managed and their value preserved for the benefit of posterity. A white paper on government policy in relation to Charitable Trusts, issued in 1955,[1] proposed that there should be discussions with the universities and colleges on whether it was necessary to retain these powers of supervision. The matter has been under discussion for some time, but no agreed conclusions have yet been reached.

AGRICULTURAL LAND OWNED BY THE MINISTER

During the war and subsequently the Department acquired some 193,000 acres of agricultural land in various ways to ensure its proper and efficient use for agriculture.

An Agricultural Land Commission was established under the Agriculture Act, 1947 to manage and farm agricultural land owned or requisitioned by the Minister and also to advise and assist him in matters relating to the management of agricultural land. The Commission does not normally farm any of the land entrusted to it by the Minister; its usual practice is to let it to suitable tenants after providing the buildings and other equipment necessary to enable it to be properly farmed. The Agricultural Land Service acts as the local land agents of the Commission for this and other purposes. The functions of the Commission in Wales are exercised by a Welsh Sub-Commission.

The acreage of land under the charge of the Commission has in recent years, however, been considerably reduced as a consequence of current government policy that such land should generally be sold as soon as it has been properly equipped and put in good working order. In particular since the Crichel Down inquiry of 1954 it has been government policy that land which has been compulsorily acquired and which is no longer required for government use should, so far as reasonably practicable, be offered back to the former owner or his successors.

[1] Cmd. 9538.

The special arrangements governing land acquired for planting by the Forestry Commission are described later in this chapter in the section on 'Forestry and Agriculture'.

SMALLHOLDINGS

'Three acres and a cow' was the slogan coined by the land reformer, Jesse Collings, some seventy-five years ago, and the idea of creating a class of peasant farmers to arrest the drift of workers from the land is one that has appealed to many in the past.

There is not the space, however, to trace in any detail the history of past measures for the provision of smallholdings, such as the large campaign, conducted mainly through county councils, to settle ex-servicemen on the land after the First World War. The current measures for the provision of statutory smallholdings can, however, be outlined. These are governed by Part IV of the Agriculture Act, 1947, which defines the purpose for which smallholdings are now to be provided as being to afford to persons with agricultural experience an opportunity of becoming farmers on their own account; in other words the present philosophy is that the smallholding is provided primarily as a stepping stone for the farmworker in the hopes that eventually he will do sufficiently well to move to a farm of his own, thus making the smallholding available for another farmworker.

There are now three categories of statutory smallholdings. First and most important are those provided by county councils with grants from the Ministry which cover three-quarters of the estimated losses incurred in providing the holdings.

County council smallholdings normally do not exceed fifty acres in size, save on poorer land, and they are normally worked without hired labour. There are three main types of council holding—dairy holdings, mixed holdings, and to a lesser extent and in suitable areas specialist market garden holdings, this last class of holdings usually being under ten acres in area, perhaps with a good deal of glass. A number of the holdings provided by county councils in earlier days were only sufficient to provide a part-time occupation for the tenant. Whilst it is recognized that such holdings are part of the established pattern of agriculture in some parts of the country, the Ministry is not now normally prepared to grant-aid the creation of new part-time holdings.

To acquire a large estate and then divide it and equip it for a number of statutory smallholdings each with its separate dwelling-house and farm buildings is today an expensive business. In a typical case the acquisition of the land and its equipment may work out at £10,000 to £12,000 per holding and the Ministry's contribution of 75 per cent of 'estimated net loss' to an average of some £200 a year spread over a period of up to eighty years. On the other hand a number of the holdings at present owned by county councils are still inadequately equipped for farming by modern standards. Accordingly in recent years the Department has generally been unwilling to agree to the payment of contributions for the creation of new smallholdings, and has encouraged county councils to devote the available resources to bringing the equipment on existing holdings up to a level capable of providing the tenant with a reasonable living. In 1961 county councils were providing some 16,400 holdings, of which 9,084 were full-time.

Secondly, the Ministry itself provides 275 full-time and 42 part-time holdings similar to those of the county councils on four estates at Bosbury in Herefordshire, Rolleston in Nottinghamshire, and Sutton Bridge and Holbeach in Lincolnshire. These started as part of the big campaign for the settlement of ex-servicemen on the land after the 1914–18 war, but are now reserved for letting to agricultural workers and the like.

The final class of statutory smallholdings are those managed by the Land Settlement Association. This body was established in 1934 with grants from the Commissioner for the Special Areas and from private sources to conduct an experiment in settling unemployed men on the land on smallholdings organized on the basis of centralized services. In the post-war days of full employment this concept of using land settlement as a means of rehabilitating unemployed workers from other industries has ceased to apply and the Land Settlement Association transferred its smallholdings to the Minister who then appointed the Association as his agent to manage them on his behalf. Most of the original settlers have retired and the holdings are now used for the same purpose as those provided by county councils, i.e. for letting to agricultural workers.

The Association now manage for the Minister eighteen smallholding estates in different parts of the country covering in all 7,400 acres and providing 835 smallholdings. Each consists of a block of land divided into smallholdings ranging from two to ten acres, together with an estate headquarters to provide the centralized purchasing, marketing and other services. Each smallholding is equipped with a dwelling-house, a heated glasshouse and a piggery and sometimes a battery house for poultry, the tenants themselves providing Dutch light structures (a kind of glasshouse made up of large sheets of glass in wooden frames) for raising horticultural crops, and other equipment. The tenants, in addition to buying most of their supplies from the Association and selling their produce through its marketing organization, can obtain under the scheme machinery on hire, technical advice, hire purchase facilities, accountancy service, a savings scheme and advice on the management of their finances. The centralized services are self-supporting being financed largely from charges made to the tenants.

Under Section 54 of the Agriculture Act, 1947, the Minister can make loans to tenants of statutory smallholdings up to an amount equal to 75 per cent of that required for the proper working of the holding.

In 1947 the Minister appointed a Smallholdings Advisory Council to advise on matters arising in connection with Part IV of the Agriculture Act, 1947, relating to smallholdings. The Council's Report made in 1949 was adopted generally for guidance to Smallholdings Authorities in carrying out their duties.

ALLOTMENTS AND DOMESTIC FOOD PRODUCTION

There has been legislation dealing with allotments since 1845 but the first important Act was the Smallholdings and Allotments Act, 1908, which made local authorities (borough, urban district and parish councils) responsible for providing allotments in accordance with local needs.

The allotments movement in its early days was a comparatively small one, fostered in the interests of what were first called 'the labouring poor' and later, in the 1908 Act, 'the labouring population'. The movement, however, received a big impetus from the war of 1914–18 and an even bigger one from that of 1939–45 with the Ministry's 'Dig for Victory' campaign. In the last war the number of allotments in England and Wales reached a peak figure of over 1,400,000 occupying some 142,000 acres which produced some $2\frac{1}{2}$ to 3 million tons of food. Numbers have now fallen to some 890,000 allotments on 91,000 acres of land (which is roughly the same as the pre-war figure).

The primary responsibility for providing allotments rests with the local authority and in peace-time the Ministry's role is a relatively limited one. The Minister's consent, however, is required before a local authority can divert to other uses land that has been acquired specifically for the provision of allotments, as well as for the compulsory acquisition of land for allotments and for the borrowing of money for the purchase or improvement of allotment land. More generally the Ministry encourages local authorities to live up to their obligations to provide allotments and to make reasonable provision in development plans under the Town and Country Planning Act, 1947.

It is becoming increasingly difficult, especially in urban areas, to find enough land for allotments in view of the high price of land and the competing demands for housing, schools, public and open spaces and the like. There are, however, few areas in England and Wales where the demand for allotments is not adequately met.

Vegetables and fruit from his allotment or garden are not the only food that the private citizen may produce in his spare time; he may also keep poultry, rabbits, pigs, goats, bees and the like. In 1951 the Minister appointed a National Council for Domestic Food Production under the chairmanship of one of the Parliamentary Secretaries to co-ordinate, in association with the government departments, the work of the various national organizations concerned with domestic food production in England and Wales, which are all represented on the Council as well as bodies such as the National Council of Social Service, the National Federation of Women's Institutes and the local authority associations.

Questions which the Council has considered in recent years include the improvement of local amenities by cleaning up allotment sites, and sheep trespass on allotments and gardens in South Wales. It has given advice to local authorities about the keeping of small livestock in council house gardens, and has published two booklets on domestic food production. It also stages exhibits at agricultural and horticultural shows.

Local education authorities provide evening classes and demonstrations for the instruction of domestic food producers. This, therefore, is something for which the Ministry is not directly responsible, but the local officers of the National Agricultural Advisory Service in practice give considerable assistance in this work.

LAND USE

One of the cardinal principles of the Government's land use policy is to protect productive agricultural land from being taken for other purposes if there is less productive land that can reasonably be used instead.

In 1942 the Coalition Government decided to set up a centrally co-ordinated system for comprehensive control of town and country planning with a view to securing the most appropriate development and use of land. This resulted in the passing of the Town and Country Planning Act, 1947, which is the basis of the Ministry's land use work.

The basis of current planning legislation is that, in general, planning consent is needed for development of land. Development is defined very comprehensively to include not only building on the land or carrying out operations such as mining or quarrying but a change in the use of the land, such as the taking of a field for a public open space. Certain forms of land use are, however, expressly excluded from this planning control, either in the 1947 Act itself or in orders made thereunder. One exception, very important for present purposes, is the use of land for agriculture or forestry. Again certain developments controlled by government departments under Statute, such as the determination by the Ministry of Transport of the route for a trunk road, do not come under the normal planning control, but approval by the department is taken as the equivalent of planning consent.

The Minister of Housing and Local Government is responsible for the administration of planning legislation. Apart from making the various statutory rules and regulations which fill in the details of the administrative framework within which the local planning authorities have to work he has certain powers to influence their operations.

When the 1947 Act came into operation planning authorities, i.e. county councils and county borough councils, had to submit to the Minister their development plans which show their intentions as to the use of land throughout their area; the plans may also designate land which is to be subject to compulsory acquisition for various purposes. By consulting these plans members of the public are able to see the likely pattern of development in their neighbourhood and to form an opinion whether any private projects they may have for using land will be compatible with this pattern. A farmer or land-owner can thus discover whether his property may be threatened in the plan by development of one kind or another and can make his arrangements accordingly. Generally if his land is left 'white' in the plan he will be able to count on being left to farm or manage it undisturbed for the period of the plan. There may be unforeseen developments which the plan cannot provide for but these are the exception. The original development plans covered a period of about twenty years up to 1971; plans come up for review every five years and the period may be extended to 1981. Before approving a develop-ment plan with or without modifications the Minister of Housing and Local Government has to consider any objections or repre-sentations which have been made to him and will normally hold a public inquiry. Approval of a development plan does not, however, in itself convey planning permission for the proposals it contains and specific permission is still needed for each particular proposal for development.

Planning permission is given by the local planning authority, but county councils have delegated much of the day to day work to municipal boroughs and urban and rural district councils. Anyone aggrieved at being refused planning permission may appeal to the Minister, who may get one of his inspectors to hold a local inquiry before giving his decision. Secondly, the Minister on his own initiative can 'call in' a planning application, i.e. take it out of the hands of the planning authority from the start. This might be done with a controversial proposal for development of national importance which needs to be looked at in a wider than local context.

When the granting of permission to a planning application would result in a substantial departure from the development plan the planning authority is required to refer the application to the Minister of Housing, who may either call it in for his own decision, direct the planning authority to refuse consent or indicate that he does not wish to intervene.

The Town and Country Planning legislation does not mention the Minister of Agriculture, Fisheries and Food, but he and his department are naturally very much involved in the practical administration of that legislation. The part that the Ministry plays in the safeguarding of good agricultural land is in fact a good example of the way in which the Department may be very closely involved in questions affecting the industries with which it deals, even when these questions are the statutory responsibility of another department.

Planning authorities consult the local members of the Agricultural Land Service in the first instance on the effect on agricultural land both of draft development plans and of individual applications for planning consent.

The planning authority is not obliged to accept the land commissioner's advice. If, however, the land commissioner and the planning authority are unable to reach agreement about the balance that should be struck between agricultural and other considerations the land commissioner would refer the matter to Ministry headquarters who would then consult the Ministry of Housing and Local Government on whether, for example, the application should be called in.

The land commissioner also represents the Ministry at public inquiries into appeals against refusal of planning permission when the refusal was based substantially on his advice and the appellant, or exceptionally the planning authority, asks for his attendance. He may similarly have to give evidence at inquiries into planning proposals which would cause considerable damage to agriculture and which for this or other reasons have been called in by the Minister of Housing and Local Government.

The basic concept of steering development on to land that is of the least value agriculturally is a simple one; to give effect to it in development plans or individual cases is often by no means simple.

Assessment of the relative value of different parcels of agricultural land is comparatively easy for the expert, though even here there may be room for a difference of opinion; land may be valuable not so much for the intrinsic quality of the soil or the standard of cultivation but because it is needed for the economic running of a particular holding. It is, however, often much more difficult to balance the agricultural value of the land against other planning considerations that may have to be taken into account, such as the social and other advantages of putting a housing estate or a factory in a particular place or the extra cost of development on poorer land. Good agricultural land is very often the easiest and cheapest to develop; it is generally fairly level and well drained and it may often be the most conveniently placed of the various alternatives.

The land commissioner, therefore, has not only to be an expert in questions of estate management and farming; he must also be well versed in general planning technique and practice, and be able to understand and appraise the arguments in favour of development on good agricultural land and to decide whether the agricultural objections ought to be pressed despite the other advantages of the proposal.

The Land Use Division of the Ministry at headquarters formulates general instructions for the guidance of the Agricultural Land Service; these have to take account of the need for consistent decisions in the local organization throughout the country, whilst leaving sufficient flexibility to enable the bulk of the more routine work to be dealt with locally. The instructions have to be sufficiently comprehensive to avoid a multitude of references to headquarters, but not so voluminous that they are never read; above all they must be sufficiently adapted to the practical facts of life in the administration of planning legislation.

The more important case work has to be dealt with at headquarters though naturally in the light of advice from the local members of the ALS and the Regional Controllers. Examples are consideration of alternative sites for the housing of the 'overspill' from London and the other large 'conurbations'. Such an exercise may extend to two or more of the Ministry's regions and would certainly require the weighing of the advantages and disadvantages of a number of alternatives.

The Ministry is also consulted by other departments on their proposals for taking and developing land, e.g. for defence purposes, and also about the planning aspects of proposals of the local authorities acquiring land, often by compulsory purchase, for housing, schools and the like. In all this work the same principles apply as with normal applications for planning permission; that is to say the Ministry endeavours to ensure that, when there is any choice, it is the land of least agricultural value which is taken and also that no more land is taken than is reasonably necessary. The Ministry also keeps in touch with the defence departments with a view to seeing that wherever practicable their land remains in agricultural use. For example, it is generally possible to arrange that land taken for firing ranges is still farmed, with suitable arrangements for moving any livestock out of the danger area when necessary.

No application for planning permission for the erection or enlargement of a factory or other industrial building with a floor space greater than 5,000 square feet can be considered unless the applicant has obtained a certificate from the Board of Trade to the effect that the proposed development is consistent with the proper distribution of industry. The Department is represented on the Board of Trade's Regional Distribution of Industry Panels which considers the applications for such certificates, so that the panels may be fully aware of any relevant factors affecting agricultural, fisheries or food interests.

MINING AND QUARRYING

Houses, schools, roads and the like are not the only forms of development which make demands on agricultural land. Land is still needed for opencast coal production, though not on so large a scale as a few years ago. Its use for this purpose is now governed by the Opencast Coal Act, 1958, but the Ministry continues to undertake the agricultural after-treatment of sites as agents of the National Coal Board. In certain parts of the country land is worked for ironstone by opencast methods. Land is also needed for quarrying for materials such as stone, gravel, clay (for brick-making) and limestone.

During the war and the post-war period our supplies of deep mined coal have had to be supplemented by opencast exploitation of coal seams lying near the surface. In this method instead of sinking a pit shaft the whole of the earth on top of the seam of coal is first removed then the coal itself is extracted by mechanical shovels and the earth is replaced.

In the early days of opencast coal production the land was often left in a poor condition and unfit for agricultural use. Members of the Agricultural Land Service and of the National Agricultural Advisory Service have, however, in the light of experience of those early days, been able to devise a technique for the restoration of agricultural land after opencast operations which normally ensures comparatively little permanent loss of fertility. One important part of this technique is that the precious top few inches of fertile topsoil are removed, stored and subsequently replaced separately instead of being mixed with the underlying layers of infertile clay, etc. The soil

I

must be generously manured, particularly with nitrogen and phosphate. Again, it needs to be properly drained and it is often necessary to wait a few years for the land to settle down again before the new tile drains are laid. Finally, it may often be necessary to put the land through a special crop rotation to restore fertility.

Accordingly it has been the practice for the land commissioner to agree with the local representatives of the Ministry of Power and of the National Coal Board the terms on which 'clearance' was given for taking agricultural land. These include conditions for the separate removal, storage, and ultimate replacement of the topsoil and the subsoil. Wherever possible the Ministry has tried to ensure that the whole of any farm was not taken at one time for opencast operations but that sufficient was left to enable the farmer to continue to farm, whilst receiving compensation rental from the National Coal Board for the rest of the land.

When the coal had been extracted and the soil and topsoil replaced under the surveillance of the Ministry's field officers then the land would be farmed for a period of up to five years by the Land Service, the farmer continuing during this period to receive compensation rental from the Coal Board and often having the opportunity of renting the grass keep.

In addition to opencast coal, land has also to be taken for the opencast working of ironstone and the surface working of sand, gravel and the like and for the disposal of industrial waste and refuse. The local officers of the ALS are consulted on planning applications under the procedures already described. In addition to endeavouring to steer such development on to land of least agricultural value the Ministry is concerned to ensure that wherever possible planning conditions are laid down to secure the proper restoration of the land for agriculture after surface working. Subsequent agricultural use may, however, be out of the question either because the workings are too deep and are filled with water, or because materials for filling are not available.

For all mineral workings other than opencast ironstone the developers carry out this restoration work (levelling, soil replacement, drainage) at their own expense, and the later agricultural treatment of the land is left to the owners and occupiers. For the restoration of opencast ironstone land in accordance with the planning conditions the mineral developers may in certain circumstances obtain assistance from the Ironstone Restoration Fund established by the Mineral Workings Act, 1951 (to which the mineral producers, the royalty owners, and the Exchequer contribute). Assistance may be given also for the levelling and restoration of derelict land which was worked before the introduction of planning control. The

Minister of Housing and Local Government authorizes these payments for work required before the land can be used for agriculture. The 1951 Act also authorizes the Minister of Agriculture to make arrangements with owners and occupiers and to pay grants to them for the agricultural treatment of restored land. These responsibilities are discharged in the field by the ALS.

FORESTRY AND AGRICULTURE

The experience of the last world war led to measures for maintaining an agricultural industry appreciably greater than pre-war. Similarly, it led the Government to decide that we ought to become more self sufficient in our supplies of timber.

Forestry, of course, is a much longer term process than agriculture. Hardwood trees such as the oak and the beech take a hundred, or even a hundred and fifty, years to mature, and even the quicker growing softwoods take upwards of sixty years. In these days there are not many individual landowners with the money or the land for growing trees on a large scale, and since the end of the First World War their efforts have had to be assisted and supplemented by the State. To that end the Forestry Act, 1919, provided for the appointment by the Crown of a Forestry Commission with the duty of promoting afforestation and the production and supply of timber in the United Kingdom. This it did mainly by the purchase and leasing of land for afforestation, but it also gave grants and advice to private landowners. No Minister was made responsible for the Commission's work but there was always on the Commission a Member of Parliament who spoke for it in the House of Commons. The Commission was financed by Exchequer grants to a Forestry Fund. By 1939 the Commission had planted close on 370,000 acres; private owners, with the aid of Commission grants, had planted over 125,000 acres.

Following on a report which the Commission prepared during the war on post-war forest policy[1] the Government decided that afforestation should proceed at a considerably more rapid pace than it had before the war. The Commission have in fact planted some 850,000 acres in Great Britain since 1945 and the total acreage of their plantations, including those they have acquired, is now (September, 1961) 1,350,000 acres.

Close co-operation between the Commission and the Ministry was clearly called for to enable this enlarged programme of afforestation to proceed with the least disturbance to agricultural production. The constitutional position of the Forestry Commission had in any

[1] The Report on Post-War Forest Policy, 1943. Cmd. 6447.

event been altered somewhat by the Forestry Act of 1945. Although members of the Commission were still appointed by the Crown, Members of Parliament were no longer eligible and the Commission were required to comply with any directions given them by the Minister of Agriculture and Fisheries and the Secretary of State for Scotland. Whilst the Minister thus became in effect the Forestry Minister for England and Wales it did not mean that officers of the Ministry advised him on forestry matters; the Minister, however, could in the last resort resolve any questions at issue between the Ministry and the Commission.

The 1945 Act also transferred to the Minister both the Commission's power to acquire land (in England and Wales) and the properties already vested in them. Proposals to acquire land under the Forestry Acts thus involve consultation between the Ministry and the Forestry Commission. This is mostly carried out locally with the Agricultural Land Service acting on behalf of the Ministry. Much of the land acquired under the Forestry Acts is existing woodland or felled woodland or scrub and, where bare land is involved, there will often be no agricultural objection to tree planting. But inevitably there will be occasions when the arguments for retaining land in agriculture and for planting trees are finely balanced. It is not merely a question of ensuring that it is the land of least value for agricultural production that is taken for afforestation; in their choice of areas for planting, the Departments seek ways of causing least disturbance to the farming of adjacent land. For example, in hill areas there will often be a belt of land along the side of a hill that agriculturally can never be much more than rough grazing but which may be eminently suitable for afforestation; however, it is important to avoid a solid band of forest all along the hill side without corridors to enable the sheep to get up from the fertile valley to make use of the grazing on the hill tops above the planted areas. Again, in an area of mixed forestry and farming the aim is that land left for agriculture should be such that it can be farmed in balanced economic units or amalgamated with other land to that end. Also, no land ought to be left unusable if this can reasonably be avoided.

Much of the land acquired under the Forestry Acts involves only parts of properties, and so far as possible acquisitions are limited to land which is needed for forestry. Where estates or whole properties come on the market it may not be possible to limit acquisition in this way, but whole properties are not acquired unless it is agreed that a substantial amount of the land can be put at the Commission's disposal. Where, however, it is decided that any part of the land ought to be retained in agriculture, this part is either sold or placed under the management of the Agricultural Land Commission.

COMMON LAND

Today many of us think of commons as essentially public open spaces either in urban areas, such as Clapham Common and Wimbledon Common, or on the outskirts of villages and in the neighbourhood of large towns. Actually the greater part of our commons are in remote rural areas. Of the 1½ million acres or so of common land that remains in England and Wales today nearly one-third is situated in Wales, and approximately two-thirds of the English common land is situated in Cumberland, Westmorland, Yorkshire and Devonshire.

To understand the reason for the Ministry's present responsibilities for common land we must go back to mediaeval times when the greater part of the land of this country was subject to some form of right of common.

In the simplest mediaeval village, particularly in the south and centre of England, the land would be held by the Lord of the Manor. However, apart from the Lord's own demesne, which he would treat as his private property, the land would be cultivated in association by the villagers, who between them regulated the use to which it was put. First of all there would be two or three open arable fields, in each of which each villager held one or more strips. All the strips in each field had to be cultivated in the same manner and it was usual to have a three course rotation in which in any year one field might be, say, under wheat, the second under barley, oats, beans or peas and the third would be lying fallow. Then there would be common meadows from which each of the villagers could take a certain amount of hay. The villagers could turn out their beasts into the common meadows after the hay harvest, or into the open field that was lying fallow until such time as it was needed for cultivation for the following year's harvest. Finally the uncultivated waste of the manor was available to the villagers or commoners throughout the year not only for pasturage but for such purposes as the gathering of fuel. The system was regulated throughout by communal decision arrived at at the manorial court presided over perhaps by the Lord of the Manor or his representative. Here customs interpreted by the villagers in the court determined what crops were to be grown and in what order, what beasts could be grazed and how many, and the way in which other rights of common such as taking of peat or sticks for firewood or timber for farm equipment and the like were to be exercised.

Whilst this system was well suited to a relatively primitive standard of agriculture, it had many inconveniences and disadvantages which became increasingly apparent with the development of agricultural techniques. The pace of any agricultural development could be held up by the need for common consent to any changes in methods of cultivation; root crops and clover could not be introduced as long as the arable fields were given over to common grazing for part of the year, disease was more liable to spread among stock on commons than on enclosed land, and the improvement of breeds was difficult. There were, of course, considerable changes in the pattern of agriculture from early mediaeval to early modern times as a consequence of such developments as the attractions of sheep rearing for woollen cloth and the demand of a growing population for more food for sale. One of the resulting changes was the gradual transfer of land from common use into full individual ownership by a process of inclosure. This reached its peak in the eighteenth and first half of the nineteenth century when some six million acres or so of waste and of open fields were inclosed. The inclosure was normally effected by private Acts of Parliament, under which Commissioners were appointed to divide and allot the land.

This procedure was put on a more uniform basis by the general Inclosure Act of 1845 which established a body of Inclosure Commissioners with powers to frame and present to Parliament Provisional Orders for inclosure, thus avoiding the delay and expense involved in obtaining special local Acts of Parliament.

Whilst the 1845 Act was designed to facilitate inclosure, it also reflected the growing public concern at the loss of open spaces around the growing industrial towns, and also at the hardship which inclosure frequently caused to the poorer commoners. The Commissioners were, therefore, required, when reporting to Parliament on applications for inclosure, to have regard to 'the health, comfort and convenience of the inhabitants of any cities, towns, villages or populous places' nearby and to the private interests of the commoners and others. After the passing of the Commons Act of 1876 the Commissioners not only 'had regard' to those considerations but required also to be satisfied that inclosure would be for the benefit of the neighbourhood.

The Minister of Agriculture, Fisheries and Food has now inherited the functions of the Inclosure Commissioners. Inclosure under the Provisional Order procedure of the 1876 Act has become for practical purposes a dead letter, but the Minister has further responsibilities under subsequent Acts. We shall only describe the Department's present responsibilities in general terms, without attempting to specify all the statutes relating to common land.

One general point to be made at the outset is that although the Minister is sometimes regarded as the guardian of common land, he is not responsible for taking action against infringements of the law.

Anyone with an interest who considers that there has been unlawful encroachment on a common can bring a civil action in the Courts, which can order the removal of any unauthorized buildings, etc. Generally the Minister's only function is, where he thinks it right, to give his consent for actions which would otherwise, under the statutes, be unlawful.

Inclosure of common land in its historic and legal sense is nowadays most infrequent. The procedure tends to be long and expensive. When, in 1957, a large area of Winfrith Heath in Dorset had to be taken for an atomic research station, a special Act of Parliament was necessary to ensure that common rights were properly extinguished.

Most applications to the Minister are under Section 194 of the Law of Property Act, 1925, for the erection on the common of fences, or buildings such as a bus shelter or a cricket pavilion; or under the Acquisition of Land (Authorization Procedure) Act, 1946, for land required for highways purposes.

The Minister's approval again is required to schemes prepared by the local authority for the regulation and management of a common as a place of public recreation under the Commons Act, 1899. The schemes provide for the expenditure of money on the drainage, levelling and improvement of the common and for the making of byelaws and regulations for the prevention of nuisances and the preservation of order.

The procedure in all those cases is broadly the same. The Minister causes the proposal to be advertised and invites objections. If necessary there is a public inquiry into any objections, conducted perhaps by an officer of the Ministry's Legal Department, after which the Minister announces his decision.

With the serious shortage of land in England and Wales there have in recent years been suggestions that better use might be made of our common land for agricultural production and forestry and perhaps for industrial and urban development. During the war the Minister was in fact able under emergency powers to sanction arrangements for the cultivation of various commons either by the war agricultural executive committees or by associations of commoners or sometimes, in towns, as allotments. Cultivation and improvement, however, is much more difficult for those with an interest in the common, whether as owner of the soil or as commoner, to arrange in peace-time owing to uncertainties about the legal position and the disappearance of the machinery through which those with such interests could co-operate together. Proposals for making better agricultural use of a common may be held up because of uncertainty whether all the remaining commoners whose consent is necessary (and sometimes the owner of the soil) have been traced. In addition to the use of common land for pasture and public recreation, many commons are also in use for military training and as water gathering grounds.

In December, 1955, a Royal Commission was appointed under the chairmanship of Sir Ivor Jennings 'to recommend what changes, if any, are desirable in the law relating to common land in order to promote the benefit of those holding manorial and common rights, the enjoyment of the public, or, where at present little or no use is made of such land, its use for some other desirable purpose'.

The Commission in their report published in 1958[1] recommended that, as the last reserve of uncommitted land in England and Wales, common land ought to be preserved in the public interest. The public interest, it considered, included both the creation of wider facilities for public access and an increase in the productivity of the land. The Commission's seventy recommendations were designed to carry out these principles. They proposed the extension of public access to commons and of schemes of management and improvement for public enjoyment or increased productivity. To protect the rights of the public, owners of commons, and commoners, it also recommended that claims to rights in respect of commons be registered, disputed claims being referred to legally-qualified Commons Commissioners. Other matters which the Report dealt with included the vesting of 'unclaimed' commons, the vesting and regulation of village greens, roadside waste, litter, animals straying on the highways from commons, and parking on commons.

The Government has since been consulting with the numerous bodies concerned with these recommendations. On November 6, 1961, the Minister of Agriculture, Fisheries and Food announced in Parliament that legislation would be prepared for a scheme for the registration of common land, generally on the lines recommended by the Royal Commission. It is hoped that registration, besides being desirable in itself, will pave the way for action on the remaining recommendation of the Royal Commission.

LAND DRAINAGE

The Ministry has two sets of responsibilities for land drainage. First of all it provides grants for the drainage of farm land, this being combined with advice to landowners and farmers on their drainage problems and also (nowadays on a limited scale) it operates a contract service for the drainage of farm land. Secondly, the Department has an oversight over the work of the authorities responsible for arterial drainage and sea defences, such as river boards and internal drainage boards, and makes grants for certain of their improvement works.

[1] Cmd. 462

Farm Drainage

Good drainage is essential to the fertility of agricultural land for a number of reasons. Well drained land warms up earlier in spring, can be cultivated earlier, and generally grows much better crops. Good drainage encourages root development and thus enables the plant to withstand drought better later in its period of growth.

There are two ways of getting the surplus water off the field (under-drainage). The first method is to lay a few feet below the surface a series of lines of porous cylindrical pipes known as tiles through which the water drains away. An alternative or supplement to the tile is mole drainage carried out by a special plough which bores a cylindrical hole some two feet below the soil.

Mole drainage alone is infrequent; it is generally used to help to get the water into the tile drain. The drains need to open into a farm ditch to carry the water to the main land drainage system of the area.

Grants of 50 per cent of the cost of approved schemes of farm drainage (both under-drainage and the construction or improvement of ditches) have been available since 1940, and these are now authorized permanently by the Agriculture (Miscellaneous Provisions) Act, 1954. Grants are now administered by the divisional offices of the Ministry, individual schemes being approved after examination by the Divisional Drainage and Water Supply Officer and his assistants; in practice the Ministry's drainage staff are generally called on to give a good deal of advice to farmers and landowners in devising a technically sound scheme. In spite of the long period over which grants have been available (and the installation of a drainage system for any field is only grant aided once) thousands of new schemes continue to come forward each year, and annual grant expenditure is of the order of £2 million.

During and after the war the Ministry and county committees operated a service for the draining of private land on repayment and also for restoring land that had been worked for opencast coal. This service now only operates in eleven out of the thirty-two divisions, and in three of these operations are confined to opencast site restoration work.

Arterial Drainage and Flood Prevention

It is not sufficient to get the water off the field and into the farm ditch; it has to be carried away from there to the sea. Again agricultural land, and indeed any land, may need protection from flooding. This often is something the individual landowner and farmer cannot undertake and some form of public authority is essential. Starting in 1225 when Henry III empowered the Bailiff and Jurats of Romney Marsh to undertake drainage works for the benefit of the farmers on the Marsh, there has been a long succession of authorities established to see to the drainage of different parts of the country. For present purposes the most important are comprised in the current two-tier system of public authorities, namely, river boards, responsible for 'main rivers', and internal drainage boards, who attend to local drainage.

Any large river and the area draining into it normally cuts across county and other administrative boundaries, and the basic principle of the River Boards Act, 1948, was to bring each river system or group of river systems in England and Wales under the control of a single authority—the river board—drawing its revenue from the whole area draining into the rivers for which it is responsible. The river boards cover between them the whole of England and Wales, apart from the Thames and Lee Catchment Areas and the London area.

River boards are responsible for a good many other things relating to their rivers besides drainage and to give a coherent picture it is necessary to refer briefly to these other functions, some of which are the concern of the Ministry of Housing and Local Government rather than the Ministry of Agriculture, Fisheries and Food. A board's functions for the most part fall under five headings—

1. *Land Drainage and Sea Defence.* It is with these responsibilities of river boards that we are mainly concerned in this chapter. River boards took over the duties of the catchment boards established under the Land Drainage Act, 1930. Two catchment boards, however, survive, namely the Thames Conservancy and the Lee Conservancy, and references to the drainage activities of river boards in this chapter apply equally to those of these two catchment boards.

2. *Fisheries.* The boards have various responsibilities for the regulation of salmon and freshwater fisheries which are described in Chapter XII.

3. *Pollution.* The boards took over responsibilities for protecting rivers from pollution which previously had been exercised by local authorities and joint boards and joint committees of local authorities. On these questions the river boards are responsible to the Minister of Housing and Local Government.

4. *Conservation of water resources.* Generally river boards have the duty, in exercising their other functions, to conserve so far as practicable the water resources of their areas, and may carry out schemes for the measurement and recording of rainfall and the flow and volume of rivers and streams. This again is primarily a matter for the Ministry of Housing and Local

Government, though some aspects of it are inseparable from land drainage.

5. *Control of navigation* is normally the responsibility of some other authority but some river boards have had transferred to them by ministerial order the responsibilities of these other authorities.

The number of members of a river board normally does not exceed forty. The standard pattern is that one member is appointed by the Minister of Agriculture, Fisheries and Food and the Minister of Housing and Local Government jointly ('the Ministers'), between three-fifths and two-thirds of the remainder are appointed by councils of counties and county boroughs whose areas are included wholly or in part in the river board area, and the rest by the Minister of Agriculture, Fisheries and Food to represent drainage boards and fishery interests respectively. Where the responsibilities of a board for navigation are sufficiently important a member may also be appointed by the Minister of Transport.

The river boards get their income almost entirely from precepts on the counties and county boroughs and internal drainage boards in their areas. The Ministry can make grants, as described below, towards the cost of new works and improvements.

The drainage work that a river board can do has until recently been confined to what is called the 'main river', which in practice means any watercourse that the board with the Ministers' approval wishes to take under its control. At present there are over 16,000 miles of 'main river'.

Internal drainage boards look after various smaller watercourses not included in the 'main river' in low-lying areas which are subject to flooding or where the agricultural land is particularly dependent on local drainage works. There are approximately 400 drainage boards, most of them in eastern England. Many of the boards are in the Fens where they look after the artificial drainage channels which are a distinctive feature of that part of the country and provide and maintain the pumps necessary in many places to get the water off the land into the larger drains and rivers.

Drainage boards are elected bodies which can levy drainage rates on the owners and occupiers of land in the drainage district. They may get grants from the Ministry for new works and improvements as described below.

River boards exercise a general supervision over the drainage of the whole of their catchment areas, and in particular they may give such directions as they consider reasonable for the guidance of any internal drainage boards. In practice, of course, river boards prefer to influence drainage boards by less formal means than the issue of statutory directions. New drainage boards can now only be created or existing boards abolished or amalgamated on the initiative of the river board, who may submit to the Minister a scheme for such purposes. A river board can also petition the Minister to make an order transferring to it the powers, duties, liabilities and property of the drainage board, so that the river board becomes in fact the drainage board for that drainage district.

The drainage by-laws of both river boards and drainage boards require the approval of the Minister, as do the rating orders of drainage boards and any proposals of a river board for taking control over additional lengths of river. The Minister, jointly with the Minister of Housing and Local Government, has default powers in relation to river boards which so far have never been exercised. The Minister's power to make grants to drainage authorities does, however, in practice give the Department an opportunity of influencing their capital works.

Whilst river boards and drainage boards have to finance their expenditure on the maintenance of the main rivers and smaller watercourses wholly out of their precepts and rates respectively, the Ministry can make grants towards the cost of new works or works of improvement such as enlarging of channels, strengthening of banks and building of pumping stations. Grants to river boards are at rates which vary from board to board according to their financial circumstances. The rates depend upon a number of factors including the total rateable value of the property in the areas on which boards can precept; a river board for a predominantly agricultural area is naturally 'poorer' than one for an area which includes a substantial proportion of urban property, and thus is likely to qualify for a higher rate of grant.

River boards are also responsible for protecting low-lying land from flooding from the open sea or from tidal action in estuaries, and such sea defence works are similarly eligible for capital grants. Normally the maximum rate of grant is 80 per cent for inland waters and 85 per cent for tidal and sea defences. Since the passing of the Land Drainage Act, 1930, to June 30, 1961, grants amounting to nearly £45 million have been paid or approved to catchment boards and their successors the river boards towards the cost of capital works amounting to over £70 million. (This does not include grants of £26 million for restoring sea defences damaged by the East Coast surge of 1953 referred to later.) Grants to drainage boards and other local drainage authorities are authorized by the Agriculture Act, 1937, at a rate of 50 per cent. The total amount of grants approved since the inception of the Act up to June 30, 1961, was nearly £8½ million.

The new works and improvements executed by river boards are by
no means solely for the benefit of agricultural land. A board has to
consider the drainage of its area as a whole, including the protection
of built up areas from flooding. No rigid distinction is possible, since
any particular improvement to a main river may reduce the risk of
flooding in rural and urban areas alike.

Outside internal drainage districts the farm ditch is normally
separated from the main river by intermediate watercourses which
up till now have not been the responsibility of any drainage authority.
Neglect of these intermediate watercourses can nullify much of the
value of draining the farm land. This problem has now been tackled
in the Land Drainage Act of 1961. The essence of the new scheme is
that river boards will henceforth be able to accept responsibility for
the improvement and maintenance of intermediate watercourses
upon which they consider work is necessary. They are empowered to
levy drainage charges to enable them to undertake this additional
work. First there can be a general drainage charge levied on farmers
outside internal drainage districts. This will be roughly equivalent to
the amount paid by the general ratepayer for land drainage in a
river board's area; at present, agricultural land outside internal
drainage districts makes no contribution to drainage works. Where
additional drainage work in the interests of agriculture is necessary
the river boards can levy, in addition to the general charge, a special
drainage charge. This will also be borne by agricultural land outside
internal drainage districts, and is to be spent on intermediate watercourses specified in the schemes for levying the charge.

The above gives a picture of river boards and drainage boards looking after the drainage of their respective areas, with the Ministry in
the background exercising a certain amount of remote control. In
practice the Department both at headquarters and through its drainage engineers stationed throughout the country keeps in close touch
with these drainage authorities.

From time to time the Department is called upon to take more
positive action when widespread flooding occurs which affects a
number of river boards and calls for action beyond the resources of
the individual boards. This occurred, for example, in the spring of
1947 when heavy rain coinciding with a thaw after weeks of snow and
frost caused many rivers, particularly in eastern England, to overflow
and breach their banks with resultant large scale flooding. It fell to
the Ministry to co-ordinate assistance from the military and other
sources. The more recent floodings of the winter of 1960 were very
different, as their seriousness arose not so much from the total area
under water at any time as from the number of places, scattered over
a wide area, where flooding occurred. Most of these were in relatively

hilly areas where the flood waters retreated naturally after the rain had stopped. The amount of outside help required by drainage authorities was, therefore, much less than in 1947; indeed most of the immediate work required was not a matter of land drainage so much as repairing damage to property and clearing up the mess.

Flooding rather different in its origin and the worst of its kind in recent years took place early in 1953 in the eastern coastal areas of England where there is a considerable area of land lying below the level of the highest spring tides and which is protected by sea and tidal river embankments, most of them the responsibility of river boards.

The freak winds of the last two days of January, 1953, raised the level of the tides in the North Sea by nearly ten feet, resulting in a quite abnormal surge of water down towards the English Channel so that by the morning of February 1st, practically the whole length of the sea defences had been overtopped or damaged with breaches at more than a thousand places. Over 300 lives were lost, 160,000 acres of land flooded and the damage was estimated at over £40 million.

It was on the river boards in these areas that the main work fell for repairing the breaches and reconstructing the sea defences but the Ministry had an important role to play. Its immediate concern was to see that the gaps were filled and the sea defences reconstructed as soon as humanly possible, and to ensure that everything should be done to bring back into production the land flooded by salt water. In accordance with standing arrangements for dealing with serious floods the War Office arranged straight away for troops to assist with the emergency repairs. At one time 14,000 servicemen were engaged on this work, but they were withdrawn as soon as the civilian contractors were able to take over. Over sixty engineers from other river boards and the Ministry's own staff were sent to reinforce those on the staffs of the river boards in the flooded area. From headquarters the Ministry organized emergency assistance generally, whilst its Regional Engineers set up local emergency headquarters in co-operation with the river boards, which were linked to Ministry headquarters by teleprinters.

In accordance with the recommendations of a departmental committee under the chairmanship of Lord Waverley a flood warning system for the east coast areas now operates annually from September to April. An Admiralty hydrographer at the Meteorological Office, Dunstable, using meteorological information available at that office combined with tidal readings supplied by harbour masters of certain east coast ports is able to predict when a tidal surge coming down the east coast is likely to raise the water level at high tide to a dangerous level, and to send warnings by priority telegram to river boards, county police, the Land Drainage Division of the Ministry, and the War Office. An amber alert is issued ten or twelve hours before the time of the high water to which it refers, and where necessary this is followed by a red alert some four hours before high water to confirm the existence of a surge and forecast its magnitude and time of arrival. If damage occurs to the defences and the local resources of the river board are inadequate to deal with it assistance from the military can be obtained by telephone through the Ministry, special arrangements being made for senior officers to be available out of office hours at times when danger is likely. In an emergency a river board can seek aid direct from the local military headquarters and other government sources.

FARM WATER SUPPLY GRANTS

Under the authority of the Agriculture (Miscellaneous Provisions) Act, 1941, the Ministry pays grants to landowners and farmers for approved schemes for supplying water to agricultural land and farm buildings. Such schemes can also cover supplies to farm-houses and cottages, excluding domestic plumbing costs. Also in connection with the growing practice of spray irrigation on both horticultural and farm crops, permanent equipment and installations such as storage reservoirs are eligible for grant in schemes designed for this purpose.

Schemes are examined by the Divisional Drainage and Water Supply Officer in the same way as grant-aided field drainage schemes. The grants are at a flat rate of 40 per cent of the cost if the supply has to be taken from a private source, such as a well or bore hole, and 25 per cent when supplies are available from a public water main. The reason for the difference in rates is that additional grant is often paid towards the cost of extending a public mains to serve predominantly agricultural areas.

Assistance for public rural water schemes is given principally by grant under the Rural Water Supplies and Sewerage Acts, 1944 to 1955, administered by the Ministry of Housing and Local Government. Some of the schemes which do not qualify may be grant aided by the Ministry of Agriculture where the extension of the mains is primarily for the benefit of farms rather than dwelling-houses. The purpose is to reduce the burden that would otherwise fall on the general rates where this is more than the local authority can reasonably be expected to bear. Grant is not at a fixed rate, but depends on an assessment of the benefits which the extension will bring both to agricultural and domestic users.

CHAPTER VIII

The Agricultural Worker

THE Ministry's responsibilities in relation to the agricultural worker fall into four groups. First there is the administration and enforcement of the legislation governing wages and conditions of employment. Secondly, there are the legislative and other safeguards for the health, safety and welfare of agricultural workers, including in particular safeguards against toxic sprays and other chemicals which in recent years have been increasingly used in agriculture. Thirdly, there is the question of labour supply, which naturally assumes greatest importance in time of war. Lastly, but by no means least, there is the question of the training of the agricultural worker.

WAGES AND CONDITIONS OF EMPLOYMENT

In most industries nowadays wage rates are a matter for voluntary collective bargaining between the trade unions and the employers. There are, however, still some industries where the organization of one or both of the two sides is not sufficiently comprehensive, or where the number of workers at many of the undertakings is so small that the risk of voluntary agreements not being honoured is appreciable; in such industries minimum rates of wages are determined by Wages Councils and Boards. Agriculture is one of these industries and, accordingly, since 1924, minimum rates of wages for agricultural workers have been established under the procedures laid down in successive Agricultural Wages Acts.

In pre-war days minimum rates of wages were fixed by some forty-seven District Committees, each covering one or more counties, so that there could be quite a considerable spread in the minimum rates between different parts of the country. There was a Central Agricultural Wages Board but at that time it was mainly an advisory body. Nowadays, however, under the Agricultural Wages Act, 1948, national minimum rates of agricultural wages are fixed from time to time by the Central Board on which there are eight representatives of the employers (nominated by the National Farmers' Union) eight representatives of the workers (five nominated by the National Union of Agricultural Workers and three by the Transport and General Workers Union) together with five independent members, including the Chairman, appointed by the Minister; one of the independent members must be a woman. Separate minimum rates are fixed for men and for women and also for juvenile workers of different ages as well as hourly rates for casual or part-time employment. The forty-seven local Agricultural Wages Committees, similarly constituted, remain in being but only exercise relatively limited local functions, such as considering applications for permits of exemption to enable a lower minimum rate than the standard national rate to be paid to individual workers who through age or physical disability may be incapable of doing a normal full day's work.

The Board and the Committees are autonomous bodies which are independent of and uncontrolled by the Minister, but the Ministry provides them with secretarial services.

The Board is intended to act more as a negotiating and conciliation body than as an arbitrator. The independent members encourage the two sides to settle between themselves as far as they can any issues coming before the Board, and as far as possible seek to defer any expression of their own views or the giving of their votes until other means and processes have been fully explored. It is only to be expected that on major issues the independent members not infrequently have to exercise a casting vote, but possibly not before the two sides have come closer together than they were at the outset of the discussions.

Although the Ministry has no responsibility for the decisions of the Board, it is responsible for seeing that wages are paid at not less than the minimum fixed by the Board, and the Ministry's Safety and Wages Inspectors stationed at regional and divisional offices visit farms to investigate complaints of underpayment and to make a number of test inspections, the results of which are also used by the Ministry's Agricultural Economics Division for the purpose of their calculations of earnings and labour costs (see Chapter XIV).

The Act provides for the establishment of minimum wage rates only. So far the Board has laid down standard minimum rates applying generally to all agricultural workers, the only variations being on the grounds of age and sex and the recent arrangements mentioned later in this chapter for apprentices. At the time of writing discussions are taking place on the Board as to the possibility of prescribing higher minimum rates for recognized skills. Quite a number of the more experienced workers such as stockmen are of course, at present paid more than the standard minimum, and some are on bonus incentive schemes based, e.g. on the number of gallons of milk produced by the cows. For example for the calendar year 1960, the average earnings of adult men employed whole time in agriculture was estimated at £10 6s 4d per week, although for the greater part of the year the minimum wage was £8 per week. Again, whilst the Wages Board specifies a standard figure for the value of a house that

K

may be provided as part of the conditions of service, some farmers will provide this free in addition to the minimum wages, and indeed farmers nowadays find that if they are to get staff of good calibre they must provide housing of a considerably better standard than was considered adequate a generation ago. Today when an agricultural worker applying for a post visits the prospective employer he is very often accompanied by his wife who may look for satisfactory living accommodation, a good bus service to the nearest town and a good school locally for the children before she will allow her husband to take the job.

SAFETY, HEALTH AND WELFARE

Legislation to safeguard the safety, health and welfare of agricultural workers is much more recent than that governing the minimum rates of wages. The main Acts, namely the Agriculture (Poisonous Substances) Act, 1952, and the Agriculture (Safety, Health and Welfare Provisions) Act, 1956, both have their origin in the Report of a Departmental Committee on *Health, Welfare and Safety in Non-Industrial Employment, Hours of Employment of Juveniles* under the chairmanship of Sir Ernest Gowers.[1] The first of these Acts was introduced urgently because of the fatal accidents which were arising from the use of new kinds of spray for killing weeds. The Act empowers the Minister to make regulations which specify the protective clothing (oilskins, masks, etc.) to be worn by those working with various dangerous chemicals, and also lay down general requirements on such matters as personal cleanliness, cleansing of protective clothing and minimum age of workers to be employed in using specified chemicals. The farmer is responsible for seeing that the necessary equipment is provided for his workers and that they use it properly.

The regulations have to be kept continually under review in order to keep pace with the introduction of new poisonous chemicals or new ways of using old ones.

Since the 1952 Act was passed the Department has extended its work on dangerous agricultural chemicals to include the protection of the general public, the consumer and the wild life of the countryside (see Chapter IX).

The Agriculture (Safety, Health and Welfare Provisions) Act, 1956, gave the Minister powers to make regulations for the protection of agricultural workers against the risks of bodily injury or to health, and for the protection of children. These regulations are made after full consultation with all sides of the industry and with a great many

[1] Cmd. 7664, 1949.

other bodies, e.g. manufacturers, traders, research institutes, who may have an interest in the subject.

With the great increase in the number and variety of machines used on farms it is not surprising that a number of the regulations deal with the guarding and safe operation of machines, such as the shielding of power take-off points and shafts on tractors and similar machines and the guarding of circular saws.

Measures to protect workers against injury by falls include the Safeguarding of Workplaces Regulations, which lay down safety standards for stairways and the fencing of the edges of floors and openings; and the regulations on the safe use of ladders. The First Aid Regulations require prescribed equipment to be provided on all farms where workers are employed.

The Ministry's Safety and Wages Inspectors are responsible for seeing that the regulations are observed. The inspectors also give advice, and free leaflets explaining the regulations in detail are widely distributed. Although the regulations—apart from those about children—apply only to farms where workers are employed, all farmers are encouraged for their own protection to observe them.

Many of the accidents which happen on farms, however, are due to human error and could not be prevented by legislation. The Ministry is therefore active, with the full co-operation of farmers', contractors' and workers' organizations among others, in trying to build up safety consciousness in the farming industry by education and advice. All available means of publicity are used—advisory leaflets, the Press, sound broadcasting, television, displays mounted at agricultural shows, lectures, slides showing photographs of actual accidents and films. The co-operation of farmers was well shown when the NFU devoted a whole issue of its magazine *British Farmer* to the subject of farm safety.

The Ministry has made two films for the safety campaign— *Tractor Sense* and *Time for Thought*—which reconstruct types of accidents caused through lack of care or thought. These have been in great demand and have been shown on television and at local meetings such as those run by the farmers' and agricultural workers' unions. The Safety and Wages Inspectors have attended a great many meetings to talk about the films, show slides and talk about safety matters generally. As these films have been so successful, three more have recently been made—this time in colour—on falls, bulls, and accidents to children. The shooting of the film on bulls clearly presented a difficult problem—the lesson it was trying to get across was that all bulls are potentially dangerous animals—and the Deputy Chief Safety Inspector courageously volunteered to play a part in this film!

LABOUR SUPPLY

The Ministry of Labour is the Department responsible for the supply of labour for all industries, and the role of the Ministry is to advise that Department on the labour requirements of agriculture and the means of meeting them. For this purpose statistics and intelligence on the agricultural manpower position are obtained from the regional and divisional offices, the agricultural returns, National Farmers' Union and other sources.

Labour supply was, of course, an important question during the war and immediate post-war period when it was necessary to use to best advantage various special sources of agricultural labour such as the Women's Land Army, prisoners of war and displaced European persons. More recently the question of deferment of agricultural workers from National Service has been one on which the National Service Deferment Board of the Ministry of Labour has been advised by county agricultural advisory panels composed of equal numbers of farmers and farmworkers. This, of course, is now a thing of the past. One remaining labour supply function is that of advising the Ministry of Labour on applications for permits for the employment of foreign labour in agriculture, and this is a task which falls mainly on the labour sub-committee or labour panel of the county agricultural executive committee.

TRAINING AND THE APPRENTICESHIP SCHEME

Agriculture has lagged behind other industries in making provision for systematic training of its young workers. At one time no doubt the young worker could pick up as he went along all that he needed to become proficient at his trade, but with the increase both in the mechanization of agriculture and in the application of modern techniques this is no longer so. An attempt has been made to fill this gap by the establishment, by the agricultural industry, of a National Apprenticeship Scheme. This is administered by an Agricultural Apprenticeship Council composed of representatives of the farmers and workers unions, with officers of the Ministry, the Ministry of Labour and other government departments acting as assessors. The local administration of the scheme is in the hands of District Apprenticeship Committees on which the Divisional Executive Officer or other officer of the Ministry sits as an assessor. The scheme is open to youths and girls normally up to the age of $17\frac{1}{4}$ years, and the period of apprenticeship is three years, during which time the apprentice receives technical training off the farm (usually provided by the local education authority), at present for a minimum of thirty-five days without loss of wages.

Unfortunately, although the scheme has been in operation for six years, it has not so far obtained much positive support from the industry; up to 1961 only about 2 per cent of the annual intake of 20,000 young workers had been entering the industry by way of apprenticeship. The main reason for this lack of real progress has been the absence of adequate financial incentives either for the training employer or the apprentice. On the one hand, the farmer has had to accept considerable training responsibilities while at the same time paying full rates of wages to the apprentice; on the other, there has been no provision for any premium rate to be paid to apprentices who have taken time and trouble to become both practically and technically qualified.

To meet this difficulty the Apprenticeship Council has now agreed to revised arrangements with the Agricultural Wages Board which provide for a lower rate of wages for apprentices during training and an increased rate for qualified men and women who have satisfactorily completed their apprenticeship and have secured their certificates by way of passing a proficiency test in one of a range of skilled farm jobs. The lower rate during apprenticeship recognizes the training responsibilities of the farmer and the value of training to the apprentice, and the subsequent high rate is intended as a realistic reflection of the increased value of a qualified apprentice. In addition, the revised scheme increases the minimum period of attendance at technical classes based on nationally recognized educational standards.

The Department also assists by grant the scheme of the YMCA for training town boys for agricultural employment.

The Ministry provides vocational training (as distinct from 'agricultural education') for two classes of adults, disabled persons and ex-regular members of the Forces. Candidates for training are only accepted if they are considered suitable by a panel of the county agricultural executive committee, while their placing with training employers and their welfare while in training are supervised from divisional offices. Facilities are also provided for selected trainees to receive further training at a farm institute.

CHAPTER IX

Supplies and Equipment

SUCCESSFUL farming not only requires the land and fixed equipment provided by the landowner, the managerial and technical skill of the farmer and the work of his employees. It is also dependent on the farmer's raw materials, of which the chief are seeds, fertilizers, including lime, and animal feedingstuffs, and also on his equipment, including an ever-widening range of machinery.

During the war and for some years after, one of the Ministry's most important functions was to see that there was an adequate supply of 'tools for the job' and that they were fairly allocated. This is a question which no longer arises today, but the Ministry is responsible for legislation to assist the farmer to know what he is getting when he buys his seeds, fertilizers and feedingstuffs. This legislation can be compared with that which now requires the composition of proprietary patent medicines to be stated on the container, and also that, to be described in the next chapter, which requires purchasers to be informed of the weight and composition of certain manufactured foods.

Again, the Department pays subsidies on certain fertilizers, including lime, to encourage their increased use in agriculture.

The Department is also responsible for collecting statistics about supplies of these raw materials as well as of agricultural machinery.

Chemical weedkillers, pesticides and the like have become of increasing importance in agriculture and horticulture in recent years and the Department administers schemes both for ensuring the safe use of these products and also for helping users to choose efficient products.

SEEDS

All who garden know how seeds can vary in quality and the importance of getting them from a reliable source.

The Seeds Act of 1920 gives farmers some assurance about the quality of the seeds they are buying. The Act protects the buyer, not by forbidding the sale of inferior material as in some other countries, but by requiring the seedsman to disclose to his customers certain essential information about the seed he is selling or offering. All buyers of the main kinds of cereal, herbage and vegetable seeds, whether they be farmers, horticulturists, allotment holders or gardeners, are thus given certain necessary facts about the seeds they buy.

The details which seedsmen must declare include the analytical purity and the germination of the seed. Analytical purity refers to absence of contamination by weed seeds, inert matter and seeds of other crop plants, and is usually expressed as the percentage by weight of the pure seed in a given sample examined under laboratory test conditions. Germination, also expressed as a percentage, is the proportion of the pure seeds in a sample which produce a normal seedling under laboratory test conditions; it is a guide to the way the seeds may be expected to grow under field conditions. Actual field performance will of course be materially affected by such things as weather and soil but laboratory tests do nevertheless provide an invaluable basis for comparing different bulks of seeds. The analysis of purity and germination is carried out at the Official Seed Testing Station at Cambridge or at private stations operated by seed firms under licence from the Ministry.

The Act authorizes the Ministry to take official 'control' samples of seed offered or stored for sale, and this is done by field officers from divisional offices, a representative check being made on all kinds of scheduled seeds passing in trade. The samples are sent to the Official Seed Testing Station for check tests, and the results compared with the declarations made by the merchants at whose premises the samples were taken. The field officers also check on firms' procedures for passing on the statutory particulars to their customers.

Offenders have occasionally to be prosecuted, but by far the greater part of the work is conducted in a spirit of guidance and advice, an approach which is appreciated by the trade and ensures its co-operation when particular problems require investigation. United Kingdom seeds legislation can in fact be regarded as a basic instrument in the technical education of farmers and seedsmen alike, and one which is a material factor in raising the efficiency of agricultural production through improvement of seed quality.

Another important part of Seeds Act work is the supervision of the hundred or so private licensed seed testing stations. A technical officer of the Ministry visits regularly each station. He checks that the equipment and testing conditions are in order, and deals with technical queries. He also takes random samples of seed which the station has tested; and these are check-tested at the Official Station and the reasons for any discrepancies fully investigated.

The Ministry is concerned to see not only that the farmer should know the purity and the germination of the seeds he buys but also that he should have advice on the suitability for his purposes of new varieties of seed resulting from the work of the plant breeder.

In recent years the breeders have produced varieties of cereal with yields per acre considerably in excess of anything that was possible, say, twenty years ago. Higher yields have been combined with other desirable qualities such as resistance to fungus diseases such as rust, and short stout straw to help the crop to remain erect in conditions of wind and heavy rain which are only too often experienced while the crop is growing. Again, the pioneer work of the late Sir George Stapledon at Aberystwyth and others has in recent years led to the development of vastly improved varieties of grass and clover seeds. The testing of new varieties of all kinds of seeds, both from home and abroad, to assess their suitability for farming conditions in different parts of the country is undertaken by the National Institute of Agricultural Botany at Cambridge. This is a body largely financed by grants from the Ministry and governed by a Council which includes representatives of the Agricultural Departments of the United Kingdom, Cambridge and other universities, the Seed Trade Association, the National Association of British and Irish Millers, the National Association of Corn and Agricultural Merchants, the Royal Agricultural Society of England and the National Farmers' Union. Promising new varieties of seeds and seed potatoes are tried out not only at the headquarters trial grounds at Cambridge but also at fourteen regional trial centres in England and Wales, and secondary trials are also carried out at a number of private and public establishments throughout the country. The Institute issues periodically lists of recommended varieties of seeds for different conditions of soil and climate based on the results of these trials.

The farmer needs not only advice on the varieties of seed most suited to the conditions in which he farms but also an assurance of getting seed that is true to that variety. To that end the NIAB, in close association with the Ministry, administers various seed certification schemes. Certified seed has to be grown and harvested under conditions, such as precautions against cross-pollination, which ensure that it is true to variety.

COMMITTEE ON SEED TRANSACTIONS

In 1954 the Agricultural Ministers appointed a Committee on Transactions in Seeds, which included representatives of all sides of the industry, to review the working of the Seeds Act, 1920.

In their first report[1] the committee endorsed the broad principles of the Act but suggested a number of amendments to make it more

[1] Cmnd. 300, 1957.

effective in practice. For example, they recommended that seeds merchants should be required to give a statutory warranty of some of the particulars such as analytical purity and germination which they were required to declare under the Seeds Act. This would give the buyer the right to bring a civil action for damages if seeds proved to be not up to description.

Most of the Committee's recommendations were only of direct concern to commercial agriculturists and horticulturists, but one which is of interest to the amateur gardener was that information similar to that at present required for farm seeds should for the future be given for flower seeds and for grass seeds intended for lawns, playing fields and the like.

In their final report[1] the Committee considered whether plant breeders should be granted some form of right in their new varieties such as is provided by schemes in various overseas countries. They recommended that plant breeders should be given the opportunity to register their new varieties with an independent statutory authority, somewhat analogous to the Patent Office, and to acquire rights in them for a period not exceeding twenty-five years. To qualify for such rights the breeder would have to satisfy the authority that the variety was distinct, uniform and stable and that there was no evidence of major weakness.

Seed producers, merchants and nurserymen would then need to have a licence from the breeder and to pay him a royalty on the seeds, etc. of the registered variety which they produced or sold. The licence would be available on reasonable terms and conditions to anyone competent to produce or trade in a protected variety, and in the event of dispute the independent authority would settle the terms of the licence.

The Committee advanced three arguments in favour of their proposal. Firstly, as a matter of equity, plant breeders in common with inventors, authors and other creative workers ought to have an opportunity of earning a proper remuneration for their work and should be protected against exploitation and piracy. Secondly, agriculture and horticulture would benefit from the increased private investment in plant breeding which a royalty system would encourage. Thirdly, it would then be possible to conclude reciprocal agreements with other countries to enable the rights of our plant breeders to be protected abroad.

In December, 1961, the Minister announced that the Government had decided to accept and give effect to most of the Committee's recommendations and that plans were being made for the necessary legislation.

[1] Cmnd. 1092, 1960.

FERTILIZERS AND FEEDINGSTUFFS

Just as it is the object of the Seeds Act, 1920, that the farmer should be informed of the purity and germination of the seeds he buys, so the Fertilizer and Feeding Stuffs Act of 1926 (which is the successor to legislation which dates back as far as 1893) and the regulations made under it are designed to let the farmer know what he is getting when he buys his fertilizers and feedingstuffs, particularly when they are compounds containing a number of ingredients.

The Minister and the Secretary of State for Scotland are jointly responsible for making regulations under the Act which prescribe (among other things) the information that must be given to the purchaser. The principal information required by the current regulations are the neutralizing value of lime; the percentages of nitrogen, phosphoric acid and potash in other fertilizers; and the percentages of oil, protein and fibre in feedingstuffs. The Act provides for a Standing Advisory Committee, which includes representatives of farmers, manufacturers, agricultural analysts and local authorities; the Committee must be consulted on the making of any regulations.

Unlike the Seeds Act, enforcement is primarily in the hands of the local authorities (county and county borough councils) who are responsible for appointing inspectors and official samplers to take samples at various points and analysts to analyse them, these appointments being subject to the Minister's consent. The local authority is also responsible for the prosecution of offenders, again generally subject to the Minister's consent.

The sale without veterinary prescription of feedingstuffs containing small quantities of antibiotics such as penicillin, aureomycin and oxytetracyline (for fattening of pigs and poultry) is governed by the Therapeutic Substances Regulations of 1953 and 1954, since these antibiotics can be harmful if fed in the wrong quantities or to the wrong sort of animal. The regulations accordingly require the seller of such foods to give on the label details of the type and quantity of antibiotic included, and instructions to ensure that it is used properly. The regulations themselves are made by the Ministry of Health but the Minister is responsible for prescribing the form and the content of the label. The Pharmaceutical Society is responsible for enforcing these regulations.

THE FERTILIZER SUBSIDY

In addition to the legislation which helps the farmer to know what he is getting when he buys his fertilizers, the Department also administers subsidy schemes to encourage the greater use of fertilizers, including lime.

During the war, and for some years afterwards, subsidies to meet increases in costs were paid to fertilizer manufacturers so that the fertilizers could still be sold at 1940 prices. Although price control continued until 1953, retail prices were raised in 1950 and 1951 so as to eliminate the subsidy. Prices subsequently rose still further because of big increases in freight rates and in the cost of imported materials. Farmers' purchases, particularly of phosphatic and compound fertilizers, declined considerably in consequence. To counteract this the Agriculture (Fertilizers) Act, 1952, was passed authorizing the Ministry to contribute up to one-half of the cost to farmers of fertilizers applied to agricultural land.

Under the Act a scheme is made for fixing the rates of subsidy for each 'fertilizer year' (July–June). Subsidy is paid on nitrogenous fertilizers (such as sulphate of ammonia) and also on phosphatic fertilizers (such as superphosphate) and on compound fertilizers containing such ingredients. No subsidy is paid on fertilizers such as sulphate of potash which supply the third main plant food, potash, since supplies of these are entirely imported, mostly through one source, and it would accordingly be difficult to be sure that the farmer rather than the overseas supplier was getting the benefit of any subsidy on potash.

Since the subsidy was reintroduced in 1952 consumption of phosphates, which had fallen sharply when the previous subsidy was withdrawn in 1951, has now recovered to above the previous level. The consumption of nitrogenous fertilizers has been rising steadily and is now nearly double what it was in 1952. The consumption of potash has also risen steadily and at about the same rate as nitrogen; although potash is not subsidized a large proportion of the supply goes into compound fertilizers that are subsidized on their nitrogen and phosphate content.

It is impracticable to pay a subsidy on organic fertilizers, such as farmyard manure and fish meal, in view of the wide variations in their composition.

THE LIME SUBSIDY

The lime subsidy was first introduced as the Land Fertility Scheme, as one of the measures under the Agriculture Act, 1937, for building up in peace-time the food producing potential of our land.

The functions of lime in the soil are complex. In acid soils there is a shortage of readily available calcium and this is made good by liming. But lime is not a fertilizer in the sense of being itself a plant food. It is an alkaline which corrects the balance of acidity in the soil and thereby releases the plant foods that are already present there and thus enables the plant to make use of them. If it is to do this efficiently the lime must be of sufficient particle fineness and neutralizing value, and the Ministry specifies the standards of fineness and quality of all agricultural liming materials which it approves for the subsidy.

As lime is relatively bulky, transport costs normally form a considerable part of the cost at farm, and consequently it is important that the farmer should draw his supplies from a nearby source. The subsidized nitrogenous and phosphatic fertilizers are supplied by relatively few manufacturers, whose prices, fixed on a national basis, can be, and have been, investigated by the Monopolies Commission. Lime supplies on the other hand, are drawn from some hundreds of widely dispersed natural deposits of limestone and chalk, and cost of production and quality of the deposits can vary very considerably from one supplier to another—and even within the same quarry. Many lime producers are in a small way of business but because of the importance of transport costs they are still, in remoter areas, the most economic source of supply. The United Kingdom is well endowed with natural deposits of limestone but they vary greatly in workable depth and accessibility as well as in their neutralizing value. We rely for the finished product on an agricultural lime industry which is essentially a quarrying, and sometimes a mining, undertaking.

For these and other reasons lime is a commodity which presents different production and distribution problems from those that apply to fertilizers, and consequently the Ministry exercises a degree of control over the materials and prices charged by individual suppliers as a condition for the lime subsidy. The Ministry also encourages the development of new sources of supply, and the production from time to time of new liming materials to standards recommended by the advisory soil chemists.

To qualify for a subsidy under the scheme, lime suppliers and the prices they charge for their products must be individually approved by the Ministry. Before a supplier is approved the Ministry satisfies itself that the prices to be charged are fair and reasonable, and any subsequent adjustments in price are related to changes in the quality or production costs of the product.

Liming is one of the oldest, as well as one of the most necessary, agricultural practices, but in times of low farming incomes it has suffered some neglect. The lime needs of the United Kingdom arise from the need to make good accumulated lime deficiency that occurred between 1900 and 1940 as well as the additional, or 'maintenance', liming required to replace the annual losses of lime leached out of the soil by rain. Supplies of lime were quite inadequate to meet these needs when the subsidy scheme was introduced and the Ministry has encouraged the production in quantity of new grades of ground limestone, and of ground and screened chalks and the utilization of suitable industrial waste limes and calcareous sea land. The members of the Ministry's lime technical service inspect and test these materials regularly.

The rates of lime subsidy have varied from time to time, but it is now at a uniform rate of 65 per cent of the approved total cost of the lime (subject to certain limits to the cost of transporting it to the farm and of spreading it on the land).

DANGEROUS CHEMICALS

One important way in which the scientist has helped the farmer in recent years has been the development of an immense variety of new chemicals for the control of weeds, pests and diseases of crops. Other chemicals have been developed for protecting grain and other food in store from insect and other pests. Many of these chemicals are poisonous and need to be used with proper precautions.

The previous chapter mentioned the legislation for the protection of the workers who handle these chemicals. Since then the Agricultural Departments have concerned themselves with the safety not only of the man who applies these chemicals on the farm but also of passers-by and of animals and wild life generally, and also of those who ultimately eat food made from material to which these chemicals have been applied at one stage or another.

In all this work the Departments are assisted by an Advisory Committee on Poisonous Substances used in Agriculture and Food Storage. This includes representatives from the Agriculture, Food and Health Departments of Great Britain, the Medical and Agricultural Research Councils, the Nature Conservancy, the Board of Trade and the Government Chemist's Laboratory, as well as eminent scientists from outside the government service, one of whom is its Chairman.

The Committee's task is to keep under review all risks arising from the use of poisonous substances in agriculture and food storage, whether to the person preparing or applying the spray, etc., the consumer of the food made from the treated crop, passers-by, domestic animals or the wild life of the countryside. There is a scientific sub-committee with members selected for their expert knowledge in the various branches of science involving toxicology, biochemistry, plant pathology, entomology, medicine, veterinary science, natural history and so on. The agricultural chemical industry is not represented on either committee.

Apart from the regulations for the protection of agricultural workers under the Agriculture (Poisonous Substances) Act, 1952, described in the previous chapter, the Department and the Committee proceed by way of a voluntary notification scheme designed to promote the safe use of agricultural chemicals. All sides of the industry are naturally anxious to make the use of agricultural chemicals safe, and the willing co-operation which they have given in the working of the voluntary scheme has rendered unnecessary legislation, which in any event would be difficult to enforce.

When a manufacturer proposes to put a new chemical on the market, or to introduce a new method of using an established one, which he thinks may be attended by some risk whether to user, passer-by, food consumer, domestic animals or wild life, he submits to the committee details of his proposals together with detailed evidence of the results of his experimental work on the chemical.

These details cover the physical, chemical and biological properties of the product, including its persistence, the products into which it breaks down, its mode of action, and its toxicity to various forms of life. The method of application of the chemical, its indicated use, methods of analysis, medical data, effects on different kinds of plants, practice in other countries and all information about possible risks from using it must also be notified. All information about the proposal has to be very carefully handled at every stage to guard against the risk of secret information leaking out and being used by the proposer's competitors. The details are first considered by the Scientific Sub-Committee. Firms can, if they wish, and they often do, send a representative to explain the firm's intentions and to answer the sub-committee's questions.

When the sub-committee has examined a proposal it submits draft recommendations to the main Committee. If these are approved they are referred to the Departments, and after the firm has been notified of them the recommendations are published for the attention of all whom they affect.

The recommendations cover the measures necessary for the protection both of operators and of consumers. They include the crops on which the chemical may safely be sprayed, the number and frequency of applications per crop per season, and the minimum period that should be allowed between spraying and harvesting. The recommendations also deal with the protection of animal life and cover general hygiene in the use of chemicals including precautions to avoid contaminating neighbouring crops, ponds, streams, rivers and watercourses, and safeguards in the storage and disposal of containers.

The Committee also examines as necessary more general questions arising from the use of dangerous chemicals, and where appropriate sets up for this purpose special panels which may include members from the industry and specially co-opted experts. The questions considered in this way have included methods of chemical analysis, safety advice to be included in the labels of containers, and precautions against the poisoning of birds by the chemical dressings now applied to cereal seeds as a protection against soil pests.

AGRICULTURAL CHEMICALS APPROVAL SCHEME

Farmers (and horticulturists) not only want to know what precautions they must observe in the use of insecticides, fungicides and weedkillers; they also want an assurance that these crop protection chemicals will be effective in use.

To this end the Agricultural Departments of the United Kingdom run a voluntary scheme for the approval of such chemicals which is analogous to the statutory arrangements for seeds, fertilizers and feedingstuffs mentioned earlier in this chapter. The present scheme was introduced in 1961 and replaced a similar one which had been in existence nearly twenty years. It is operated on behalf of the Agricultural Departments by the Agricultural Chemicals Approval Organization at the Ministry's Plant Pathology Laboratory. Proprietary brands of products are approved on application from the manufacturers only if there is adequate evidence that they will act efficiently against the pests and diseases they are designed to control. This evidence is obtained from the results of field trials carried out by the manufacturers, supplemented as may be necessary by independent field trials carried out by the Advisory Services of the Agricultural Departments.

No product containing a toxic chemical can be approved until it has been submitted to the Advisory Committee on Poisonous Substances used in Agriculture and Food Storage and agreed by them and by the Departments to be safe to use.

One of the main advantages of the new scheme as compared with its predecessor is that a new product can be approved before it is ready to go on the market. Thus, from the first announcement of the appearance of a new product, users will know that there is reliable evidence of its efficiency.

The Agricultural Chemicals Approval Organization is advised by a Scientific Advisory Committee composed of experts in plant pathology, entomology, weed-killing, chemistry and crops. They come from universities, research stations, the National Agricultural Advisory Service and the Agricultural Departments jointly responsible with the Ministry for the scheme.

Approved products can be recognized by an identification mark, known as the Approved Mark, on their labels and containers. A list of approved products is issued each February, and anyone interested can obtain a copy on application to the Agricultural Chemicals Approval Organization at the Plant Pathology Laboratory, Hatching Green, Harpenden, Herts.; the Publications Branch of the Ministry at Ruskin Avenue, Kew; or from any of the Ministry's regional or divisional offices. Copies can also be obtained from the offices of the Agricultural Departments of Scotland, Northern Ireland, Channel Islands and Isle of Man.

AGRICULTURAL MACHINERY

There has been no more striking development in agricultural practice in this country in recent years than the development of farm machinery. The tractor has now virtually replaced the horse as a source of mobile motive power, and in fact has been developed to the stage where it can do many things that the horse could never do, such as rotary cultivation with the assistance of the power take-off from the machine. The combine harvester has now taken the place of the reaper, binder and thresher wherever cereals are grown on any large scale, the problems of devising machines for mechanical harvesting of sugar-beet have now largely been solved and the majority of our cows are now milked by machine.

It was only the use of machinery on a large scale which enabled agricultural production in the last war to be maintained and increased with a reduced and diluted labour force, and as mentioned in Chapter II one of the many important tasks of county agricultural executive committees was the running of a machinery service to undertake ploughing, harvesting and other operations for farmers as well as for the land farmed by the committees. The National Institute of Agricultural Engineering, then directly administered by the Ministry, was concerned with the testing of machines, and the development of new machines.

With the return to normal conditions the Ministry's responsibilities in relation to agricultural machinery are now much less than they were at one time. The need for a State-operated machinery service has largely ceased, and in those comparatively few counties where it has been continued it has now been amalgamated with the field drainage service (Chapter VII). The National Institute of Agricultural Engineering is now an independent research institute grant aided and supervised by the Agricultural Research Council (Chapter V). It still tests and develops agricultural machinery but the tests instead of being made at the request of the Ministry are carried out for the manufacturers and the reports are confidential unless publication is agreed by the manufacturer.

Advice on the use of agricultural machinery and on mechanization continues to be an important part of the work of the NAAS, which contains a group of Machinery Advisory Officers. Increasing attention is being paid to the part to be played by mechanization in the general farming plan.

CHAPTER X

Agricultural Marketing and Co-operation

MARKETING

EVEN in the days before there was a Ministry of Food, the Ministry of Agriculture concerned itself not only with helping farmers in various ways to produce better crops, livestock, milk, eggs and so on but also with the marketing of their produce once it had left the farm. The present day appreciation of the importance of marketing may be said to date from the various reports of 1923 and 1924 of the Departmental Committee on Distribution and Prices of Agricultural Produce (the Linlithgow Committee).[1]

These reports showed that British farmers were in a far weaker position than farmers overseas because they had failed to combine co-operatively in large-scale trading units mainly because they lacked the economic incentives such as existed in exporting countries. Moreover, although British farm produce was frequently superior in quality to imported produce, it often compared unfavourably in packing, grading and presentation and failed in these respects to meet the needs of the consumer.

There have been two main lines of development since the Linlithgow Committee. The first was an attempt to standardize and improve quality, culminating in the Agricultural Produce (Grading and Marking) Act, 1928, which was the parent of the pre-war National Mark Schemes. These efforts were more successful than the relatively small amount of produce sold under the National Mark suggested. The idea of grading took root, fruit and egg packing stations began to be set up and private grading schemes developed alongside the official schemes. The latter were suspended when war broke out and have not been revived.

The second line of development lay in producers' marketing organizations. At first attention was concentrated on voluntary co-operation, but the evident weakness at a time of agricultural depression of large-scale voluntary marketing combinations of producers such as British Hop Growers and the arrangements for the negotiation of milk prices led to the conclusion that such marketing organizations should be on a statutory basis. Statutory authority was accordingly provided by a series of Agricultural Marketing Acts

[1] Cmd. 1854, 1892, 1927, 1971 and 2008.

dating from 1931 which are now consolidated in the Agricultural Marketing Act, 1958. The marketing schemes can be studied in detail by examining the accounts of the operation of the individual marketing schemes contained in the annual reports of Ministers to Parliament under Section 30 of the Agricultural Marketing Act, 1958,[1] together with the biennial volumes of the Agricultural Register published by the Oxford University Press for the Oxford Agricultural Economics Research Institute.

One point must be made clear at the outset in this necessarily summary account of the system. The responsibility for promoting a marketing scheme rests with producer interests, and the operation of the scheme when approved is the responsibility of the marketing board, essentially a producers' organization. The Minister's role is to 'hold the ring', and in particular to see that schemes operate with due regard to the public interest.

A scheme can cover the whole or part of Great Britain and may also extend to Northern Ireland. For a scheme applying only to England and Wales (or part of it) 'the Minister' means the Minister of Agriculture, Fisheries and Food. If it covers only the whole or part of Scotland (there are, for example, no less than three Scottish Milk Marketing Boards covering different areas in Scotland) then 'the Minister' means the Secretary of State for Scotland. For a scheme covering Great Britain 'the Minister' means these two Ministers acting jointly. When a scheme extends to Northern Ireland, 'the Minister' includes the Home Secretary also.

The promoters of any scheme must satisfy the Minister that they are 'substantially representative of the persons who produce the product in the area to which the scheme is applicable'. All the marketing schemes now in operation were in fact promoted by the Farmers' Unions operating in the area concerned. The Minister can, however, appoint a Reorganization Commission to prepare a scheme for the consideration of producers, and the pre-war Pigs and Bacon Marketing Schemes (now defunct) and also the Milk Marketing Scheme for England and Wales originated in the reports of such Commissions, though all these schemes as submitted by the producers differed somewhat from those prepared by the Commissions.

When a draft marketing scheme is submitted to the Minister he must first of all satisfy himself that it comes within the scope of the Agricultural Marketing Act. Thereafter, before it can be approved, it must go through a procedure designed to ensure that the effects it would have on producers, distributors, and others are fully considered. First a notice of the submission is published in the

[1] The Report for the period 1959/60 was ordered by the House of Commons to be printed on July 26, 1961; Parliamentary Paper 253 (HMSO 6s 6d net).

London Gazette (and where appropriate the corresponding Scottish and Northern Ireland Gazettes). Objections and representations are invited and unless the Minister proposes to modify the scheme to meet the objections he must arrange for an independent Commissioner, normally a barrister, to hold a public inquiry into them and to report. In practice there have been such inquiries in connection with all the schemes now operating.

Following the Commissioner's report the Minister may make such modifications as he thinks proper. Provided these are acceptable to the promoters and provided the Minister is satisfied that the scheme, as modified, will conduce to the more efficient production and marketing of the product concerned then he can proceed to the next step of presenting it to Parliament for approval by affirmative resolution of both Houses. (A draft scheme extending to Northern Ireland requires affirmative resolutions of both Houses of the Northern Ireland Parliament before it can be submitted to the Parliament at Westminster).

If the scheme receives the necessary parliamentary approval then the Minister makes an order bringing it into force. The main provisions of the scheme remain in suspense pending a poll of producers registered under the scheme (that is all the producers in the area of the scheme except those specifically exempted), and the scheme will in fact lapse unless at this poll at least one-half of the registered producers vote, and at least two-thirds of those voting (measured both by number and by productive capacity, e.g. for an egg marketing scheme the number of laying hens) are in favour of the scheme continuing in force.

The members of a marketing board are for an initial period nominated by the promoters of the scheme itself. Subsequently the majority are elected by the registered producers. The remainder—not more than one-fifth of the total (with a minimum of two)—are appointed by the Minister. The Minister is required to appoint people who have experience and capacity in commerce, finance, administration, public affairs, or the organization of workers, or who are specially conversant with the interests of consumers of the regulated product. These members are not ministerial watchdogs on the board. They are appointed rather to add to the collective wisdom of the board by making available knowledge and experience gained in a wider field than the production of eggs, milk or whatever it may be.

There are at the moment (1961) no less than four Milk Marketing schemes in force in Great Britain, one covering England and Wales and the remainder three different areas in Scotland. There are five other schemes, namely, schemes for eggs, and for (fleece) wool, each covering the United Kingdom;

schemes for potatoes, and for tomatoes and cucumbers, each covering Great Britain;

a scheme for hops, covering England only.

The different schemes vary considerably in the extent and manner in which they regulate the marketing of the product concerned. In any classification of the schemes the main distinction to be drawn is between those with trading boards, such as the eggs, wool and hops schemes, i.e. where in general, unless specifically exempted, a producer *must* sell his produce through the board and, on the other hand, those schemes which are wholly or mainly regulatory such as those for potatoes, and for tomatoes and cucumbers, where the board may prescribe conditions of sale but there is no obligation to sell to the board itself. The Tomato and Cucumber Marketing Board has in fact no trading powers at the moment, and the trading activities of the Potato Marketing Board are largely concerned with the purchase of surplus potatoes in a year of glut in order to keep them off the market though some may be resold for human consumption if a market can be found.

The main features of the marketing schemes for milk, eggs, wool and potatoes have been indicated in the various sections of Chapter IV which describe the part which the boards administering these schemes play in the implementation of the price guarantee arrangements for these products. The boards for eggs, milk and wool have in fact (subject to certain important exceptions) a statutory monopoly for the sale of these products, and the Government makes a payment to the board to bring the average return up to a figure calculated in accordance with an agreed formula. The Hops Marketing Board also has a statutory monopoly but no government price guarantee. Although the price guarantee for potatoes is operated through the Potato Marketing Board, producers are not in fact required to sell to the board. The board can, however, determine the conditions on which potatoes may be sold by registered producers (particularly the size of potatoes that can be sold for human consumption) and minimum prices, and in this way in a year of glut it is able to regulate the volume of supplies coming on to the market.

The Tomato and Cucumber Marketing Board exercises only limited regulatory powers (for example, laying down what descriptions of tomatoes and cucumbers may be sold by producers) and undertake certain development work (such as the publication of marketing intelligence, advertising and the promotion of research).

The other marketing boards also engage in a variety of 'nonmarketing' functions, such as promotion of research designed to increase efficiency of production.

Once a scheme has been voted into full operation its terms are binding on all registered producers, and contraventions (such as selling produce in a manner not allowed by the scheme, or failing to make returns required by the board) are considered and penalized by a disciplinary committee made up of members of the relative board under the independent chairmanship of an experienced lawyer approved by the Minister. This system of domestic discipline is in accordance with the self-governing nature of a scheme but is subject to various safeguards for the producer, including a right of appeal to arbitration.

In view of the wide powers that can be conferred on marketing boards the Act provides a number of safeguards for the public interest.

First of all, of course, the scheme itself has to be approved by Parliament as well as by a majority of the producers. Then the Minister may give the board directions if it uses certain of its powers restrictively and in a way contrary to the public interest, and he may, moreover, in the public interest revoke the scheme at any time subject to the approval of Parliament.

The operation of schemes is also subject to scrutiny by standing Consumers' Committees and Committees of Investigation (separate committees for England and Wales, for Scotland and for Great Britain, with representatives from Northern Ireland added when the committees are considering schemes that extend to that country).

The Consumers' Committees report to the Minister on the effects of agricultural marketing schemes on consumers, and consider any complaints made to them by consumers. The first post-war reports of the Consumers' Committees, published in 1958, dealt with all the marketing schemes in operation apart from the eggs scheme, which was covered in a separate report published in 1960; a further report on the Potato Marketing Scheme was published in 1961 (copies of all reports are obtainable free from the Agricultural Departments). The reports drew attention to various points to which the committees suggested the boards might give consideration, but the general conclusion reached was that the marketing schemes had not operated adversely to the interests of consumers. The Committees of Investigation consider and report at the Minister's direction on any report made by Consumers' Committees or on any complaints from other than consumer interests which the Minister may refer to them, or, if the board so requests, on any directions which the Minister for his part proposes to issue to the board. Where a Committee of Investigation finds that some feature of the scheme is contrary to the complainer's interest and is not in the public interest the Minister may put the matter right by issuing directions to the Board or amending or revoking the scheme.

Only three complaints have been referred to a Committee of Investigation in recent years. A complaint against the operation of the British Wool Marketing Scheme, made by two organizations of wool merchants acting as agents of the board in the collection and handling of wool from producers, was referred to the Great Britain Committee in 1957, and on the recommendation of the committee the Minister, after considering representations submitted by the board, issued directions to the board and made an order amending the scheme. In 1959 a complaint by an individual merchant about the British Egg Marketing Board's arrangements for the sale of frozen eggs was not upheld by the committee. The third complaint, by certain Scottish wool interests against the operation of the British Wool Marketing Scheme, is still (January, 1962) being considered by the Committee.

PIG INDUSTRY DEVELOPMENT AUTHORITY

The pre-war marketing schemes for pigs and bacon which covered only pigs sold to bacon curers and not those purchased for fresh pork or for manufacture into sausages, pork pies, etc.) were not revived after the war. In accordance, however, with a recommendation in the Report of a Reorganization Commission for Pigs and Bacon,[1] a Pig Industry Development Authority for Great Britain was established under the Agriculture Act, 1957, with wide powers for securing improvements in the whole field of pig production, processing and distribution from the farm to the retailer. The seventeen members of the Authority are all appointed by the Agricultural Ministers. Three, including the Chairman, are quite independent of the industry whilst the remainder are appointed after consultation with various sections of the industry, such as pig farmers and breeders, workers and the bacon, pork and manufacturing trades.

The various schemes (some of them inherited from the Ministry) which the Authority operates for the production of better pigs, such as pig recording, progeny testing and premium boars have been referred to in Chapter VI. The Authority finances research at various Research Institutes and University Departments of Agriculture, as well as giving research scholarships. The Authority has also started a scheme for Accredited Herds as a source of good quality breeding stock.

On the processing and distribution side the Authority has prepared

[1] Cmd. 9795, 1956.

a code of practice on bacon curing which has been agreed with the British Bacon Curers Federation and recommended to all firms for voluntary adherence. They are launching a PIDA mark for home bacon as a guarantee of quality. They have also set up an advisory bureau to provide an information service for the public on British pig products generally.

The Authority gets its income from a levy on producers and purchasers of pigs. For convenience this is at present collected by a deduction from the Exchequer price guarantee payment to the pig producer.

AGRICULTURAL CO-OPERATION

In addition to its responsibilities for statutory schemes under the Agricultural Marketing Acts, the Department has always sought to encourage voluntary co-operative action on the part of producers in the purchase of their supplies, the marketing of their produce and the provision of various services.

Agricultural co-operation is firmly established in this country and steadily increasing in importance, though it has never attained such a predominant place as in some continental countries. In particular, there has been virtually no development of a co-operative credit service apart from the normal provision of merchants' credit by co-operatives. The total turnover of English and Welsh co-operative societies registered under the Industrial and Provident Societies Act is of the order of £140 million a year; well over half of this represents sale to members and others of requirements such as fertilizers and feedingstuffs. Marketing of members' produce, particularly eggs, poultry, livestock, bacon, horticultural produce and wool account for roughly one-third of the turnover. The Department makes grants to the Agricultural Central Co-operative Association and to the Welsh Agricultural Organization Society, whose functions are to promote agricultural co-operation in all its forms in England and in Wales respectively and to look after the interests of their member societies, e.g. by the provision of a work study service.

In recent years the Agricultural Central Co-operative Association has helped with the development in England of farmers' machinery syndicates which buy and operate collectively farm machinery, such as tractors and combine harvesters. The Ministry now makes a grant of one-third of the cost of erecting or converting buildings for use by such syndicates for the drying, cleaning and storage of grain and for the storage of machinery.

The English and Welsh bodies have also both taken a leading part in recent years in the organization of rabbit clearance societies (see Chapter VI).

MARKETING OF HORTICULTURAL PRODUCE

As was explained in Chapter IV, horticultural production is not covered by the price guarantees of the Agriculture Acts, 1947 and 1957, but instead is assisted by protective tariffs. Horticulturists are eligible for a number of the farming grants and subsidies, such as the fertilizer subsidy and farm water supply grants, and like other farmers are entitled to various other services provided by the Ministry such as the advice and help of the NAAS. However, from the nature of things, horticulturists cannot benefit from a number of the farming grants and subsidies directed to other branches of agriculture such as the silo subsidy and the grants for the ploughing of grassland, and in practice they are excluded also from the Small Farmer Scheme. Again, the assistance they can get under the Farm Improvement Scheme is limited by the statutory test which confines grant to items which a prudent landlord would provide for an average tenant, bearing in mind the long term needs of the land. This often rules out buildings designed for specialist or intensive production.

Horticultural production in this country accounts for some 10 per cent of our total agricultural output expressed in terms of wholesale value or, say, some £125 million annually. As with the rest of agriculture there are a wide variety of products. Vegetables range from the cabbage that may be produced on the normal farm as part of the ordinary arable rotation to such specialized products as asparagus which require special cultivation. In fruit we have at the one extreme the apple with a potential storage life sufficiently long to enable its marketing to be spread over many months and at the other highly perishable soft fruits such as the strawberry. Flowers range from annuals grown in the open to blooms such as the carnation which require special cultivation under glass.

One of the greatest problems that all horticulturists have had to face in recent years is that of marketing, including the preparation of their produce for the market. There are two reasons in particular for this. Firstly, so many horticultural products are highly perishable. Secondly, the chain of marketing and distribution from primary producer to shop is not broken, as with so much other farming produce, by an intermediate processing or manufacturing stage, such as the manufacture of wheat into flour and bread or turning the pig into bacon.

The measures which the Government announced in a recent white paper,[1] *Horticulture. A Policy for the Improvement of Production and Marketing of Horticultural Produce* are concerned predominantly with marketing, and should therefore be described in this chapter.

[1] Cmnd. 880, November, 1959.

The white paper programme constituted what the Minister described at the time as a three pronged attack covering capital grants to help growers to improve the presentation of their produce for market, the establishment of a Horticultural Marketing Council, and the modernization of Covent Garden market.

THE HORTICULTURAL IMPROVEMENT SCHEME

The Horticulture Act, 1960, provides for expenditure of up to £8 million (which with Parliamentary approval can be increased to £8¼ million) on grants to cover one-third of the cost of specified capital expenditure on horticultural holdings or by co-operative horticultural marketing associations in accordance with proposals which may be submitted over a five-year period. This scheme is thus in many ways similar to, though in a number of important respects different from, the Farm Improvement Scheme (Chapter VII).

The main differences flow from the fact that whereas the object of the Farm Improvement Scheme is essentially to improve the efficiency of *production* on the holding, the primary object of the Horticulture Improvement Scheme is to improve the facilities for storing and preparing for market the produce from the holding. This is in accordance with the Government's view that the economic position of the horticultural industry can best be helped by improvements in the quality and condition of produce consigned to market and by better timing of marketings. Thus although grants are available for a limited range of improvements to increase production efficiency (such as the removal of hedges and banks and other obstacles to production, and the improvement of existing glass-house heating systems) they are not available for the reclamation of waste land in order to bring it into horticultural use nor (with a relatively few exceptions) for the provision of buildings, such as glass-houses, in which crops are actually grown. Moreover the scheme offers grants not only for permanent buildings for the grading and packing of produce and its storage under controlled conditions of temperature and atmosphere, but also for the plant and equipment necessary for such purposes. This means that whilst the Farm Improvement Scheme covers improvement to the *land*, the Horticulture Improvement Scheme is also concerned with the *business* carried out on that land.

Like the Farm Improvement Scheme (and the Small Farmer Scheme) the present scheme is restricted to holdings that can be expected to provide a reasonable living for at least one man, but the actual tests for eligibility are rather different and are designed also to confine the grants to land that is already used for horticulture and likely to remain so. The main test is that the holding should have not less than four acres of 'eligible land' which has been in use for horticultural production for at least two years. In assessing this qualifying acreage any area occupied by glass-houses, mushroom houses or rhubarb sheds is multiplied by twenty, and land cropped under movable lights or used for growing watercress is multiplied by four, to take account of the greater intensity of production. There is also a subsidiary 'intensity of cropping' test designed to exclude land used for growing vegetables as part of a normal arable farm rotation. A further condition is that the holding must, after completion of the approved proposals, be capable of providing a reasonable living to any person carrying it on with reasonable efficiency and as a full-time occupation.

Grants under the Farm Improvement Scheme are for landlord's equipment, although either landlord or tenant can carry out the work and get grant. The grants under the present scheme are made either to the occupier of the holding or to his landlord, and to reduce the risk of public money being used to improve holdings that subsequently go out of horticultural production the occupier must satisfy the Department that he has adequate security of tenure; that is to say, he must either own the freehold of the land or occupy it under an agricultural tenancy (see Chapter VII) or under a lease with an unexpired term sufficient to cover the useful life of the proposed improvements.

Another difference from the Farm Improvement Scheme, the reason for which is obvious, is that the Horticultural Advisory Officers of the National Agricultural Advisory Service advise the Department on the technical merits of all improvement proposals, although the Agricultural Land Service is associated with them on proposals relating to buildings and other fixed equipment.

One entirely new departure is that grants for some improvements can be made not only to individual growers but also to growers' co-operative marketing associations. For a number of smaller growers it may not be economic to instal buildings for grading and packing their fruit and vegetables or to have gasproof and temperature controlled chambers for storing apples until the new year. Many, even of the larger growers, have found that it has paid them best to do their grading, packing and marketing co-operatively, especially where this has enabled the packing station to have a sufficiently large output to establish its 'brand name' in the wholesale markets as a reliable source of high quality produce.

Accordingly the provision by such co-operative associations of premises and equipment for the grading, packing and storage of its members' produce is also eligible for grant, provided the members between them have not less than the minimum of four acres of 'eligible land' mentioned above.

THE RUNCIMAN COMMITTEE AND THE HORTICULTURAL MARKETING COUNCIL

We read from time to time of instances of growers getting for their produce, whether it be lettuces, tomatoes or apples, what seems only a derisory return and certainly only a fraction of what the public are paying in the shops. Horticultural produce is very perishable and yields very variable so that when a spell of fine weather brings on ample crops some degree of glut and wastage is unavoidable. Even so the critic is left wondering whether there is not something fundamentally wrong with the present system of marketing.

It was these sort of considerations which led the Government in 1955 to appoint a committee under the chairmanship of Lord Runciman to consider whether the present arrangements for the marketing and distribution of home produced and imported vegetables, fruit and flowers could be improved.

After a very thorough examination the committee reported[1] their conclusion that many of the criticisms made of the present system of marketing and distribution were misconceived and many of the proposed solutions impracticable. They went on to say 'The costs of distribution, having regard to the services performed, are not excessive; and the profits of distributors, compared with those in other trades, are not high. We have reached the conclusion that the system, though by no means perfect, is better than any other which could take its place at present.'

The committee went on, however, to make two main recommendations for improving the present position. The first was the establishment of a Horticultural Marketing Council on which all sections of the industry should be represented, charged with the task of encouraging and fostering improvements in the marketing and distribution of vegetables, fruit and flowers, and of promoting research. This recommendation was accepted by the Government and after the practical problems involved had been examined by a non-statutory Horticultural Marketing Advisory Council the Horticulture Act of 1960 established such a Horticultural Marketing Council, with an independent chairman and deputy chairman.

The main functions of the Council will be to compile and publish information about supply, demand and prices; to encourage the grading of produce and the standardization of containers; to promote

[1] Cmnd. 61, January, 1957.

research into demand, the preparation of produce for market and methods of marketing, storage and transport; and to promote publicity. The Council has no power to regulate sales such as an agricultural marketing board might have and no powers to trade except for purposes of experiment or demonstration. The Government's intention is that the Council should eventually be financed by the industry and for this purpose it must submit to the Minister within three years a scheme for imposing charges. During this period, however, the Act authorizes contributions from public funds for the Council's expenses up to a maximum of £250,000.

The Council is now getting down to its task, but it has been established too recently for any detailed account to be given of its activities.

COVENT GARDEN MARKET

The other main recommendation of the Runciman Committee was about the fruit and vegetable markets of the London area and in particular Covent Garden. The history of Covent Garden as a fruit and vegetable market dates from 1670, when Charles II granted a Charter to the Earl of Bedford to hold a market in the square at Covent Garden. The charter rights still exist, and have passed by purchase into the hands of Covent Garden Market Ltd. The layout of the original market is still determined by an Act of Parliament which was passed in 1828 to enable the market to be improved to meet the conditions existing at that time. Conditions today of course are very different, particularly with the growth of motor traffic, and the congestion which the market causes at the present time is notorious. Another difficulty has been the piecemeal development of marketing activities over some thirty acres surrounding the area covered by the Charter and the Act of 1828.

The Runciman Committee concluded that the only body that could satisfactorily reorganize Covent Garden would be a public authority invested with the wide powers needed to accomplish this difficult task. The Government accepted this view, and the Covent Garden Market Act, 1961, has been passed by Parliament to give the Government the required powers.

The essence of the proposals to which the Act gives effect is the appointment by the Minister of a Covent Garden Market Authority which shall have the duty of acquiring the market and, later on, of building a new and up-to-date market on or near the site of the present one. The Authority, which was formally constituted in October, 1961, has power to control by licensing and regulation all marketing activities carried on throughout the area. Initially it will be financed by a loan from the Exchequer, but ultimately it will be expected to raise the necessary funds by commercial borrowing.

The present traffic congestion in the Covent Garden Market area (and, incidentally, a very serious fire risk) arises to a large extent from the large number of wooden boxes used for the conveying of produce to and from the Market which are at present stored in unsuitable premises in the vicinity. The first step proposed for relieving the congestion is that the Authority should acquire suitable accommodation outside the market areas for the storage and handling of these empty containers.

It will, of course, be some time before the new Authority will be able to develop the full plan for the reorganization of the market.

CHAPTER XI

Food

MANY of the present activities of the department described in earlier chapters could be labelled 'food' just as much as 'agriculture', if only because the agriculture of this country is almost exclusively a food producing industry (wool, flowers and nursery stock are the only important exceptions). Again, much of the work involved in administering the various agricultural price guarantee schemes described in Chapter IV, was before the amalgamation the responsibility of the Ministry of Food.

This chapter describes various part of the Ministry's work which are predominantly 'food' rather than 'agriculture'. The whole apparatus of rationing and government trading in food has of course now disappeared, and today the Government, in general, does not intervene in the activities of the food trades to nearly the same extent as it does with farming. There are, however, two main fields in which the department still intervenes. First of all, there are what may be called hygiene and consumer protection measures to ensure that certain foods, more particularly milk and meat, are protected from contamination and infection, and legislation to safeguard the consumer's interests by ensuring that he is informed of the ingredients, weights, etc. of certain of the foods he buys. Secondly, there is the task of keeping up to date the plans for safeguarding food supplies in the event of war, and any action that may be called for to safeguard food distribution in peace-time emergencies such as strikes and floods.

There are also the very general 'food' responsibilities of the Department nowadays. During and since the war it has come to be a widely held opinion that the Government has a general responsibility for food in terms of quantity, quality and price; and that not only producers but consumers, distributors and manufacturers as well have a claim on ministerial attention. Thus the Minister and the Department have had to be prepared for practically any important item of food or drink to become a burning issue.

Again there may be a call for the Government to take action if shortages result in substantial price increases, notwithstanding the fact that the Department no longer has the powers of control over stocks, prices and distribution which it had during the period of

175

control. In 1953, for example, bad weather reduced very considerably the size of the Indian tea crop, and the retail price of a representative popular blend rose from 4s a pound at the beginning of 1953 to 5s a pound a year later, and as a result of serious flooding in India in the summer of 1954 and a hold-up of supplies through the London dock strike the price by the beginning of 1955 had gone up to 7s 8d a pound.

Although the Government of this country could hardly be held responsible for this doubling of price over a period of two years, Ministers were under continued interrogation in the House of Commons on the price of tea and some seventy to eighty questions were asked over a period of twelve months.

The various commodity divisions of the Ministry therefore study all developments in the food world which may affect the feeding of the nation; and, through the National Food Survey, watch is kept on domestic consumption.

The exercise of the Minister's responsibilities for food questions often calls for scientific advice, or research which may be undertaken within the Ministry itself or through some appropriate outside organization.

FOOD STANDARDS

The adulteration of food and drink and the issue of short weight are frauds that are as old as recorded history, and measures for the protection of the consumer are among the earliest examples of social legislation. Our earliest food legislation seems to be an Act passed in 1266 to protect the purchaser against short weight in bread and the sale of unsound meat. Later on there were numerous Acts for safeguarding the quality of particular commodities such as bread, hops, butter and wine and for checking their adulteration. The first general Act designed to check the adulteration not merely of particular foods but of food generally was passed in 1860; this Act among other things enabled district boards and town councils to appoint and pay public analysts, a provision essential to the enforcement of any pure food legislation.

The governing statute is now the Food and Drugs Act, 1955, and many of the powers under this Act are exercised jointly by the Minister of Agriculture, Fisheries and Food and the Minister of Health.

Broadly two methods of control, not necessarily mutually exclusive, are possible under the Act. The first method is to specify what may and what may not be contained in a particular food, class of food, or in foods generally; the second is to specify how a particular food is or is not to be designated, labelled or advertised, and in particular what information about its composition should be given to the purchaser. If the departments consider that there may be a case for regulations to control the composition, description, etc. of any food, they usually seek the advice first of all of the Food Standards Committee which includes trade and scientific members, representatives of consumer interests and enforcing authorities, as well as members appointed in a personal capacity. After hearing evidence from the trade and those responsible for enforcement the Committee normally issues a report making recommendations. If these recommendations are accepted by Ministers as a basis for action then all the interests substantially affected are consulted on detailed proposals for regulations. The Ministers then decide whether or not to make the regulations, with or without amendment of the proposals. If made, the regulations have to be laid before each House of Parliament and for a period of forty sitting days can be annulled on a motion from either House. Some regulations provoke considerable controversy and whilst actual annulment would be very rare it is quite usual for a motion to be put down to enable them to be debated.

The regulations which now prescribe standards for ice cream provide a good example of the sort of controversy that can arise. Before the war most ice cream contained milk fat, though there was some made from margarine. During the war the use of cream or milk in ice cream was prohibited and all manufacturers used other fats, such as those derived from whale oil, palm kernel oil or coconut oil.

When ample supplies of milk, cream and butter became available it was argued by some that it was wrong to describe as ice cream something that contained no milk fat at all. To this the rejoinder was made that no one expected, say, salad cream or peppermint cream to contain milk solids (though it is reputed that an over-zealous official had at one time sought to stop a well-known brand of sherry being sold under the name 'Bristol Milk') and that people had for many years become used to ice cream that contained no milk fat at all and the continuation of this practice was not likely to mislead the public. Ministers eventually accepted the recommendation of the Food Standards Committee that products which did not contain any milk fat (but had minimum quantities of other fats and certain other ingredients) could continue to be sold as 'ice cream', and not under some new and unfamiliar name such as 'frozen dessert'. New standards were, however, introduced for products to be known as 'dairy ice cream' and 'milk ice' which were not to be made from other than milk fats. As a further safeguard, however, the Ministers decided that where pre-packed ice cream contained vegetable or other non-milk fat the fact should be indicated on the label or

M

container. The Ice Cream Regulations are therefore an example of those that control both the ingredients in the article and the information to be supplied about the ingredients.

It should not be supposed that standards need to be established by regulations for all foodstuffs. Very often the consumer is adequately protected by the general provision that has been part of Food and Drugs legislation since 1875 that it is an offence to sell to the prejudice of the purchaser any food which is not of the nature, substance and quality of the article demanded by the purchaser. If, for example, some unscrupulous person sold as 'marzipan' a product consisting of almond flavouring added to a paste made from nuts other than almonds he would be guilty of an offence, and the local authorities responsible for enforcement would expect no difficulty in securing a conviction.

A regulation must not only be necessary to supplement the more general provisions of the Act; the standards it lays down must be such as can be verified by analysis of the article after it has been purchased.

There is, for example, much to be said for an ice-cream standard which takes account of the amount of air whipped into the liquid mix as it freezes; this may vary considerably and hence affect the amount of nutriment in a given volume of ice cream. So far, however, the difficulties of enforcement have precluded a standard based on the volume of the products as sold. For instance, the act of sampling from bulk may change the physical condition of the sample taken. Again, under the statutory sampling procedure, a part of the sample must be held available for examination by the Government Chemist in the event of a prosecution. This means that it must be stored in its original condition for as long as six months, and a reliable way of doing this has still to be found in the case of this product.

Food and Drugs authorities (namely county councils, and councils of borough and urban districts with a population of over 40,000) are responsible for the enforcement of the Food and Drugs legislation (in some cases the Minister has concurrent powers of enforcement). Each Food and Drugs authority is required to appoint a public analyst (who is obviously a key person in the enforcement of the Act) and the appointment and discharge of this officer is subject to the Minister's approval.

Legislation dealing with weights and measures is the responsibility of the Board of Trade, but the Ministry keeps in close touch with that department on everything concerning food.

The aim of the Merchandise Marks Acts is to prevent goods from being sold under false or misleading descriptions, and in particular to safeguard purchasers from being misled into thinking that imported goods are home produced. Orders in Council can be made to prohibit the sale of certain imported goods unless they bear a specified mark to show that they are imported. Here again the Board of Trade is the department normally responsible for the administration of the Acts, but the Ministry is responsible whenever it is a question of food, such as bacon. Orders in Council requiring the marking of imported goods can be made only after a public inquiry by a standing committee set up under the Act and there is a separate committee for agriculture or fisheries produce. The orders are laid in draft before Parliament and are not made until after a period of forty sitting days, during which either House could pass a resolution against the making of the order. In general responsibility for the enforcement of the Acts and of the Minister's Orders thereunder lies with local authorities, but the Ministry has independent power to take action itself.

SLAUGHTER-HOUSES AND MEAT INSPECTION

The majority of the provisions of Food and Drugs legislation concerned with hygiene and public health are primarily the responsibility of the Ministry of Health. There are, however, two foods, meat and milk, where for various reasons the Ministry of Agriculture, Fisheries and Food has special responsibilities.

Slaughter-houses have been very much the concern of the Ministry of Food ever since the Department became responsible early in the war for the purchase of all fatstock and for controlling the distribution of meat.

Before the war there were in England and Wales some 12,000 slaughter-houses, most of them old, small and badly sited. During the period of control all fatstock was purchased by the Ministry of Food at a limited number of 'collecting centres' and all slaughtering was concentrated in about 500 of the pre-war slaughter-houses, to which were added, after the war, a few new ones built by the Ministry. This was done as a necessary part of the system for distributing and allocating meat supplies under the rationing system, but it had the incidental but very real benefit that the general standard of hygiene in slaughter-houses was raised, the beasts were treated more humanely, slaughtering methods were more efficient and better use was made of the offals and other by-products. Moreover, all meat had to be inspected before it left the premises.

When the Ministry of Food ceased to control distribution in 1954 the slaughter-houses which had remained in operation during the control period were no longer sufficient to meet the requirements of the butcher who wished to do his slaughtering locally, and a number of the old slaughter-houses were reopened and some new ones were built. The total used at one time amounted to some 4,400 but has since fallen to about 3,500.

The aims of government policy are adequate facilities, humane conditions and high standards of hygiene in slaughter-houses. Accordingly new standards of construction and practice for humane and hygienic conditions in slaughter-houses were established from January 1, 1959, by regulations made by the Minister under the Slaughter of Animals Act, 1958, and, jointly with the Minister of Health, under the Food and Drugs Act, 1955. Some of these standards were immediately applied to all slaughter-houses, full compliance with the remainder was required from the outset for any new slaughter-house. For existing slaughter-houses full compliance was required from a date appointed by the Minister for each local authority area in the light of a report from the authority on the slaughter-house requirements and facilities of the area. After the date appointed by the Minister the local authority cannot renew the licence of any slaughter-house which does not comply fully with the regulations and it is anticipated that the total number of slaughter-houses will fall to about 2,500. The local authority is responsible for enforcing the regulations but the Ministry's veterinary staff co-operate with advice and assistance.

After the local authority has submitted to the Minister its report on the slaughter-house requirements and facilities in its area, any application for a new slaughter-house licence must be referred to the Minister, who directs the authority to grant the licence if he is satisfied that the new slaughter-house premises are needed for securing adequate slaughtering facilities in the area, or to refuse the application if he is not satisfied on this point. The Minister may also direct the authority to grant a licence for special reasons.

A closely connected question is that of inspection of meat by local authorities at the slaughter-house to see that it is fit for consumption. The Food and Drugs Act gives local authorities the necessary powers for this, but at the moment leaves them free to decide the amount of inspection, and in fact some meat still leaves slaughter-houses uninspected. The Minister's objective is to secure that all meat is inspected by local authorities; the shortage of qualified meat inspectors has been a difficulty, but this is being gradually overcome.

Imported meat also should be inspected before it reaches the consumer. It would be a physical impossibility to inspect the meat when it arrives at the ports, and therefore the Department needs to be satisfied that a satisfactory inspection is carried out in the exporting countries. Accordingly under the Public Health (Imported Food) Regulations no meat or meat products may be imported for human consumption unless accompanied by an official certificate in the form of a label or stamp recognized by the Minister to certify that the meat (whether in carcase form or made into meat products such as canned meat) has been produced from healthy animals, inspected before and after slaughter, and that it has been handled, processed and packed in a hygienic manner. Before the official certificate of any country is accepted one of the Ministry's veterinary officers normally visits the country to satisfy himself that there is a satisfactory system for the inspection of meat and for ensuring hygienic conditions in slaughter-houses and meat product factories.

Some meat, for example the products of knackers' yards, or meat rejected by inspectors at slaughter-houses, is clearly unfit for human consumption, and it is the Ministry's business to see that it is not sold for that purpose. Regulations have, therefore, been made under which unfit meat from slaughter-houses must be sterilized, and so rendered harmless, and all knacker meat must either be sterilized, or be stained to make it recognizable as such. Unfit meat which goes into manufactured pet food, or is used for manufacturing purposes not connected with food, is rendered harmless to human health by the processing it undergoes.

MILK PRODUCTION AND DISTRIBUTION

Milk is claimed to be a perfect and complete food for man. It is indeed, but there are also many bacteria and other harmful organisms which could thrive and multiply in it. Precautions are therefore taken to prevent milk being infected at any stage before it leaves the cow until it reaches the consumer, or as a result of the condition of the cow.

Since 1885 there have been regulations, now called Milk and Dairies Regulations, requiring all dairy farms to be registered and specifying the hygienic precautions to be observed in the production and distribution of milk at all stages from the farm to the retail dairy or milk round. The current regulations provide for the inspection of cows, and lay down standards for buildings where cows are milked or where milk is handled and stored to ensure that the interior is light, well ventilated, easy to clean and properly drained. They also prescribe special conditions to be observed in the milking of cows and in the cleansing of appliances and vessels used for milk. Where the Medical Officer of Health suspects that any milk may be infected he may prohibit the sale of the milk or require it to be pasteurized or sterilized in order to destroy any harmful organisms in the milk. He may also prohibit a milker or other worker who handles milk from attending his employment if he has reason to believe that the worker is suffering from an infection which may contaminate the milk.

Originally the enforcement of the Milk and Dairies Regulations was wholly in the hands of local authorities, but in a white paper, *Measures to Improve the Quality of the Nation's Milk Supply*,[1] published in 1943, the Government announced their intention to take further steps to ensure that milk reaching the public was of good quality and free from harmful infection. One of the proposals announced was that the responsibility for administering the Milk and Dairies Regulations at the farm should be transferred to the Ministry of Agriculture and Fisheries. The reason for this was that the diffusion of responsibility between the different county and district councils was open to serious criticism on grounds of lack of uniformity, especially where the supplies, say, of a big London wholesaler were drawn from farms scattered perhaps over a dozen counties. Another argument for this transfer of responsibility was that, as large quantities of milk were being supplied to schoolchildren and other priority classes of consumers under government schemes, the central authority ought to accept a greater degree of responsibility for controlling the conditions under which milk was produced and handled. Statutory authority for the transfer was provided by the Food and Drugs (Milk and Dairies) Act, 1944, and by the Milk (Special Designations) Act, 1949. The local Medical Officer of Health still retains the power, referred to above, to deal with infected milk or with persons who may be the cause of infection of milk, wherever it may arise.

The white paper emphasized that the production of tuberculin tested (TT) milk should be encouraged. As the name implies, tuberculin tested milk must be produced from cows which have been shown to be free from tuberculosis. (As mentioned in Chapter VI, bovine tuberculosis has now been virtually stamped out in the United Kingdom under the Attested Herds Scheme). A farmer wishing to sell TT milk must, of course, comply with the Milk and Dairies (General) Regulations. But quite apart from these requirements his milk supply is sampled and must periodically pass a statutory test of keeping quality. The greater part of our milk supply is now of TT standard.

Over almost the whole of England and Wales, milk sold by retail is required to be bottled and to be either heat-treated (pasteurized or sterilized) or, if sold raw, of TT standard. Pasteurization or sterilization destroys any harmful organisms and makes the milk keep better without any serious impairment of its flavour or nutritive value. Most milk is heat-treated before retail sale.

[1] Cmd. 6454.

The improvements envisaged in the 1943 white paper have thus been largely achieved.

The Ministry's Milk Service, under its Chief Milk Officer, is responsible for technical work on the administration of the Milk and Dairies Regulations and for other work arising on the Government's clean, safe milk policy. Like most other technical services of the Ministry its officers are for the most part based on the regional and divisional offices.

Milk Officers inspect farms as necessary to see that they comply with the Milk and Dairies Regulations. This 'statutory' work is combined with advice to farmers on buildings, equipment, and production methods—all with the objective of assisting them to produce clean, safe milk. Farm visits are supplemented by lectures to groups of farmers and by farm and other demonstrations designed to arouse greater interest in all aspects of clean milk production. The Service works in close association with the Ministry's Regional Advisory Bacteriologists, who advise on the suitability of water supplies in use on dairy farms and on any other problems requiring a bacteriological investigation.

Some Milk Officers also supervise laboratories at which samples of TT milk are tested for keeping quality and other laboratory tests arising from clean milk work are carried out.

THE AUSTRALIAN MEAT AGREEMENT

During the war and the immediate post-war period the Ministry of Food made a number of long term agreements or contracts with overseas governments or producers' organizations in order to ensure our future supplies of important foodstuffs. Only two of these remain in force today, the Commonwealth Sugar Agreement, which has been described in Chapter IV, and the Australian Meat Agreement.

The object of the latter agreement, which runs from 1952 to 1967, was to increase the production of meat in Australia and consequently the export of meat to the United Kingdom. The United Kingdom agreed to take all of Australia's exportable surplus of beef, mutton and lamb at guaranteed minimum prices, while Australia undertook to encourage increased production and to accept restrictions on exports to countries other than the United Kingdom or British Dependencies during part of the period of the agreement.

The minimum prices are negotiated periodically (normally at three-yearly intervals) between the two governments for up to six years in advance for beef and up to three years in advance for mutton and lamb. When the United Kingdom Government ceased to trade in meat in 1954 an alternative method had to be devised of implementing the minimum prices in the free market (just as the ending of State trading and control meant finding alternative means to implement the price guarantees to the home farmer). Under the present arrangement the seven largest importers of Australian meat on Smithfield market provide the Ministry each week with details of average prices at which different classes and grades of beef, mutton and lamb have been sold, wholesaler to retailer. These returns are considered by a small committee consisting of representatives of the Ministry and of the Australian Government, with an independent chartered accountant as chairman, and a figure is agreed for the average price of Australian beef, mutton and lamb, for each week converted to a f.o.b. basis. If over the year as a whole (running from November to October) the weighted average price for either beef, mutton or lamb is below the minimum, then the deficit on the total tonnage of that meat (i.e. beef, mutton or lamb) received during the year is paid to the Australian Government. For the purpose of this calculation a surplus on one type of meat cannot be used to offset a deficiency in another. Deficiency payments are passed on to exporters through the Australian Meat Board by means of bounty payments on exported meat.

FOOD RESEARCH

The Department's work in the field of food research and the responsibilities of its Chief Scientific Adviser (Food) are now broadly governed by the recommendations of the first annual report of the Government's Advisory Committee on Scientific Policy[1]—

'a. That executive departments should be responsible for identifying problems requiring research, settling their order of priority, deciding where the various investigations should be carried out and applying their results.

b. That executive departments should, as a rule, appoint a Chief Scientific Officer whose functions should be to advise generally on the scientific aspects of departmental policy, and, in particular, to define the problems calling for research, to make the necessary arrangements for its conduct and to watch the application of its results; and that he should be provided with an adequate staff capable of undertaking operational research covering the economic, technical and other factors affected by scientific advances.'

Most of the Ministry's own scientific work is connected with questions for which the department has specific executive responsi-

[1] Cmd. 7465, 1948.

bility. There are, for example several lines of work directed towards ensuring food supplies in war-time. In 1950 a Research Establishment and Experimental Factory was established at Aberdeen for the development of dehydrated foods, and a new technique, known as Accelerated Freeze Drying, was evolved. The new lightweight, stable foods produced by this process have been found to be more palatable than anything previously available. The Ministry has now ceased to operate the Aberdeen establishment as it was decided that the process had reached a stage at which private enterprise should take over; some of the research projects, however, have been transferred to various food research establishments under the aegis of the Agricultural Research Council. The researches into new dehydration processes at Aberdeen have included fundamental work into flavour, quality, etc., which has application to other forms of food preservation.

The Department has also carried out research on the long-term storage of essential foods which might be included in the strategic stockpile. This has included work on questions such as warehouse climate, the compression of foodstuffs and the effects of containers on contents and vice versa which are of more than defence interest.

Research work on atomic energy in which the department takes part includes studies on the effects of radioactive materials on growing plants and animals and on stored foods; design of monitoring instruments to determine the levels of radioactivity in foods; and methods of protection and decontamination.

Other work arises from the Department's responsibilities for food hygiene and standards. For instance, studies have been made on the micro flora of meat at a slaughter-house as a basis of studying changes during the distribution of meat and during manufacturing processes. Work is also done in collaboration with the Ministry's experimental centres and agricultural scientists to see what effects new methods of breeding, feeding and management of livestock may have on the quality of meat and of eggs. The Department also studies the nature and occurrence of chemical additives and of contamination in food.

The Ministry's scientific staff are also concerned with more general questions of nutrition. Information about the amounts and nutritional value of the foods consumed in this country is available from the records of domestic food consumption collected by the National Food Survey and also from estimates of the amount of food available for consumption. This information is used as a guide on matters of nutritional policy and aspects of national diet which require investigation. The nutritional problems revealed by these data are dealt with by Nutrition Section of the Ministry's scientific staff usually in collaboration with the Ministry of Health and the Medical

Research Council. They also study the nutritive value of new foods and of familiar foods presented in new forms.

The Chief Scientific Adviser (Food) and the other scientific staff concerned with food need to be aware of the facilities for food research available elsewhere and of the research work in progress. New lines of work for which a need is established are placed, so far as possible, with the appropriate research establishment; the Ministry itself only undertakes research and investigation which cannot be placed elsewhere.

The Department of Scientific and Industrial Research was until recently responsible for the bulk of government-financed research on food questions. In 1959, however, the Agricultural Research Council took over three of the DSIR food research establishments, namely, the Low Temperature Research Station at Cambridge (basic research into changes in animal and plant tissue under conditions not only of cold storage but of other methods of food treatment and preservation, such as curing, drying and canning), the Ditton Laboratory at East Malling (problems of storage of fruit and vegetable, such as the storage of apples in refrigerated chambers with a controlled atmosphere), and the Pest Infestation Research Laboratory at Slough. The DSIR remains responsible, however, for the Torry Research Station at Aberdeen which studies problems of the storage and processing of fish and its by-products.

There are no grant-aided Food Research Institutes corresponding to the Agricultural Research Institutes such as Rothamsted. On the other hand, there are Research Associations, each with its own laboratories, which are financed jointly by the industry and by the Department of Scientific and Industrial Research; these are concerned respectively with problems of flour milling, baking, food manufacture (more particularly meat products, chocolate and confectionery), and fruit and vegetable canning and quick freezing. In addition there is the British Industrial Biological Research Association which was formed at the end of 1960 to investigate the possible effects upon human health of chemicals present in food and drink. The Ministry keeps in touch with the work of these research bodies, and also takes part in the planning of the food research projects of international bodies such as the Food and Agriculture Organization and the Organization for European Economic Co-operation.

When the Agricultural Research Council assumed their new responsibility for food research the Minister and the Secretary of State for Scotland established a Food Research Advisory Committee under the chairmanship of the Permanent Secretary of the Ministry with membership drawn from persons with experience in the food industry or qualified in the allied sciences; the Secretary of the ARC is a member *ex officio*. The Committee's terms of reference are—

'To advise on those problems (except fish, which is dealt with separately) requiring investigation or research which should be undertaken with the aid of public funds, and to make recommendations as to the priorities to be accorded to such problems.'

This Committee can, therefore, be regarded as filling the same role in relation to State-financed food research as that of the Agricultural Improvement Council (see Chapter V) in relation to agricultural research.

DEFENCE PLANNING

In Chapter II some idea was given of the work undertaken prior to September, 1939, in preparing plans both for a food production campaign and also for food control in the event of war. Similarly the Ministry, like other departments, has to plan against the possibility of another war, although all engaged on this task most sincerely hope that the need to bring their plans into operation will never arise.

The Ministry's Emergency Services Division has general responsibility for preparing defence plans and for co-ordinating them with those of other departments, but all headquarters divisions are responsible for devising and developing plans within their own particular spheres, and Regional Controllers are responsible for considering how the plans could be implemented in their respective regions. The Ministry is responsible for food defence questions, apart from emergency feeding, in Scotland and Northern Ireland. The Ministry has a small defence staff located in Northern Ireland under a Food Defence Officer, and an officer of the Department of Health for Scotland, designated as Food Defence Officer for Scotland, is responsible to the Ministry for defence planning work in that country.

Local food officers designate (in general one for each local authority area, though some areas have combined for this purpose) are being appointed to plan the local organization.

Under conditions of nuclear war communal feeding might be necessary on a scale far exceeding that of the last war, as a result of hurried evacuation, the destruction of homes, interruption of gas, water or electricity services, or the breakdown of the normal peacetime arrangements for food distribution. This would be undertaken by local authorities (county and county borough councils) as part of their civil defence duties and the Ministry is reimbursing the whole of their expenses of peace-time training and exercises in communal feeding.

The Ministry has laid in stocks of emergency feeding equipment, such as Soyer boilers and field cookers for providing quickly supplies of soup, stew, or tea, and some of this is on loan to local authorities. The 'Queen's Messenger Convoys' which in the last war did such splendid work in providing emergency meals after air raids have been continued under the title of 'Food Flying Squads' staffed by members of the Women's Voluntary Service in England and Wales and Scotland, and by members of the Women's Institutes in Northern Ireland. These would be the shock troops of emergency feeding to provide hot drinks and light meals as soon as possible after an attack until such times as the local authority was able to cope with the situation from its own resources. These Flying Squads gave invaluable assistance in looking after those who were driven from their homes by the east coast floods of 1953, and the vehicles concerned proudly display this in their legend of battle honours. They have continued to render similar services in civil emergencies such as those produced by the widespread floods in the winter of 1960.

PEACE-TIME CIVIL EMERGENCIES

The organization for safeguarding food supplies in peace-time 'emergencies' was one of the few continuous links between the first and the second Ministry of Food and this continues to be one of the responsibilities of the present department.

'Emergency' is sometimes thought of as a bureaucratic euphemism for war. However, in the Ministry 'civil emergency' is a useful bit of shorthand for any happenings which may interrupt seriously the production or distribution of food. The term covers 'Acts of God' such as the east coast floods of 1953, industrial disputes such as the railway strike of 1955, or special shortages such as that which led to petrol rationing at the time of the Suez dispute of 1956/57. The Emergency Services Division is responsible for co-ordinating within the Ministry the arrangements for maintaining essential supplies and services during such peace-time emergencies.

ATOMIC ENERGY

In spite of the importance of atomic energy nowadays, it may at first sight seem a little surprising that the Department should need both administrative and scientific staff for work arising from peace-time uses of atomic energy and radioactivity. So far the only important application of atomic energy to agriculture is the use of radioactive tracers and other devices for research work. In the food industry some applications such as low dose treatments for the destruction of insect pests or of harmful micro-organisms are ready for technical development. The sterilization of foods with ionizing radiation is still at the research stage.

The main task of the Ministry, however, is to safeguard the agricultural, fishing and food industries and the consumer from harmful effects which may arise incidentally from the use of atomic energy.

All establishments at which nuclear reactors are sited are capable of producing substantial quantities of radioactive wastes. Unless the disposal of these wastes is properly controlled there is a risk that food, feedingstuffs and fish will be contaminated with consequent risk to human beings and to livestock. The Minister of Agriculture, Fisheries and Food has accordingly been given specific powers to control the disposal of the radioactive waste from such plants, which may take the form of a gas or airborne dust emerging from a chimney, a liquid perhaps carried by pipeline to the sea, rivers or brooks, or solid materials buried in a special dumping ground. (The Minister of Housing and Local Government has similar powers to deal with hazards to the public through drinking water or breathing the atmosphere). The operator requires an authorization from the Minister for disposing of these radioactive by-products, and before the authorization is given the Department will need to be satisfied there is no danger to the agricultural or fishing industries or food production. The operator is required to keep records of the action taken under the authorization, and scientifically qualified inspectors from the Department visit the installation from time to time to make certain that the conditions of the authorization are being complied with. In addition, the Ministry's own radiobiological laboratories carry out various biological analyses, such as the assessments of the radio-iodine content of sheep thyroids and of the uptake of radio-active matter by fish and marine organisms, to make certain that the amount of radioactive contamination is not exceeding the accepted limits.

The Department is also responsible for co-ordinating plans to deal with any hazards to agriculture, fisheries or food which might arise from an accident at a nuclear installation. For example, when the accident occurred in 1957 which put the United Kingdom Atomic Energy Authority's reactor at Windscale out of action there was a risk that herbage in the neighbourhood would be contaminated with radio-active materials and that this, if eaten by grazing cows, would make their milk dangerous. As a result the Ministry arranged for any milk produced from the areas affected to be safely disposed of until the risk was over. The Ministry is, of course, very closely interested in the survey which the Agricultural Research Council is carrying out on the effects of radioactive fallout from atomic explosions, and with the other UK Agricultural Departments has assisted the Council in the assembly of samples for this survey and has also co-operated in experimental work on such questions as the amount of radioactivity in the milk of cows which have grazed on pastures which have been treated to reproduce the conditions resulting from different degrees of contamination by radioactive fallout.

CHAPTER XII

Fisheries

THE Fisheries Department (comprising two divisions under an Under Secretary, the Fisheries Secretary) is very much of a Ministry in miniature. It has a general responsibility for fisheries, both sea and fresh water, in England and Wales. Its interests cover all kinds of marine life—from the oyster to the whale. Its responsibilities can be considered under three headings. First, there are the sea fisheries ranging from the distant water fleet fishing as far afield as the Arctic waters to the small inshore boats fishing round our own coasts, Secondly, there are the salmon and freshwater fisheries which include not only small commercial fisheries but the waters fished by a vast army of amateur anglers. Thirdly, there is the small but important whaling industry with its catchers ranging the waters of the Antarctic.

SEA FISHERIES

The Fisheries Department is concerned with all aspects of the fishing industry from the catching of the fish in the sea to its appearance on the fishmonger's slab. We do not eat quite so much fish as do some other nations but nevertheless over a £100 million worth of fish and fish products are consumed each year. Of this about half is imported—mostly canned fish such as salmon—and about half comes from our own fishing fleets.

Our fishing fleets are made up of three main groups. First, there is the distant water fleet of some 240 vessels which fish mostly for the cheaper kinds of fish such as cod, haddock and plaice in the waters around Iceland, in the Barents Sea and off the coasts of North Norway, Spitsbergen and West Greenland, and occasionally off the Canadian coast. They bring back about half of the home caught fish. Then there are the middle and near water vessels—about 650 of them, which fish the waters around the Faröes; also in the North Sea and other waters around the British Isles, where in addition to cod, haddock and plaice, higher quality fish such as sole is caught. Included in the near water group are the seiners, which specialize in catching prime fish.

Thirdly, there are about 4,000 small inshore boats which catch a large variety of fish including shellfish, pilchards and sprats.

Some of the near water and inshore vessels driftnet for herring in the North Sea and Irish Sea, and the English Channel. This is a seasonal and highly specialized section of the industry.

These three sections between them land over £50 million worth of fish in our ports each year. All the distant water and most of the middle water boats come from the major fishing ports of Hull, Grimsby and Fleetwood, while the rest of the fishing fleet come from ports all round our shores ranging in size from Lowestoft, Milford Haven and North Shields to the small fishing villages like Robin Hood's Bay or St Ives. The fish when landed is mostly sold by auction to the wholesale merchants in the ports or for some form of processing such as drying, smoking, canning or conversion into quick frozen fillets or fish sticks. From the port wholesaler the fish is transported either by road or by rail to the retail fish merchant or to the fish and chip shop, much passing through inland wholesale markets like Billingsgate or through the hands of inland wholesalers. Rapid transport is essential for such a highly perishable commodity as fish and the industry is proud of the fact that most fresh fish is on sale in the retail shop the morning after it has been landed.

This is a brief picture of our sea fishing industry. It throws up a great variety of problems both great and small. Many of the questions affect other government departments such as the Scottish Office and the Home Office who are responsible for the fishing industries in Scotland and Northern Ireland respectively; the Admiralty on fishery protection questions; the Foreign Office and the Commonwealth Relations Office on international questions relating to fisheries; the Ministry of Transport on safety at sea; and the Board of Trade and the Customs as regards imports.

In addition to these questions for which the Fisheries Department has a primary responsibility for government policy it also has to concern itself with other matters particularly of commercial and economic policy in so far as they affect the fishing industry. Thus the Fisheries Department has to see that the interests of the industry are fully taken into account when tariff and trade agreements are being negotiated, and must give advice. It takes part in the discussions of international bodies concerned with trade such as the Organization for Economic Co-operation and Development and the General Agreement on Tariffs and Trade when fish and fish products are being considered.

Reorganization and Development

The Government's role in relation to the fishing industry has widened considerably in recent years. The first step in this direction was taken when, in accordance with the Sea-Fishing Industry Act, 1933, a Sea Fish Commission was appointed under the chairmanship of Sir Andrew Duncan to investigate matters relating to all branches of the industry from the catching of the fish to its sale, and to report whether, and if so what, steps should be taken towards reorganization.

The first report of the Commission led to the establishment of a Herring Industry Board consisting of a chairman and two other members who have no financial or commercial interest in the industry, appointed by the Fishery Ministers (i.e. the Minister of Agriculture, Fisheries and Food, the Secretary of State for Scotland and the Home Secretary), with powers (transferred to the Fishery Ministers by subsequent legislation) to make schemes for the reorganization and development and regulation of that side of the industry. The current activities of the Board under such schemes (which need to be submitted to Parliament by Ministers and approved by affirmative resolution of both Houses) include the operation of factories for processing surplus herrings for the manufacture of fertilizers and animal feedingstuffs, the making of rules governing minimum prices of first hand sale of herrings and the setting of minimum standards for processed herrings and herring products.

The final Report of the Duncan Commission led to the establishment under the Sea Fish Industry Act, 1938, of a White Fish Commission which for practical purposes had to be wound up on the outbreak of war in 1939 before it had time to do very much.

The years immediately following the war were busy and profitable for all sections of the deep sea fishing industry. Trawlers were returning from their war-time duties—those of them that survived—and the demand for fish was strong as long as other foods were scarce. It was not until 1949 that the industry once more found itself in difficulties, this time more acutely than before. For one reason and another the price obtainable for fish fell far below production costs; the catching side of the industry lost money heavily; trawlers were laid up in large numbers; and the future looked black indeed for both owners and men.

To meet these difficulties the Government came forward with plans differing somewhat from those of the 1938 Act. These met with full agreement in the industry and were embodied in the Sea Fish Industry Act, 1951. Under this Act the Fishery Ministers appointed a White Fish Authority consisting of five members with no commercial or financial interest in the industry on much the same lines as the earlier White Fish Commission. As under the 1938 Act the Authority was assisted by an Advisory Council which contained representatives of all sides of the industry. The Act gave the Authority considerable executive powers to use its finances to undertake certain commercial activities and to assist people engaged in the fishing industry.

N

In addition, however, the Authority is authorized, after consulting the interests concerned, to prepare schemes to enable it to do virtually anything it thinks necessary for the better organization, development or regulation of the white fish industry or any section of it. Any scheme of this kind has to be published in draft and is open to objections and, if necessary, to public inquiry; and it requires the approval not only of the Ministers but also of both Houses of Parliament. This procedure was deliberately adopted because it was recognized that many of the problems of the industry were so complex that they would require much further investigation before there could be any hope of propounding solutions for them. In the exercise of its powers the White Fish Authority has undertaken various measures designed to improve distribution and the quality of fish reaching the market; to increase consumption of fish; to discover new fishing grounds; and to improve the efficiency of fishing gear. For example, with the co-operation of the other interests concerned the Authority has carried out a scheme for controlling the quality of fish landed at Hull and is examining the problem of mechanizing landing and handling of fish at Grimsby. Valuable information on methods of freezing fish at sea has also been gained from experiments made by the Authority.

To finance its activities the Authority can impose a statutory levy, at present $\frac{1}{2}$d per stone, on every person purchasing white fish at first hand sales. In its experimental projects the Authority is aided by grants from the Government and also by contributions from the industry, and it keeps in the closest touch with the scientific staff employed by the Fishery Departments.

The 1951 Act enabled the Authority to make loans for the purchase of fishing vessels and gear, and for plant for processing white fish. There was small response to the offer of these loans, and the near and middle water sections of the fishing fleet continued to diminish at a fairly rapid rate until the White Fish and Herring Industries Act, 1953, gave the White Fish Authority and the Herring Industry Board power to make grants as well as loans, although only for inshore, near and middle water vessels. One of the difficulties of the industry was the higher costs of the older fishing vessels with coal-fired engines, and the White Fish and Herring Industries Act, 1957, authorized grants towards the cost of converting such engines to either diesel or oil-fired steam propulsion.

The Fisheries Department of the Ministry and of the Scottish Office exercise a general supervision over the activities of the White Fish Authority and the Herring Industry Board both through the estimates for expenditure each year and through keeping in close touch with the two bodies. Again, for example, the approval of

Fishery Departments is required for any experimental project for which government financial assistance is wanted. In the last resort the Fishery Ministers can give either body such general directions as they consider necessary in the national interest.

Apart from the oversight over the affairs of the White Fish Authority and the Herring Industry Board the Fisheries Department is directly responsible for the administration of the fishery subsidies. The 1953 Act gave specific authority for a subsidy on white fish (from which the distant water fleet was excluded), which has in fact been paid since 1950, and the 1957 Act extended it to include herrings. The rates of subsidy are fixed annually in the light of a general review of the previous year's fishing and the prospects for the coming year, and are embodied in schemes requiring parliamentary approval by affirmative resolution. A total of approximately £2½ million (UK) was paid in all, in the financial year 1960/61. The White Fish and Herring Industries Act, 1961, extended the subsidy to the distant water fleet.

The subsidy to the near and middle water fleet, and also now to distant water vessels, takes the form of a payment varying according to the size and nature of the vessel for each day spent at sea. This is also the arrangement for the larger herring vessels. For the smaller herring vessels and for the inshore industry the subsidy is based on the weight of fish landed.

In August, 1961, a white paper[1] was issued giving the Government's proposals on various recommendations in the Report[2] of the Committee under the chairmanship of Lord Fleck which had been considering the size and pattern and implications of an economic fishing industry in the United Kingdom. The Government accepted, in principle, the Committee's recommendation that there should be continued financial assistance for the whole of the fishing industry both by way of operational subsidies and by way of grants and loans for the construction and modernization of vessels, for a period of ten years, and said that it would be an objective of Government policy that the trawler section of the industry should become self-supporting by the end of that period. A Bill to give effect to the Government's proposals is at present (January, 1962) before Parliament.

Inshore Fisheries

In England and Wales there are special arrangements for looking after our inshore fisheries. These, while they now account for less than 7 per cent by value of all landings, are nevertheless of considerable economic importance to a number of small communities around our coast.

[1] Cmnd. 1453.   [2] Cmnd. 1266.

Under the Sea Fisheries Regulation Act, 1888, and subsequent legislation there are now eleven local sea fishery committees which regulate the inshore fisheries in their respective districts of England and Wales. At least half the members of each committee are nominees of the principal local authorities of the district, and the remainder are appointed by local river boards and by the Minister. The committee's expenses are met by the Local Authorities of the area. In addition, there are nineteen river boards (see Chapter VII) which have the powers of local sea fishery committees within parts of their areas, but only nine of them have made by-laws relating to sea-fisheries.

Committees can make by-laws to restrict or prohibit any particular method of fishing or the use of any particular instrument, and to prohibit or regulate the discharge into the sea of substances that may harm fish. They also have powers for keeping down the numbers of predatory fish, marine animals such as seals, and birds, when this is necessary for the preservation and improvement of the fisheries and is not prohibited by other legislation. They can also contribute towards the cost of maintenance or improvement works at small fishery harbours.

The Minister also can make grants to harbour authorities towards the cost of works of construction, improvement or repair of fishing facilities.

The local committees appoint Fishery Officers to enforce their by-laws. The by-laws require the approval of the Minister and this means the Fisheries Department must keep in close touch with the committees. Where objections are lodged to proposed by-laws local enquiries may need to be held before a decision is taken about confirming them. Representatives of all the committees have a meeting each year with the Fisheries Department in London to discuss questions arising from their work.

The Sea Fisheries Inspectorate

The Sea Fisheries Inspectorate is the link through which the Fisheries Department maintains contact with the fishing industry, not only at the principal deep sea fishing ports in England and Wales but also at the many small harbours and landing places along the coasts.

The Chief Inspector and his deputy are stationed at Headquarters. The coastal areas of England and Wales are divided into nine districts and a District Inspector is stationed at the principal fishing port in each of these areas. Most District Inspectors have a Fishery Officer as deputy. In the larger districts with a coastline of more than about 400 miles the Fishery Officer may be stationed at another port in order that the area as a whole may be covered more conveniently.

The inspectors keep in touch with all sections of the industry, from the associations representing owners, skippers, crews, merchants and insurers, to the individual fisherman, owner or merchant. The inspectors have to maintain many other contacts such as with the officers of the Fishery Protection Squadron of the Royal Navy and foreign fishery protection vessels, the officers of local sea fisheries committees, local authorities and the regional officers of various government departments. Again they must maintain liaison with officers of the three Fighting Services over gunnery and bombing ranges, mine-sweeping exercises, air-sea rescue and other matters affecting fishing and fishing vessels. In general the inspectors should know all that is going on in their areas affecting fisheries and they need to keep abreast of technical developments. They work with the Ministry's scientific staff in carrying out surveys and investigations, and visit other laboratories in particular those of the DSIR, for the same purposes. As a result of their liaison work the inspectors are the intelligence officers of the Department, providing not only information but assessing the trends in the industry and advising on future departmental policy.

Inspectors deal with local enquiries and explain departmental policy and practice. Where necessary they enforce legislation; for example, they inspect the nets of fishing vessels and also the catch to see that the orders which specify the minimum sizes of fish to be taken and the minimum mesh of nets are being observed.

The Fisheries Department is responsible for the collection and publication of statistics about our commercial sea fisheries as is explained at greater length in the final section of Chapter XIV below. The staff for the collection of statistics and certain scientific data are stationed at the offices of the District Inspectors, whilst at other ports the information is obtained by part-time officers.

Regulation of Fisheries on the High Seas

Apart from its work on the home side of the industry the Fisheries Department does a great deal of international work on fisheries problems. This century has witnessed a great increase in the proportion of our fish coming from the distant areas. The main reason has been the growing demand for cheap fish, especially for the fried fish trade, coupled with the great advance in the capacity and power of modern trawlers which makes it economical for them to travel long distances. The waters round Iceland supply more fish than any other distant-water ground, followed in order by Bear Island, the Barents Sea, North Norway and West Greenland. The relative importance of these grounds fluctuates with the season, however, and all are needed if a constant supply is to be maintained throughout the year.

The United Kingdom has always upheld the principle of the freedom of the seas. According to this principle a State may exercise certain rights, including the right to exclusive fishing, only within a narrow area round its coast. All the waters lying beyond this area are high seas, and it is only by agreements between the countries concerned that fishing within any of these areas can be controlled, limited or reserved for the nationals of a particular State.

In recent years, however, some countries have been claiming a wider area of fisheries jurisdiction than is, in the United Kingdom view, allowed by international law. The United Kingdom has continually protested against such claims. For example, in 1935 Norway introduced along part of her coast a system of measuring the extent of her fisheries jurisdiction from straight lines joining points of the mainland or offshore islands, instead of from low-water mark as previously. When Norway decided to enforce this system in 1948 it was agreed to submit the question to the International Court of Justice, which gave judgement in Norway's favour in 1951. Again, Iceland in 1948 passed a law stating that all the fisheries lying above the Icelandic continental shelf were subject to Icelandic control, and between 1950 and 1958 she unilaterally extended the limits within which she claimed exclusive fisheries jurisdiction from three miles to twelve miles. The problems raised by Iceland's action were all the more serious because the grounds off Iceland are so important to the distant water section of the British industry. The Fisheries Department has been closely involved in the negotiations dealing with these and other problems arising from the claims of countries off whose coast we fish to extend their fisheries jurisdiction. The agreements reached include those of 1959 with Denmark relating to the Faröe Islands, of 1960 with Norway, and of 1961 with Iceland.

The Fisheries Department has also been concerned with attempts to codify by agreement the customary law of the sea and to settle outstanding problems. Following an abortive conference at the Hague in 1930, one held in 1958 under the auspices of the United Nations resulted in four conventions, to which the United Kingdom is a party. The first defines the extent to which a coastal State may exercise sovereignty over its territorial waters and areas beyond them; the second deals with rights on the high seas; the third provides for international collaboration in measures to conserve the living resources of the high seas; and the fourth gives a State the right to exploit the plants or animals on the sea bed of the continental shelf surrounding its coast as well as mineral resources such as oil beneath it. The conference did not, however, reach agreement on the crucial question of the extent of the territorial sea or the breadth of exclusive fisheries jurisdiction. Neither did a further conference which was convened in 1960 in another attempt to solve this problem.

It also follows from the principle of the freedom of the high seas that those who fish there are subject only to such fisheries regulations as may be provided by the laws of their own country. Here again, therefore, international agreement is necessary if any common measures to control fishing vessels on the high seas are to be adopted. During the nineteenth century a number of conventions were brought into force to deal with this problem. The most important of these for the United Kingdom is the North Sea Convention of 1882 between the United Kingdom, Belgium, Denmark, France, Germany and the Netherlands, embodies in English law by the Sea Fisheries Act of 1883 (as modified by later Acts and supplementary agreements). The Convention provides general rules to govern the conduct of vessels fishing on the high seas, lays down methods of identifying fishing vessels and their gear by means of letters and numbers, and provides for their enforcement through authorized officers—usually naval officers—of the member governments.

As can be imagined, disputes between fishermen on the high seas may easily arise, especially when the parties concerned are of different nationalities and are practising different methods of fishing. In 1934 an agreement between the United Kingdom and Norway set up machinery for dealing with such disputes. In each country there is a Trawler Enquiry Board which considers claims between British and Norwegian vessels resulting from damage to fishing gear occurring in the waters of that country. Each board investigates the cases submitted to it and tries to get both parties to come to an agreement. If this proves impossible, the board submits a report suggesting an appropriate amount of compensation. The boards have successfully disposed of many cases, and the Fisheries Department is concerned to see that the process works as smoothly as possible.

The Fishery Protection Squadron, which consists of ships of the Royal Navy, is responsible for seeing that foreign fishermen do not fish within our territorial waters and for safeguarding the interests of our fishermen wherever they may fish on the high seas. The Fisheries Department also keeps in close touch with the Ministry of Transport about the regulations made by that department relating to safety and good order at sea and to the marking of vessels and gear for identification purposes.

Conservation of Fisheries

As national populations grew and with them the scale and efficiency of the deep sea fishing industries many of the best fishing grounds were being depleted. It was clear that the fish population was going to fall to a very low figure unless the extent and manner of fishing could be regulated by international agreement. The United Kingdom is now a party to two international conventions providing for this. One covers the fisheries in the North Sea and north-east Atlantic and the other the north-west Atlantic fisheries. The conventions are designed mainly to prevent the taking of immature fish, and to this end minimum sizes of mesh are prescribed for the fishing nets and the landing and sale of immature fish is also prohibited.

Under each convention member governments appoint a commission with certain executive powers, and the Fisheries Departments provide the United Kingdom representatives. Each commission meets periodically to review the working of the convention and to recommend any changes in its provisions. Any such changes do not, of course, automatically become the internal law of the various participating countries. United Kingdom practice has been to frame its enabling legislation (such as the Sea Fish Industry Act, 1959) in general terms so that amendments can be made by issuing fresh orders or regulations.

Research

The Fisheries Department is also directly responsible for a considerable amount of fisheries research work which is often closely allied to its work in the international field.

The chief centre for this is the Fisheries Laboratory at Lowestoft. The main object is the better exploitation of commercial fisheries. A large proportion of the work is, therefore, devoted to studies on the stocks of fish in the sea; how they are influenced by their environment and by fishing; how they reproduce, grow and die, and how they are caught by fishing gear of all kinds. Much of this work must inevitably be done at sea, and for this purpose the department maintains four fishery research vessels, three based on Lowestoft and one on Grimsby. These vessels are designed and equipped basically for fishing, but have special laboratories and accommodation for scientists and can undertake a variety of tasks. The largest is used for research in the distant water fisheries, in the north-east Arctic, off the Faröes, and as far west as Greenland. The two vessels of intermediate size work in the North Sea and off the south and west coasts of the British Isles. The smallest is used for inshore and shellfish research. In addition to the processing and analysis of the information collected at sea, work at the laboratory includes research into the physiology, feeding and behaviour of fish, the rearing of fish and the development of electronic instruments for the detection of fish and for the continuous measurement of the temperature and salinity of sea water. Much of the information on the state of the fish stocks is obtained by sampling the landings at the ports; nearly three-quarters of a million fish, of many different kinds, are examined every year for this purpose. Regular age-censuses are obtained for a number of the major stocks, and are used in conjunction with commercial statistics of landings and fishing effort to measure the effects of fishing and to forecast future trends in the fisheries.

There is a subsidiary laboratory at Hamilton Dock, Lowestoft, whose main task is to advise the Minister on safe levels of discharge of radioactive wastes to streams and to the sea, and to conduct the fundamental research on which such advice must be based. Research on inshore and shellfish fisheries, including control of diseases and pests and the cleansing of shelfish from sewage contamination, is done at separate laboratories at Burnham-on-Crouch and Conway.

More fundamental work is undertaken at institutions such as the Plymouth Laboratory of the Marine Biological Association which receive grants from the Development Commission based on recommendations from the Department. On the other hand the Department of Scientific and Industrial Research at the Torry Research Station and now the Herring Industry Board and the White Fish Authority investigate practical questions of handling storage, processing and freezing and their effect on quality and the life of fish.

The Development Commission at the request of the Fishery Ministers has appointed an expert committee of eminent scientists and men with practical fishery experience which reviews and advises on the research programmes of the Ministry, the Department of Agriculture and Fisheries for Scotland and the grant-aided Institutions, The International Council for the Exploration of the Sea, a body established at the end of the last century to which nearly all the western European countries belong, co-ordinates fisheries research in the main waters worked by our fishing fleets. The Council has a meeting each year for the exchange of knowledge and the formulation of future research plans, and works in close conjunction with the international commission concerned with conservation in the North Sea and north-east Atlantic.

SALMON AND FRESHWATER FISHERIES

There are in England and Wales about 2,000 men engaged in commercial fishing for salmon, sea trout and eels. In addition, about 850,000 anglers take out licences to fish. The main value of rod and line fishing today lies in the sport it provides for so many people, but it is none the less important.

The salmon is, and has always been, a commercially valuable fish with a rather curious life history which often places it in need of public protection. It normally breeds in the upper reaches of rivers, and the young fish after one, two or three years in fresh water migrate to the sea to return as mature fish weighing up to 50 lb. or more. Thus each generation of salmon may traverse a river twice or more during its lifetime, and a riparian owner by selfish and greedy action could for immediate gain quite easily ruin the fishery not only for himself but for his neighbours as well.

For some 700 years local bodies have been responsible for the regulation and conservation of our inland fisheries. Originally they were conservators appointed by the local Justices, but now they are the river boards whose constitution and functions have been described in Chapter VII.

Under the Salmon and Freshwater Fisheries Acts 1923 to 1935, and other legislation the boards are responsible for the maintenance, improvement and development of trout and freshwater salmon fisheries in their areas. They can impose licence duties and make by-laws and orders covering a wide variety of subjects, such as close seasons, the kinds of nets and other instruments that may be used for fishing, the size of the fish that may be taken, the regulation of fishing in public waters, the licensing of coarse fish anglers and so on. Such by-laws require the Minister's approval given through the Fisheries Department. The Minister's approval is also required for the making of fish passes and the construction and placing of gratings to prevent salmon and trout entering unsuitable channels. The river boards can prosecute those who pollute rivers and have power to control the discharge into their river of new effluents which may be harmful to fish. The Salmon and Freshwater Fisheries Acts have recently been reviewed by a committee under the chairmanship of Lord Bledisloe, whose recommendations are at the time of writing under consideration.

The visitor who descends into the basement of the Ministry's headquarters at Whitehall Place may be surprised to find there a small laboratory devoted to research on freshwater fisheries. Among the tasks performed there is the testing of samples to determine the extent to which effluents are harmful to fish. The laboratory also acts as a headquarters for field investigations into pollution problems and into practical questions of the maintenance and development of fish population in natural waters. The major part of the research work on freshwater fish, however, is conducted by the Freshwater Biological Association at its headquarters on Lake Windermere, with a grant from the Government.

WHALING

The Fisheries Departments in England and Scotland are also concerned with the affairs of the whaling industry in the United Kingdom. Before the last war the United Kingdom was one of the larger Antarctic whaling countries. Eight expeditions consisting of factory ships with their attendant catches were sent south during each Antarctic summer, and in addition three land stations were operated, two from South Georgia and one from South Africa. During the war the factory ships were pressed into service ferrying fighter planes across the Atlantic and all eight of them were torpedoed and lost. Immediately after the war three new 'expeditions', as the factory ship plus the catchers are known, were built, and these, together with the land stations operated until 1960 when one of the expeditions was sold to Japan. The United Kingdom is now, therefore, one of the smaller Antarctic whaling countries. Nevertheless, the industry continues to provide an important part of the whale oil supplies required for margarine manufacture in this country as well as processing the meat for various purposes such as pet food.

The main problem in connection with Antarctic whaling is the severe depletion of whale stocks. An International Whaling Convention accordingly limits the length of the whaling season and the size and numbers of whales that may be caught, in order to conserve whale stocks. The United Kingdom and the other major Antarctic whaling countries Norway, Japan, USSR and the Netherlands, are members of the convention together with a number of other countries. The Fisheries Departments represent the United Kingdom at the meetings of the Commission which supervises the working of the convention, and in addition are responsible for seeing that the regulations are carried out by the United Kingdom whaling industry. For this and other reasons the whaling expeditions have to be licensed annually before they may operate, and must also carry government inspectors on board.

CHAPTER XIII

International Aspects

ROUGHLY half our food requirements are met from home production; the rest have to be imported. About half our imports come from the Commonwealth, about a quarter from Western Europe and a fifth from North and South America (excluding Canada).

Some of these imports, such as tea, coffee, cocoa, oranges and lemons are not produced at all in this country and we have to import all our supplies. At the other extreme we produce at home in normal seasons all that we need of various other foodstuffs, such as liquid milk and maincrop potatoes. For very many foodstuffs, however, home production has to be supplemented by imports to meet the country's requirements.

The United Kingdom provides the principal market for a number of overseas suppliers. For example, roughly 50 per cent of the beef, 90 per cent of the mutton, 95 per cent of the bacon and 75 per cent of the butter entering into international trade comes to these shores. We take over 90 per cent of the butter and cheese, and about the same proportion of the mutton and lamb, exported by Australia and New Zealand and almost all of the bacon exported by Denmark. The Ministry is, therefore, inevitably very much involved in questions of international trade and commercial policy. The department's interests in what happens overseas go wider than this, however. There is for example the work of the Food and Agriculture Organization of the United Nations (FAO), as well as a great variety of topics already mentioned in earlier chapters, such as international collaboration in the control of animal and plant diseases, and the international conventions for the regulation of fisheries.

This chapter outlines the questions of international interest with which the Ministry is concerned, particularly in the field of international trade, and describes the organization within the Ministry for dealing with them.

COMMERCIAL POLICY

The Ministry and its predecessors were not always involved to any great extent in questions arising from international trade. During the second half of the nineteenth century and the first three decades of the twentieth the basis of the United Kingdom's international commercial policy was free trade and the elimination of duties and other protective devices on imported foodstuffs and manufactures alike.

In spite of the forebodings expressed at the time of the repeal of the Corn Laws in 1846 this policy of free trade did not at first adversely affect British agriculture; on the contrary with the expanding market provided by an urban population growing both in numbers and wealth the period from 1850 to 1875 was one of general prosperity for the home farmer. From about 1875 onwards, however, the exploitation of the virgin wheat lands of North America and Australia and the development of railways overseas, shipping and refrigeration subjected our agriculture to ever-increasing competition, and a period of agricultural depression set in.

In the early thirties of this century the institution of a general protective tariff for industry marked a fundamental change in this country's commercial policy, which as mentioned in Chapter II included tariffs and import restrictions on a wide range of foodstuffs.

This policy of protection for home industry and agriculture has, however, to be reconciled with the need to maintain and expand our export trade, a need that has become the more vital since the war with the loss of our earnings on our former overseas investments.

In fact the reduction of impediments to international trade has in the post-war years been a cardinal feature of this country's international commercial policy, as exemplified by its support of the General Agreement on Tariffs and Trade (GATT) concluded in 1947; the signatory countries (at present about forty) are between them responsible for some 80 per cent of world trade. Under the agreement member governments undertake to be bound in their commercial policies by various general principles, including the elimination of quantitative import restrictions as a normal method of protection, the limitation of subsidies on exports and generally a reduction in other barriers to trade. Mutual tariff concessions between member governments have been agreed at various international conferences arranged by GATT.

As mentioned in Chapter III, government support for our home agriculture nowadays is predominantly through exchequer subsidies rather than tariffs, import restrictions or other protective devices. The same is true of fisheries. Nevertheless tariffs remain the main instrument for the protection of our horticulture and they also apply to various other foodstuffs. Accordingly the Ministry has been very much involved in all international negotiations and discussions, under GATT or otherwise, affecting the country's trade policy.

Negotiations at GATT tariff conferences and elsewhere on agricultural produce can be particularly difficult. Nearly all countries nowadays protect their home agriculture in one way or another, and it has been found difficult in GATT to apply rigidly to agricultural produce many of the principles and general undertakings set out in the agreement.

Again, whilst this country has accepted the need for maintaining, in the words of the Agriculture Act, 1947, 'a stable and efficient agricultural industry capable of producing such part of the nation's food and other agricultural produce as in the national interest it is desirable to produce in the United Kingdom', the maintenance and expansion of our export trade is also vital. In farming policy it is a question of striking a sensible balance between different objectives.

Second only in importance to GATT as an international organization for removing restrictions on trade has been the Organization for European Economic Co-operation (OEEC). This was created in 1948 to operate the Marshall Plan for United States aid to rehabilitate the economy of Europe. Its distinctive contribution in the field of trade between the countries of Europe was the formulation between 1948 and 1951 of a code of liberalization under which member countries undertook by stages to dismantle the various systems of quantitative import restrictions which they had felt obliged to adopt as a means of alleviating their immediate post-war difficulties. The OEEC has now been replaced by the Organization for Economic Co-operation and Development, of which the United States and Canada are also full members. This new organization will continue and develop the work of its predecessor but with more emphasis on assistance to countries in the process of economic development.

Apart from occasions where special balance of payments difficulties (as in the United Kingdom in 1951) forced individual member countries to take emergency measures to protect their currencies, most European countries had by the mid-fifties reduced very considerably their quantitative restrictions on imports of industrial goods. Because of the intractability of the domestic problems that complete liberalization would have raised, member countries did not find it possible to go as far for agricultural as for industrial products. Nevertheless, in conformity with its obligations under GATT and other international agreements this country has, with the improvement in its balance of payments position, removed the great bulk of restrictions on imports from countries other than Eastern Europe and mainland China.

The difficulty with these latter countries is that since the State is normally the sole importer or exporter, an adequate reciprocity in the volume of trade can only be secured by its regulation under bilateral commercial agreements. In the main these countries want from us capital goods and other industrial products and in return wish to send us a wide range of agricultural and horticultural produce and some manufactures and industrial raw materials. It is frequently a matter of nice judgement to weigh the advantage of securing a market for our industrial products against the effect on our farmers (and possibly on the cost of the Exchequer guarantees) of taking, say, so much bacon from Poland.

In recent years agriculture and fisheries have been involved in many of the questions raised by the movement towards greater European economic unity. In 1957, by the signature of the Treaty of Rome, six European countries (France, West Germany, Italy and the Benelux countries) began the process of building a European Economic Community. In 1961 Greece became associated with the Community. An integral part of the Community's arrangements is to be a common agricultural policy. Later came the European Free Trade Association in which the United Kingdom joined with Norway, Sweden, Denmark, Switzerland, Austria and Portugal. Finland has recently become an associate member. EFTA is essentially an industrial free trade area, but there are general trade provisions for agricultural and fishery products in the EFTA Convention. Agreements covering agricultural products have been concluded between member countries. The United Kingdom has concluded one with Denmark under which we have eliminated our tariff on bacon and certain other agricultural produce in favour of all members of the Association. The dangers of economic division with Europe have always been recognized by both the EEC and the EFTA. At the time of writing the latest developments are that the United Kingdom, Denmark and the Irish Republic have applied to negotiate for membership of the EEC, while Sweden, Switzerland and Austria, the three neutral members of EFTA, have also applied to negotiate for association with the EEC. The negotiations between the United Kingdom and the EEC and between Denmark and the EEC began in Brussels before the end of 1961.

INTERNATIONAL COMMODITY AGREEMENTS AND COMMODITY SURPLUSES

The periodical occurrence of world surpluses in different agricultural products have led to international agreements for securing a better balance between production and consumption.

One possibility is to make these surpluses available to poorer countries with a low standard of nutrition. Some countries have been able to do this on a substantial scale, but it raises very considerable problems, such as the impact on normal commercial trade.

There remains the possibility of international agreements for regulating the production and trade in individual commodities with a view to keeping production broadly in line with demand. The United Kingdom Government has approached the question of whether to associate itself with proposals for a particular international commodity agreement essentially from the point of view of whether they can be expected to moderate short term price instabilities, arising from fluctuating supplies, whilst taking account of long term trends in supply and demand.

The two most important current international commodity agreements on specific articles of foodstuffs to which the United Kingdom is a party are those on sugar and wheat.

The International Sugar Agreement is concerned with all trade in sugar apart from exports to the USA and exports from Eastern European countries to the USSR. Much more than half of the international trade, however, is governed by preferential arrangements of one kind or another such as United States Sugar Acts and the Commonwealth Sugar Agreement (see the section on sugar in Chapter IV). There have been a series of such agreements dating from 1931 which have aimed at assuring supplies of sugar to importing countries and markets to exporting countries at equitable and stable prices. The United Kingdom has been a party to these agreements since 1937. Since in normal times some 90 per cent of the sugar we eat is provided by home production and by Commonwealth supplies bought at prices unrelated to the world price, it is not as an importer of free market sugar that we are primarily interested in the agreement. Rather our membership is an indication of this country's interest in seeing a reasonable degree of stability in world prices of primary commodities, and again of our sense of responsibility towards the sugar exporting colonies and other Commonwealth countries.

The latest agreement was negotiated in 1958 at a conference convened by the United Nations. Most of the important exporting countries acceded to the agreement as well as a large number of importing countries. The agreement operated mainly through export quotas which vary with the world sugar price, backed by production controls. The Commonwealth countries had a single export block quota. As an importer from the free market the United Kingdom Government undertook under the agreement to limit imports of sugar from any non-member country to the maximum imported in any of the years 1951, 1952 or 1953. At the time of writing the future of the agreement is uncertain owing to the breakdown of the negotiations for future quotas.

The other important international agreement to which the United

Kingdom is now a party is that on wheat. Here again, dating from 1933, there is a long history of efforts to deal by international action with the problems of world surpluses or shortages, and an uninterrupted series of agreements has been in force since 1949. The United Kingdom Government has not always felt able to accede to these agreements. It has, however, with most other nations having a major interest in world trade in wheat, adhered to the current International Wheat Agreement which was concluded in 1959.

This agreement differs from its predecessors not only in the range of its objectives but also in the nature of its operation. It brings within its purview a greater proportion of world trade and contains provisions for the examination of wheat problems in all their aspects.

Under that part of the agreement which deals with commercial trade (as distinct from concessional or special transactions) we and the other importing countries undertake to purchase not less than a specified proportion of our total imports (for the United Kingdom 80 per cent) from exporting member countries at prices within the prescribed price range. This price range, related to No. 1 Northern Manitoba wheat in bulk in store Fort William/Port Arthur, is $1·50 to $1·90 per bushel. The exporting countries for their part undertake, in association with one another, to ensure that sufficient wheat is made available at prices within the range to satisfy the commercial requirements of the importing countries. At the maximum of the price range importing countries have the right to purchase, and exporting countries the obligation to offer, specific quantities of wheat determined by reference to recent patterns of trade at not more than the maximum price.

An important new feature of the 1959 agreement is the obligation laid upon the Council which administers the agreement to make an annual review of the world wheat situation and to inform its member governments of the implications for the international trade in wheat of the facts which emerge. In addition to this study of the major problems of surplus accumulation and disposal and their underlying causes, the agreement provides for the study of the factors affecting wheat consumption and the means of promoting increased consumption.

In September, 1960, the United Kingdom acceded to an International Coffee Agreement on behalf of the commonwealth territories of Kenya, Uganda and Tanganyika. The agreement provides for export quotas to existing markets and for a programme of activities to stimulate coffee consumption. The Ministry also participates in the discussions which take place from time to time on proposals for international commodity schemes for other items such as cocoa and copra.

O

THE FOOD AND AGRICULTURE ORGANIZATION

The Food and Agriculture Organization was established as a specialized agency of the United Nations in 1945 as a sequel to the Hot Springs Conference on Food and Agriculture of 1943. Its headquarters are now in Rome, and nearly all the countries of the world, except those of the Soviet bloc, are members.

The Organization has three main tasks. First of all it collects, analyses and distributes a wide variety of important information on various aspects of nutrition, agriculture, fisheries and forestry; and it keeps under constant review world commodity developments and problems. Secondly, it is a means of providing technical assistance to the less developed member countries with the aid of funds supplied under the United Nations Technical Assistance Programmes. Thirdly, it arranges meetings and gatherings of representatives of member governments not only for the interchange of information and for the study of commodity problems but also to concert inter-governmental action on other problems in FAO's field, such as international measures for the control of foot-and-mouth and other animal diseases and the conservation of fisheries.

The United Kingdom is the second largest contributor to the funds for the Organization and takes an active part in its work. The Ministry is constantly being asked to find experts to serve on its committees or undertake assignments in giving technical assistance to under-developed countries.

ORGANIZATION OF WORK

It will be clear from what has been said earlier in this book that there is scarcely a division of the Ministry whose work does not have international implications. The preparation for say a GATT tariff conference involves consideration not only of possible concessions in our own tariffs but also what reductions we should want to secure in the tariffs of other countries. These are questions which need consideration (and often consultation with outside organizations) by not only the various commodity divisions and the Fisheries Department but also the divisions responsible for, e.g. agricultural machinery and seeds. The Animal Health and Horticulture Divisions are very much interested in international bodies and conventions concerned with animal and plant health respectively. In the negotiations for, say, the Polish bacon import quota the Meat and Livestock and Fatstock Marketing Divisions would be concerned with the possible effects on home production and also on the cost of the guarantees. The Advisory Service Division may have to find many of the experts wanted for various FAO assignments.

However, there clearly needs to be some part of the Ministry with overall responsibility for these international questions to act as a co-ordinator and clearing house. This is the task of the External Relations Group comprising three divisions under an Under Secretary. One division, recently established, is concerned principally with co-ordinating work for the negotiations with the European Economic Community, another division is concerned with European organizations (other than the EEC) and with individual European countries, and the remaining one with other international organizations and with countries outside Europe. There can, of course, be no hard and fast line, and the divisions work closely together.

The Group is the normal channel of communications with other departments, such as the Foreign Office and the Board of Trade, on international questions and is responsible for seeing that all other parts of the Ministry are kept informed of such questions as interest them and for ascertaining their views. Where there is a difference of views between different parts of the Ministry then the Group must see that they are resolved in discussion or alternatively put up to higher authority for a decision.

The Group normally represents the Ministry in inter-departmental discussions on questions of commercial relations with Commonwealth and foreign countries and the work of international organizations such as GATT. The Group is, of course, assisted as necessary by representatives from other divisions of the Ministry who may have a particular interest in the questions being discussed. Sometimes, as for example with the International Wheat and Sugar Agreements, or the International Whaling Convention, it is the specialist division of the Ministry concerned which is primarily responsible for providing representatives.

The Scottish and Northern Ireland Departments of Agriculture and Fisheries also need to be brought into the consideration of many of these international questions. This may be done either by the External Relations Group or by some other division of the Ministry according to circumstances.

The Group provides the secretariat for the inter-departmental committee concerned with FAO questions such as the briefing of the delegation to the annual meetings of the FAO Council. It is also the channel of correspondence with the FAO headquarters at Rome. One section within the group is responsible for providing advice and help to visitors who may come from overseas as students or representatives of foreign governments or private persons interested in British agriculture.

AGRICULTURAL AND FOOD ATTACHÉS

Officers of the Ministry are stationed as Agricultural and Food Attachés or Advisers at the Embassies or High Commissioners' Offices in various countries important to the Department, particularly Australia, New Zealand, Canada, the USA, Denmark, France and Argentina. The job of the attachés is to keep the Department fully informed on agricultural and food matters in those countries, and the External Relations Group for its part sees that the attachés are kept fully briefed on developments in this country within the Ministry's sphere of interest. The attaché in Paris also represents the Ministry on the UK delegation to the Organization for European Economic Co-operation and Development, which has its headquarters there.

In addition to its Food Attaché in Buenos Aires the Ministry also has a Veterinary Attaché and two other veterinary officers stationed in South America. They are there primarily to co-operate with the authorities in Argentina, Chile and Uruguay in reducing to the minimum the risk of meat infected with the virus of foot-and-mouth disease being exported to this country. They regularly visit the frigorificos (a frigorifico is a combination of slaughter-house, packing plant and cold store) which have been approved as suitable to export meat to Great Britain, and advise on those which wish to be added to the approved list.

The precautions taken by these South American governments against the risk of export of infected meat include the inspection of farms and also of animals before they are moved to the frigerificos, disinfection of any places and vehicles which may have become infected, and ensuring that only clean new packing and wrapping material is used for exported carcase meat.

CHAPTER XIV

Statistics and Economics

THE Ministry probably has a larger statistical organization than any other department of comparable size, and statistics play a greater part than in many other departments in the formation of policy. The Department's food, agricultural and fisheries statistics are indeed published in considerable detail, but their range and content have been determined mainly by policy uses.

The Ministry is concerned with the problems and welfare of the food producing and distributing industries. Statistics are thus required for measuring progress, identifying problems, and devising and administering the solutions. Up to a point this must mean not only the problems and solutions that are found to be of importance or utility at any particular moment, but all possible problems and solutions from which choices may have to be made on the basis of the statistics available.

The fixing of the farm price guarantees is one leading branch of policy which depends heavily on statistics, since one of the most important of the many relevant factors which have to be considered is the level of farmers' incomes. In order to assess the profits of the 'national farm' the Department prepares an aggregate profit and loss account for the industry, covering all items of farmers' receipts and expenditure. This task alone means bringing under statistical review almost everything that can happen on a farm, because of its effect on receipts or expenditure.

More generally, there has necessarily been a statistical background to almost all major policy developments such as the recent Small Farmer Scheme. Statistics are used to check the magnitude of the suggested problem—the number, kinds and whereabouts of the farms in question, and the incidence on them of whatever is being examined (such as dependence on milk as a source of income); and very often the statistical material may suggest, even though it cannot determine, the most useful solution. Similarly, statistics often play an important part in the implementation of the policies adopted; thus the agricultural census returns may be used in the checking of claims for ploughing grant or for cereals subsidy.

The Fisheries Department also require statistics to enable policy to be laid down fairly; levels of assistance to the industry are determined with the aid of figures showing catches taken by the various types of vessels. In addition, measures for the conservation of fisheries must be based primarily on statistics about the stocks of each species of fish in the various sea areas and the effect of fishing on it.

The result of all this, therefore, is that the Ministry's statistical organization has developed to a rather unusual degree, and has done so very largely as a form of common service to the department, as a tool to be used in the consideration and execution of specific policies.

The Ministry is not, of course, the only user of its own statistics. Anyone, for example, who looks at the markets section of the farming weeklies, or wakes up in time to listen to the 6.45 a.m. market reports on the BBC will have a practical acquaintance with one of the uses made of the Ministry's market price statistics.

AGRICULTURE

The agricultural census, which has been held every year since 1866, is the most important source of information about all branches of agriculture. Every occupier of a holding of over one acre with any appreciable output of agricultural produce is required every June to fill in a detailed form whose 'vast scheme of 140 questions' has been described by Mr Paul Jennings as having 'all the lucidity of a great philosophical intellect striving to fit the teeming facts of the universe into a towering monistic system'.[1] In more prosaic terms, the farmer has to give the acreage of principal crops, numbers of livestock and of the labour force both whole-time and seasonal. Similar censuses are now taken in March, September, and December based on a sample of one-third of all farmers (so that each farmer has to fill in two general census forms in all in the course of the year). Special censuses are also taken twice a year for glasshouse crops (January and July), and for vegetables grown for human consumption (September and December), annually (from contractors) for agricultural machinery, and every five or six years for orchard fruit. A special 'world agricultural census' was held in 1960/61 on behalf of the Food and Agriculture Organization of the United Nations, ten years after the last world agricultural census.

The census form is a lengthy document with some 150 questions in the June form, and about half that number in the other quarters. Proposals are constantly coming up from outside as well as inside the Department for additions to the list. A nice balance has to be maintained between collecting information that is really important on the

[1] 'Marshman as at June 30th' in *Even Oddlier*, Reinhardt, 1952.

one hand and not putting an unnecessary burden on occupiers on the other. To help the Department in the discharge of this delicate responsibility there is an Agricultural Statistics Advisory Committee with representatives of farmers, landowners and farmworkers, and every proposal for adding to the list of questions is subject to the scrutiny of this committee.

The census forms are sent to the Data Processing Division of the Ministry at Guildford (see Chapter XVII). Queries on any census form which require a special visit to the holding are referred to the divisional office. Although the forms are assembled by hand the census material is now processed on an electronic computer.

There is a statutory ban on the disclosure of individual census figures to anyone outside the Department and those handling individual census forms are required to observe strict security precautions.

The census returns yield figures for the acreage of various crops. Figures for total production are derived from estimates of yield made by local officers of the Department, who also supply a regular series of reports on crop conditions throughout the year which are used for a monthly series of reports on agricultural conditions in England and Wales that is issued to the Press.

The census results are used not only for estimates of production but also for studies on the structure of the agricultural industry. Thus as part of the study of the problem of small farmers (see Chapter V) the census results were analysed with the help of a punched card installation for studying how many farms of different sizes are producing various kinds of crops and livestock and, carrying analysis a stage further, for an estimate, for example, of how many small farmers produce enough to be likely to receive a reasonable living from their holding.

The normal regular census returns obtained under compulsory powers may need to be supplemented from time to time by special enquiries. The pig, for example, is a prolific animal with a relatively short life. Variations in the farmer's expectation of the profitability of pig production in the immediate future not infrequently lead to fluctuations in the pig population which can be the cause of much concern to Ministers, Members of Parliament, farmers and bacon factories alike. The Department, therefore, with the support of the NFU now conducts each month a small sample survey of pigs on agricultural holdings, which requires a personal visit from a field officer on each occasion to be certain of getting prompt and up-to-date information not only of the present but also of prospective pig numbers. Again the Ministry, farmers and the grain trade all want to have up-to-date and reliable estimates of stocks of cereals remaining on farms month by month to give them some idea of the amount of grain that remains to be marketed or to be consumed on the farm. Accordingly monthly returns are obtained each year from a random sample of about 2,000 holdings throughout the country.

Prices realized at the different markets for livestock are provided by market reporters, and special officers are employed to collect information on current prices to growers of fruit and vegetables. In addition under the Corn Returns Act, 1882, all dealers in grain in certain towns in England and Wales are required to make weekly returns of the prices and quantities of wheat, barley, and oats purchased. A wide variety of statistics are collected also from animal feedingstuffs manufacturers, slaughter-houses and the like.

The Agricultural Economics Division of the Ministry is required to produce an estimate of farm income and output for the annual review. For this purpose the whole of agriculture is treated as one large farm—the 'national farm'—whose incomings and outgoings are estimated. For some of these estimates information derived from sources such as the agricultural census returns have to be supplemented by special detailed inquiries. In estimating, for example, how much farmers spend on wages in the course of a year, it is no use multiplying the statutory minimum wage by the number of workers. Overtime, payments in kind, the effect of casual labour, the number of workers who are paid more than the minimum wage and so forth—all these factors complicate the situation. The calculation is, therefore, based on a random sample for the whole country collected by the Safety and Wages Inspectorate; this sample enquiry is also the basis for the factual memoranda prepared by Agricultural Economics Division when the Agricultural Wages Board is considering claims from the Agricultural Workers' Unions. Similar, though in some cases less firmly based, estimates are made for all the other items of farm expenditure. Estimates are also made of farm output not only for the purposes of the price review but also for such purposes as estimates of the future cost of the agricultural price guarantees, which are so dependent on the level of production and on market prices. From time to time forecasts have to be made even further ahead. International organizations in particular have a habit of wanting to know what is likely to be happening five or ten years ahead even if making such estimates is very much akin to crystal gazing.

Agricultural Economics Division maintains close contact not only with the Commodity Divisions of the Ministry, who supply a lot of most useful information, but also with other departments, particularly the Department of Agriculture and Fisheries for Scotland

and the Ministry of Agriculture for Northern Ireland who are both suppliers and consumers of the statistics prepared by the Ministry and the Central Statistical Office.

THE PROVINCIAL AGRICULTURAL ECONOMICS SERVICE

The Provincial Agricultural Economics Service in England and Wales is the sole survivor today of the pre-war Provincial Advisory Service based on university departments of agriculture. As mentioned in Chapter II the rest of the Provincial Advisory Service was absorbed into the National Agricultural Advisory Service when the latter was established in 1946, but in order to maintain their independent status the Agricultural Economists remained in the employ of nine universities, covering between them the whole of England and Wales. One reason for this is that the provincial economists are responsible for the collection and analysis of financial and economic data from farmers. For example, some 2,500 farmers make their accounts available to the PAES by co-operating in the 'Farm Management Survey', which gives a picture of the relative profitability of different types and sizes of farms. As this information is considered at the annual price review (see Chapter III) it was felt desirable that the selection of farms and collection of information should be in 'neutral' hands: again it was thought that some farmers would be more willing to make their accounts available to a university investigator than to the Ministry.

The work of the PAES is not, however, confined to undertaking investigations into farm incomes and farm costs on behalf of the Ministry. It also includes independent research and participation in the universities' teaching. In addition the Service gives specialist advice on agricultural economics matters generally and acts in a consultative capacity to the NAAS in their farm management advisory work.

The salaries and other expenses of the PAES are met by direct grant from the Ministry to the universities instead of becoming part of the general university expenses covered by the Treasury grant made on the recommendation of the University Grants Committee. The Ministry controls the size of the staff complement through its administration of the grant but the members of the PAES are employed by the several universities and enjoy the salary scales and conditions of service of other university staff. There are at present about 250 persons in the PAES of whom 110 are in academic grades or their equivalent.

There is an independent committee to advise the Ministry on the general development of work in agricultural economics and of the PAES. This committee includes representatives of the universities but the Minister appoints its chairman and independent members.

FOOD

The Ministry of Food naturally wanted the fullest information about food from home and abroad, and since it either purchased all the principal foodstuffs or controlled their purchase, processing and distribution, it had access to a wealth of statistics not previously available. With decontrol many of these statistics ceased to be available in their original form, but where they continue to be necessary they have been replaced by returns from food manufacturers and processors provided by individual firms or trade associations either voluntarily or under the Statistics of Trade Act, 1947.

The loss of statistics following decontrol was partly made good by the Ministry's analyses of data obtained each year from some 10,000 households in Great Britain under the National Food Survey which the Central Office of Information conducts for the Department. This gives for all foods information on household expenditure, consumption, prices and free supplies which enables the adequacy of the diet of all sorts of groups to be assessed. The Survey was originally started for the purpose of studying how people were faring under rationing and food control. Nowadays the main interest of the survey is economic—what kinds of foodstuffs are people spending their money on, what are the trends, and why? At a time when most people in this country are getting at least enough to eat, the total energy value of their diet hardly increases from year to year. This means that future expansion of the market is (apart from that arising from an increase in population) likely to take only the form of the substitution of higher valued for lower valued foods—for instance animal protein foods for vegetable protein, better qualities of each kind, and more tinned or other processed foods at the expense of the fresh article. But though the general picture has never been more favourable, it is still important to watch the position of the more vulnerable groups, such as the larger families living on relatively low incomes, who have not fully shared in the general rise in the standard of diet. The Survey is the only instrument available for examining the position of such special groups, whether they are defined in terms of income, occupation, age, location or family size. The Survey as a whole is thus a mine of information for workers in such widely separated fields as applied economics, social medicine and market research. University departments, marketing bodies and commercial agencies all have plenty of interest in the commodities covered by the Survey, which account for some 30 per cent of the public's total expenditure.

FISHERIES

Statistics about commercial sea fisheries are collected at all ports in England and Wales where fish is landed. At the major ports, which account for over 95 per cent of the landings, full-time officers employed by the Ministry do the work. At the smaller ports, where landings are lighter and less frequent, the work is undertaken by part-time collectors who may be fishermen, fish salesmen or others closely connected with the industry.

Collection of fishery statistics started in 1886 and in the earlier years was confined to a simple record of the landings of sixteen kinds of fish. Today the Ministry's collectors cover all varieties of sea fish and shellfish normally landed at our ports, and for the principal varieties of fish such as cod, hake and haddock, the catch is divided into large, medium and small fish.

Unlike their counterparts in the agricultural industry fishermen do not have to complete a form of 150 or even twenty questions. For vessels over 40 ft. in length collectors make a return showing for each voyage the weight of each variety of fish landed, the price it realized at first sale, the method by which the catch was taken, the number of hours spent fishing, the number of days spent at sea, and the precise area in which fishing was undertaken. The weight and value of the catch are, at the major ports, taken from records compiled by the collector whilst on the market, supplemented and checked by sales notes furnished by the vessel owners. The rest of the information is obtained from the mate or skipper of the vessel. For the small, under 40 ft. vessels individual returns are not required; the collector for the port at which such landings are made normally submits one monthly return giving the total weight and value of all fish and shellfish landed during the period. No record is made of the commercially unimportant amounts of fish taken by anglers.

The forms when completed are forwarded to the Fisheries Department of the Ministry in London who after scrutiny pass them to a punched card installation for processing. The monthly and annual tabulations produced give a comprehensive picture, not only of the quantities and values of each kind of fish landed at each port, but also of the overall activities of each type of fishing on the various grounds frequented.

Some of the statistics are published monthly in the form of a brief *Monthly Statement of Sea Fisheries* and annually in the *Sea Fisheries Statistical Tables*. Both published and unpublished figures are available to and extensively used by administrators, scientists and research workers.

The Ministry, in common with the departments responsible for the fishing industry in many other countries, gives two international organizations extremely detailed information on the catches taken. For the areas extending from the coasts of western Europe to the longitude of Cape Farewell information is supplied to the International Council for the Exploration of the Sea, whilst information on fish taken in waters farther west is reported to the International Commission for the North-west Atlantic Fisheries. Statistical information given to these bodies is supplemented by information obtained by this country's research vessels. All these statistics are published and freely available to all nations.

In the United Kingdom there is no legislation requiring the provision of fishery statistics; since the earliest days of their collection they have been obtained through the good will of the industry, and collectors rarely experience any difficulty in obtaining all the information they require. There is no statutory bar to the disclosure of information collected, but whilst the Ministry is anxious to meet all bona fide requests for statistics it is at pains never to disclose information from which the earnings of an individual firm or vessel could be ascertained.

In addition to collecting statistics of fish landed the Ministry maintains a record of each registered fishing vessel showing its length, year of construction, the types of gear carried and the engine power, etc. This information is valuable in the formulation of policy as regards grants and loans towards vessel construction and the modernization of obsolescent vessels. In conjunction with the statistics of fish taken, it is indispensable material for the fishery scientists whose duty it is to advise the Ministry on the state of the stocks of fish and on any changes in the national and international measures for conserving them.

CHAPTER XV

The Ordnance Survey

IT may come as a surprise to learn that the Ordnance Survey is a part of the Ministry. The Ordnance Survey is responsible to the Minister, who is advised by the Permanent Secretary of any new or out of the ordinary occurrences concerning it. The day to day affairs of the department are administered by the Director-General, who consults the Ministry when any major changes in administrative or technical policy are proposed or when senior civilian vacancies have to be filled. The Director-General is a Major-General on the active list appointed by the Minister with the concurrence of the Army Council.

Under the Director-General are three functional Directors. Two of them—the Director of Field Survey and the Director of Map Production—are Brigadiers, whilst the third—the Director of Establishment and Finance—is a civilian holding the rank of Assistant Secretary in the Administrative Civil Service. A number of the senior staff on the technical side are are also officers of the Royal Engineers survey service who are normally posted to the Department for a period of three years. The rest of the staff are all civilians, although at one time a large proportion were soldiers.

The Ordnance Survey has its own parliamentary vote for which the Director-General is the accounting officer. The gross annual cost of the Department is about £4,500,000, against which sales of maps realize about £350,000, royalty payments £70,000 and repayments for services rendered to public departments and outside bodies about £480,000. Sales of maps have risen steadily since the war—some 2,300,000 copies in 1960/61 compared with about 1½ million ten years ago.

The man in the street usually connects the Ordnance Survey with the familiar one inch to the mile map, but this popular series is but one of the many produced by the Department, whose main task is to provide large-scale plans of this country. It also carries out mapping services for other departments such as the War Office, the Land Registry and the Geological Survey.

History

It was the need for accurate maps in the measures for the pacification of the Highlands of Scotland after Culloden, and subsequently in the preparations to meet the threat of invasion from France, which led to the establishment of the Ordnance Survey in 1791, working under the Board of Ordnance. It remained under military control until 1870 when responsibility for its administration passed to the Commissioner of Works and then in 1889 it came under the newly formed Board of Agriculture.

The original task of the department was a survey of the whole country on a scale of one inch to the mile. In 1858, however, following the recommendations of a Royal Commission, the Government decided that the whole country should be mapped on a scale of 1/2500 or approximately 25 inches to the mile, apart from mountain and moorland areas for which a scale of 6 inches to the mile was considered adequate. A national survey at this large scale was needed because of the rapid pace of building and other development which followed the industrial revolution and growth of the railways system. The value of reliable large scale plans both for planning and for the transfer of land was widely recognized by the public and by the professions, who won their demand for the 1/2500 survey against some Parliamentary opposition. This was a very important development and no other country had, or for that matter has since, endeavoured to map such a high proportion of its area on such a large scale.

All the smaller scale maps today such as the 1/25,000 (2½ inches to the mile), the inch to the mile, the ½ inch and ¼ inch were derived from the original 25-inch or 6-inch survey. All those who have used the locally produced maps on walking holidays overseas will probably agree that our present day 1-inch maps compare very favourably in clarity and wealth of detail with the corresponding maps available elsewhere.

The original 25-inch and 6-inch survey was eventually completed in 1895. Since then regular revision has been needed to keep the maps up to date with the continued growth of our towns and other changes in the landscape. These revisions have naturally been interrupted by the effects of two world wars, when the Survey was almost entirely engaged on military tasks, including the mammoth job of helping to provide for the invasion of Normandy some 120 million maps, many of which were compiled, drawn and printed by the Ordnance Survey.

Surveying

It was realized during the war that with the amount of damage to property by enemy attacks up-to-date maps were going to be urgently needed for post-war building and development. It was accordingly decided in 1944 that after the war all the major towns in Great

Britain should be resurveyed on a scale of 1/1250, or roughly 50 inches to the mile. Experience had shown that the 1/2500 scale was too small for plotting the layout of public services and utilities and for the other purposes for which plans are required in urban areas today. For the rest of the country the old 25-inch series (6 inch for mountain and moorland areas) were to be revised.

This task was larger and more complex than anything the Ordnance Survey had had to tackle since 1800, and meant the training of a considerable number of new staff. To date the Department is about three-quarters of the way through the survey of urban areas on the 50-inch scale and hopes to complete the work by about 1966. The revision of the maps for rural areas on the 25-inch or 6-inch scale is a much longer task which will not be finished before 1980 at the earliest. The work is being planned to avoid, so far as possible, the survey becoming so out of date in the future as to require any repetition of the present prodigious effort to bring it up to date. For example, in all areas where further development on any scale is likely small teams of surveyors known as continuous revisers are left behind after the area has been surveyed so that new developments can be added to the plan as they take place.

The Ordnance Survey has always paid particular attention to archaeological sites. Its special maps, such as those of Roman Britain and Monastic Britain, are well known. It is perhaps not so generally recognized that by showing archaeological information on its large scale plans the Ordnance Survey has produced a geographical record of the archaeology of Great Britain which has no counterpart in the world and which is the envy of foreign archaeologists. No doubt from time to time users are puzzled if not irritated by the wealth of archaeological information appearing on some maps, but at a time when the face of the country is changing with such rapidity as at present it is more necessary than ever to record archaeological sites.

There are three stages in the making of a map; the surveying of the land, the drawing of the map, and its reproduction by lithographic and photographic processes.

The first stage in a survey is the preparation of a rigid framework within which are fitted the roads, rivers, buildings and all other detail appearing on the plan. Distances and angles for this framework were formerly measured with steel tape and theodolite, but these are now to some extent giving way to the tellurometer and tacheometer. The tellurometer uses the known speed of radio waves to measure the distance between two points. It is very accurate, especially over longer distances; tests have shown the magnitude of errors to be as little as from one to eight parts in one million over distances of twenty miles. The tacheometer is an instrument which when set up over a point whose position is known is used to find the bearing and distance of nearby objects by simple measurement of angles and intercepts on a graduated staff; it is used extensively in fixing the position of features such as house corners, from which further detail can in turn be measured by simple tape measurements.

The development of aerial photography for surveying purposes has been rapid, and many different types of what are termed photogrammetric instruments are now being used to make precise measurements of air photographs in order to determine heights and distances on the earth's surface; they are also used for the plotting of ground features. Helicopters, too, have been used to great advantage by the Ordnance Survey in recent years to carry men, materials and equipment to inaccessible mountain peaks for the construction of triangulation points and for carrying out observations. Much time is now saved by using electronic data processing and computing machines to reduce the data obtained in the field and from the aerial surveys to terms suitable for use by the cartographer.

Map Making

Considerable changes have taken place over the years in the medium used in the fair drawing of Ordnance Survey maps. Originally they were engraved on copper but nowadays the usual process is to draw them on enamelled metal or on specially coated glass. It is not without regret that the Department has, in the interests of economy, all but given up the writing of names which today are normally printed, cut out and then stuck down on the final drawing. Gone is the special skill in the writing of names of the old Ordnance Survey draughtsman who could so often boast of his ability to write the Lord's Prayer in the space covered by a threepenny bit. Whilst some may regret the loss of artistic character from the 1-inch and smaller scale maps, this must be weighed against the clarity achieved by modern drawing and printing techniques. Without them it would be impossible to produce and maintain the wide range of maps and plans in the quantities demanded by our modern economy. Aesthetic tastes are not forgotten however, and in a few, in particular in sheets of the 1-inch Tourist Series, a system of hill shading is used to depict relief. Where the relief, as in the Lake District and the Highlands, is so dramatic that it cannot be adequately portrayed by contours the convention is adopted of throwing a 'graded hill shadow' on those parts of the hills which would be in shadow if the sun was in the north-west. The success of this method depends largely on the skill of the draughtsman, even though today his task is made easier by the stereoscopic examination of air photographs of the area.

The Ordnance Survey has its own printing works in which are

printed all Ordnance Survey maps and plans, as well as those of some other government departments including a large proportion of the War Office map requirements. The lithographic processes involved in map production are numerous. In brief the draughtsman's fair drawings, one for each colour on the finished map, are photographed and from the glass negatives a set of zinc printing plates is prepared by photo-mechanical methods. The printing plates are used in rotary offset printing machines in which an impression is transferred in colour from the plate to the sheets of paper. Nowadays multi-coloured maps are usually printed on machines capable of printing two colours at a time. Even so the 1-inch map, which has ten colours, passes through the printing machine five times and a run of 40,000 copies may take several weeks in the machine room.

The fruits of all this labour are available in the form of maps and plans to suit a variety of purposes at agents and booksellers in most towns in Great Britain.

CHAPTER XVI

The Royal Botanic Gardens, Kew

TO the average man Kew Gardens means a pleasant park on the outskirts of London where at any time of the year he can see one of the most beautiful and varied displays of plants in the country. Comparatively few know that Kew is part of the Ministry and that it has one of the largest and finest botanical collections in the world or that its main function is scientific research. The work there includes the accurate identification and classification of all kinds of plants, the provision of information on the way that plants can be used for the economic benefit of mankind, and research into plant anatomy and physiology.

Just over 200 years ago, in 1759, Princess Augusta, mother of George III, established in the grounds of her home at Kew House a garden of some nine acres which was at the time unique. Up to that time plants had been grown in gardens either for their medicinal properties or for the scented beauty of their flowers. In Princess Augusta's garden plants were grown simply as plants and thus came into being one of the first truly botanical gardens in this country. The head gardener, William Aiton, had had a botanical training and within three decades was cultivating as many as 5,500 different species of plants. The grounds were embellished with a number of buildings designed by the famous architect, Sir William Chambers, some of which, including the Orangery and the Pagoda, are prominent features of the Gardens today.

After Princess Augusta's death in 1772 George III united the grounds of Kew House with the neighbouring gardens of Richmond Lodge and appointed as his botanical adviser Sir Joseph Banks. Under his direction men trained at Kew were sent out to new lands to collect interesting and useful plants, to sail with Captain Cook on his voyage of discovery and to suffer with Captain Bligh in the illfated cruise of the *Bounty*. In such ways were founded the collections at Kew in which plants from all countries are represented.

After Banks's death in 1820 the Gardens went downhill and fell into a state of neglect, but in 1840 a committee which had been appointed to 'enquire into the management, etc., of the Royal Gardens' presented to Parliament a report in which they drew attention to the benefits to the community of a central and well equipped botanic garden where useful as well as ornamental plants might be received and distributed; the committee felt that such an establishment would help medicine, manufacturers, horticulture and the economical development of the colonies. In the following year the Gardens were taken over by the State and placed under the control of the Commissioners of Her Majesty's Woods, Forests, Land Revenues, Works and Buildings but since 1903 they have been under the control of the Ministry of Agriculture. The Director is appointed by the Minister with the Sovereign's approval and also acts as botanical adviser to the Secretary of State for the Colonies and to the Commonwealth War Graves Commission.

Additions were made to the Gardens from time to time and they now occupy about 300 acres. The annual cost of all the activities is now of the order of £300,000 including the cost of some sixty scientific staff but excluding the cost to the Ministry of Works of the maintenance of the buildings. A charge of 3d is levied for admission to the Gardens and this and other miscellaneous receipts brings in an annual income of about £15,000.

The Herbarium and Library

Under the Director the activities of the Gardens are divided into four departments. The first is the Herbarium and Library, primarily devoted to systematic botany, that is to say the classification and naming of plants. The Herbarium houses a world-wide collection of more than 6½ million sheets of pressed botanical specimens, together with 15,000 specimens, pickled in liquid preservative, of flowers such as orchids which lose much of their structural interest if they are pressed. There is also the library of 55,000 volumes and 80,000 reprints and separate papers, and about 150,000 drawings, paintings and photographs of plants.

Kew has long been famous for the preparation of floras and basic plant lists for all parts of the Commonwealth, including Australia, India, Pakistan, Malaya, New Zealand and tropical and South Africa (as well as some countries outside the Commonwealth). The Department is at present engaged on the preparation of floras of Cyprus and Iraq and regional floras of Africa. The botanical literature of the world is searched for all new names of plants so that they may be recorded in the *Index Kewensis*, an alphabetical list of all botanical names of flowering plants. The original two volumes were published in 1895 but new plants are being discovered or new names given at the rate of some 3,500 to 4,000 a year. Supplements to the Index are issued every five years.

The Jodrell Laboratory

The Jodrell Laboratory presented and equipped by Mr T. J. Phillips Jodrell was first opened for research into the structure and physiology of plants in 1876. One example of the distinguished work done here is that of the early researches of Cross and Bevan on cellulose and lignification which ultimately led to the foundation of the British rayon industry.

In recent years the laboratory has become known in botanical circles throughout the world as a centre for research for the comparative anatomy of flowering plants, and the vast store of anatomical knowledge available at the Jodrell Laboratory has enabled many practical problems to be solved ranging from the identification of timbers and the roots of trees to the detection and identification of adulterants in, or substitutes for, plant products of economic importance. For example, the ramification of roots sometimes makes the foundation of buildings subside and each year a good deal of identification work is done on this for local authorities, architects and surveyors. Another example of the range of work in the Jodrell is the identification of the timber used for the bookcases in the library at Trinity College, Cambridge. These were traditionally believed to be made of cedar, but microscopical examination in the Jodrell showed them to be of English oak. Again, the laboratory was able to show that material from the Sutton Hoo ship burial previously identified as human bone was in fact a piece of oak wood.

Although the laboratory has in recent years concentrated on plant anatomy it has also conducted investigations on questions of plant physiology of interest to the practical gardener, including the use of synthetic growth substances to assist the rooting of cuttings and the effect of atmospheric pollution on glasshouse plants. Work done at the laboratory has also shown that supplementary illumination from mercury vapour lamps can improve the growth of certain tropical plants.

The work of the laboratory, therefore, dovetails into that of the herbarium and museums not only in its general fundamental work on the structure and growth of plants but also in its important economic applications.

The Department of Economic Botany

It was one of Sir Joseph Banks's plans for Kew that the Gardens should serve as a nursery of useful plants for supplying territories such as Australia, New Zealand and Africa, then being opened up to commerce and development. In pursuance of this, living plants have been supplied to many parts of the world, and mention may be made of two shipments with spectacular results, the sending of cinchona (quinine) in 1861/62 to India which proved of incalculable benefit in relieving the scourge of malaria, and the introduction of Hevea seedlings in 1876 to Ceylon and Singapore, from which arose the great rubber industry of the Far East. This service continues and in recent years there have passed through Kew improved varieties of cocoa for West Africa, Malaya, Ceylon and Fiji; banana varieties for the West Indies, West Africa, East Africa, Australia and India; pasture grasses for Mauritius, varieties of cinnamon for Seychelles, and ipecacuanha plants for British Honduras.

A large number of enquiries, from all parts of the world, on economic plants and plant products are dealt with. These range from such matters as the identification of strange seeds found in canned peas to supplying information on a little known tropical American plant used locally as a narcotic and believed to be of possible value in modern medicine.

The Department also manages three museums in the Gardens which contain a wealth of material invaluable for scientific and educational purposes. The wood museum, for example, houses specimens of most of the commercial timbers now in use in the United Kingdom and is much used by carpentry pupils and those interested in timbers.

The Gardens Department

The Gardens Department maintains a living collection of some 45,000 species and varieties (considered to be the finest in the world) and supplements the information provided by the Herbarium and the Department of Economic Botany and provides living material for anatomical and physiological study in the Jodrell Laboratory. About forty student gardeners, some from overseas, are employed in the Gardens. While some, on completion of their training, fill posts in gardens and parks in this country, others, like Banks's Kew collectors of old, find their way abroad, there to use and make more widely known the skill in horticulture which they have acquired at Kew.

One offshoot of the Gardens is the National Pinetum, Bedgebury, in Kent which contains a living collection of world species of *Coniferae*. The trees grow better there than they do in the London air; in any case there would not be room for all at Kew.

PART III

The Organization of the Ministry

CHAPTER XVII

Headquarters Organization and Common Services

THE Minister of Agriculture, Fisheries and Food is the parliamentary and political head of the Department. All the Department's acts are done in the name of the Minister, who is answerable for them to Parliament. The Minister is assisted by two Parliamentary Secretaries, one of whom sits in the House of Lords and the other in the House of Commons.

Under the Minister's direction each Parliamentary Secretary takes a special interest in certain parts of the Department's work, though it is, of course, impossible to maintain any clear cut division of business between the two Parliamentary Secretaries; any subject may be raised in either House of Parliament, and the Parliamentary Secretary concerned will need to deal with it whether or not it falls within his special field of interest. Both Parliamentary Secretaries would normally attend any important discussions on policy questions which the Minister might have with senior officials.

The Minister is also responsible for the work of the Forestry Commission in England and Wales. The Commission, however, is a department quite distinct from the Ministry, and neither the Parliamentary Secretaries nor any of the staff of the Ministry take any part in its administration, though the Parliamentary Secretary (Lords) naturally deals with any forestry business arising in the Upper House (in the same way as from time to time he deals with matters affecting other departments who have not a Minister in the Lords) and the Parliamentary Secretary (Commons) deputizes for the Minister as necessary in the House of Commons.

Headquarters carries out the normal functions of a government department, namely advising the Minister on questions of policy (including such matters as drafting answers to Parliamentary Questions and Ministerial correspondence) and the execution of that policy when settled (though a large part of the latter function has now been delegated to the regional and divisional organization described in the next chapter).

The Permanent Secretary is responsible to the Minister for the operation of the whole department. The headquarters organization

HEADQUARTERS ORGANIZATION

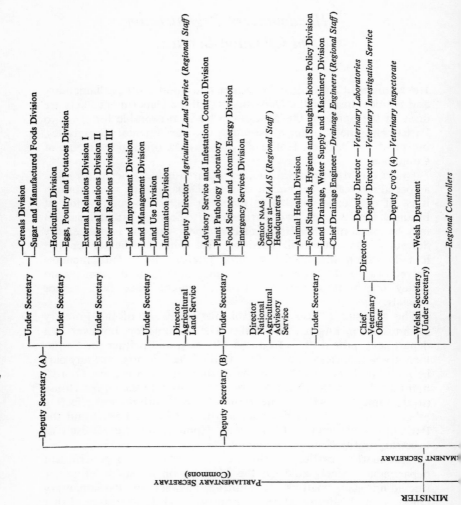

MINISTER

PARLIAMENTARY SECRETARY (Commons)

PERMANENT SECRETARY

—Deputy Secretary (A)—

—Under Secretary
- Cereals Division
- Sugar and Manufactured Foods Division

—Under Secretary
- Horticulture Division
- Eggs, Poultry and Potatoes Division

—Under Secretary
- External Relations Division I
- External Relations Division II
- External Relations Division III

—Under Secretary
- Land Improvement Division
- Land Management Division
- Land Use Division
- Information Division

—Director Agricultural Land Service
- Deputy Director—*Agricultural Land Service (Regional Staff)*

—Deputy Secretary (B)—

—Under Secretary
- Advisory Service and Infestation Control Division
- Plant Pathology Laboratory
- Food Science and Atomic Energy Division
- Emergency Services Division

—Director National Agricultural Advisory Service
- Senior NAAS Officers at—*NAAS (Regional Staff)* Headquarters

—Under Secretary
- Animal Health Division
- Food Standards, Hygiene and Slaughter-house Policy Division
- Land Drainage, Water Supply and Machinery Division
- Chief Drainage Engineer—*Drainage Engineers (Regional Staff)*

—Chief Veterinary Officer
- Director—
  - Deputy Director — *Veterinary Laboratories*
  - Deputy Director — *Veterinary Investigation Service*
- Deputy cvo's (4) — *Veterinary Inspectorate*

—Welsh Secretary (Under Secretary)
- Welsh Dpartment

— *Regional Controllers*

```
PARLIAMENTARY SECRETARY (Lords)

—Deputy Secretary (C)—
    —Under Secretary ——┬— Economic Advice and Marketing Division
                        └— Statistics Division

    —Under Secretary ——┬— Agricultural Economics Division
                        └— Agricultural Guarantees Division

    —Under Secretary ——┬— Labour, Safety and Seeds Division
                        ├— Grassland and Crop Improvement Division
                        └— Investigation Division

    —Fisheries Secretary——┬— Fisheries Division I
      (Under Secretary)    ├— Fisheries Division II
                           └— Fisheries Laboratories

    —Under Secretary ——┬— Milk and Milk Products Division
                        ├— Meat and Livestock Division
                        └— Fatstock Marketing Division

—Director of Establishments and Organization ——┬— Establishment Division I
  (Under Secretary)                             ├— Establishment Division II
                                                ├— Establishment Division III
                                                └— Establishment Division IV

—Principal
  Finance Officer ——┬— Accountant ——┬— Accounts Division
  (Under Secretary)  │  General      ├— Internal Audit Division
                     │               └— Data Processing Division
                     └— Finance Division

—Legal Adviser and Solicitor ——┬— Common Law Divisions
                                └— Conveyancing and Real Property Divisions

—Chief Scientific Adviser (Agriculture)

—Chief Scientific Adviser (Food)

—Director, Royal Botanic Gardens, Kew
```

is shown on pages 234-5. The regional and local organizations are dealt with at greater length in the next chapter.

Under the Permanent Secretary are three Deputy Secretaries, each of whom is responsible for the work of up to five Under Secretaries. The Director of Establishments and Organization and the Principal Finance Officer, as well as the Legal and Scientific Advisers, are directly responsible to the Permanent Secretary. Each Under Secretary in turn supervises the work of a number of headquarters divisions, in accordance with normal civil service practice. The divisions under certain Under Secretaries are known collectively as departments, e.g. the Establishment Department, the Finance Department and the Fisheries Department.

The Ministry, to a greater extent perhaps than any other government department, discharges almost all the functions of government in relation to the industries with which it deals, and the range of the work of the various headquarters divisions of the Ministry is very wide. Whilst, naturally, divisions doing similar work are brought under the same Under Secretary and Deputy Secretary as far as reasonably possible, the grouping is inevitably to some extent arbitrary and quite a number of variants of the present grouping would be equally logical.

The amalgamation of the Ministry of Food with the Ministry of Agriculture and Fisheries naturally led to a good deal of re-grouping of work between headquarters divisions. Straightforward amalgamation of common service divisions or departments, such as Establishments, Finance and Information, was clearly called for (though the details of such amalgamations might be anything but straightforward). At the other extreme some divisions remained unchanged as wholly 'agriculture', such as Land Use and Animal Health, or wholly 'food' such as Food Standards and Hygiene. The organization of the Fisheries Department of the Ministry of Agriculture and Fisheries was not appreciably affected by the addition of the small amount of work on fish for which the Ministry of Food had been responsible in its final days.

The re-arrangement of work on questions with which both the Ministry of Agriculture and Fisheries and the Ministry of Food had been concerned was rather more complicated. For the greater part of this was done by the adaptation of existing 'commodity' divisions of the Ministry of Food in which the two blocks of work were brought together. For example, certain branches of the Livestock Division of the Ministry of Agriculture and Fisheries had been responsible for the administration of the Milk and Dairies Regulations on farm premises, including the National Milk Testing Service, and for certain dealings with the Milk Marketing Board, whilst the Milk and

Milk Products Division of the Ministry of Food had been concerned with the administration of the Milk and Dairies Regulations in wholesale and retail premises and with the operation of the milk guarantee through the Milk Marketing Board. Both divisions were concerned in other milk questions, such as the determination each year of the guaranteed price for milk. Bringing all this work (as well as part of that previously done by the Welfare Foods Branch of the Ministry of Food) into one division has eliminated some overlapping and occasion for interdepartmental controversy, and has resulted in a better system for dealing with all the Government's responsibilities for the production, processing and distribution of milk at all stages from the farm to the consumer.

The allocation of work on the basis of commodities dealt with means that a number of divisions will be handling similar questions which arise on a variety of commodities. The Milk and Milk Products Division, for example, is primarily responsible for the Department's relations with the Milk Marketing Board, and other commodity divisions have dealings with other agricultural marketing boards, such as those for potatoes, eggs and hops. Co-ordination here is the duty of the Economic Advice and Marketing Division, which would be consulted by the Milk and Milk Products Division on any question arising with the Milk Marketing Board which might affect the Ministry's relationships with other marketing boards or which otherwise raised some general question of Agricultural Marketing Act philosophy. Again, the Milk and Milk Products Division administers one of the many agricultural price guarantee schemes, namely that for milk, and the Agricultural Guarantees Division is the co-ordinating body here.

PROFESSIONAL, SCIENTIFIC AND TECHNICAL STAFF

The Department's many responsibilities as described in previous chapters requires, in addition to the normal civil service administrative, executive and clerical staffs, a considerable cadre of professional, scientific and technical staff. The number of different kinds of jobs not covered by grades common to the whole civil service, and therefore requiring to be performed by 'departmental classes' peculiar to the Ministry (and perhaps the corresponding Scottish and Northern Ireland Departments), is very considerable, ranging as they do from masters of research vessels to nutrition chemists or, in the 'industrial' grades, from tractor drivers to stud grooms.

The highest scientific post in the Department is that of Chief Scientific Adviser (Agriculture). The holder needs to combine scientific eminence with practical farming experience, as the job requires someone who has had (and still has on occasions) 'mud on his boots', as well as a wide range of knowledge in the various branches of agricultural science. He is a member of the Agricultural Research Council, and of the Price Review Official Team and is chairman of the committee which recommends the award of post-graduate scholarships in agriculture as well as being available to give advice to the Minister and senior officials on all questions of agricultural science.

His opposite number on food questions is the Chief Scientific Adviser (Food), who is also responsible for the scientific investigations on food matters undertaken by the Ministry as described in Chapter XI. The Director of Fishery Research is the Department's principal adviser on fisheries scientific questions.

Then there are the various professional services, such as the Veterinary Service and the Agricultural Land Service, and technical services, such as the Sea Fisheries Inspectorate and the National Agricultural Advisory Service. Their duties have been described in earlier chapters, and combine in varying proportions work on the administration of various measures which calls for scientific or technical qualifications (such as control of disease and bull licensing), the provision of advice to the industry and the collection of intelligence. The officers in charge of the various services together with a small cadre of supporting technical staff are stationed at headquarters alongside the administrative divisions concerned.

The staff for these services, like all other permanent civil servants, are recruited by the Civil Service Commission. Appropriate qualifications, such as membership of a professional body or a certain standard of university degree are normally required, and subject to these candidates are usually selected by an interviewing board on which the Ministry is represented.

THE ESTABLISHMENT DEPARTMENT

The Establishment Department is under the charge of an Under Secretary, the Director of Establishments and Organization. He is the chief adviser to the head of the Department on its staff economy. He has to determine how many staff should be employed, what their grades should be, where and how they should be used. He is guided by the Treasury on such questions as their rate of pay and their conditions of service but on other matters he has a relatively free hand.

The Establishment Department carries out its functions under his direction. The Department as in any other Ministry has to recruit, select and appoint candidates to fill the posts available, to provide for their salaries and allowances to be paid, to give them special training in certain circumstances, to promote them as vacancies occur, to grant them leave when they are entitled to it, to keep watch on their efficiency and conduct, to transfer them from one post to another when occasion demands, to arrange for their retirement or discharge, to calculate their pensions and gratuities. It is also the responsibility of the Establishment Department to issue office instructions and circulars, to consider and suggest improved work methods and organization, to provide the domestic housekeeping services such as accommodation, cleaning, communications, registry, typing and messengerial assistance and to keep the Ministry's archives and official papers.

The work of the Establishment Department is allocated between four divisions. With a staff of nearly 15,000 to look after, including 4,000 in 'departmental grades' peculiar to the Ministry the Department has a multiplicity of special problems. Only about a third of the staff are stationed at headquarters offices. The remainder work mainly in eight regional offices, thirty-two divisional offices or in one of the numerous experimental centres or other specialized outstations in England and Wales. Because of the dispersal of so many staff the Establishment Department has delegated some of its functions within defined limits to the Regional Controllers. The main concern of two of the divisions at Headquarters, however, is the staffing of ex-headquarters offices and the maintenance of liaison with the regional organization respectively.

What the Establishment Department has to do is not only to staff the Ministry economically and efficiently but to do so with sympathy. In order to do this it sets great store on adequate consultation with representatives of the Staff Side of the Departmental Whitley Council.

THE FINANCE DEPARTMENT

The Finance Department is responsible for general control over the financial policy and expenditure of the Ministry, as well as for the accounting and audit work of the Department. While the various administrative divisions are responsible for the financial implications, as well as all other implications, of their policies and for the preparation and submission of estimates of expenditure, the Finance Department examine and criticize all proposals and estimates from the financial point of view and exercise general control over approved expenditure.

The scale of the Ministry's expenditure is indicated by the following list of the Votes for which the Permanent Secretary accounts to

Parliament, showing how the provision for some £278 million in the original Parliamentary Estimates for 1961/62 is made up.

Vote	Service	Net Provision in Original Parliamentary Estimates for the Financial Year 1961/62 £
1.	Ministry of Agriculture, Fisheries and Food	21,228,915
2.	Agricultural and Food Grants and Subsidies	234,753,230
3.	Agricultural and Food Services	11,410,065
4.	Food (Strategic Reserves)	2,274,000
5.	Fishery Grants and Services	8,672,190

Vote 1 is mainly salaries. Vote 2 is the cost of agricultural support given through the agricultural price guarantees and production grants (a substantial part of the support cost in Scotland is borne on the Vote of the Department of Agriculture and Fisheries for Scotland but the Ministry accounts for most of the expenditure in respect of Northern Ireland as well as for all of that for England and Wales). Vote 3 covers a wide miscellaneous range of other services for the benefit of agriculture and horticulture, ranging from over £4 million for grants for land drainage, and £3·2 million for compensation, etc. for animals slaughtered under the Diseases of Animals Acts (mainly on account of bovine tuberculosis and fowl pest) down to such items as £4,000 for the maintenance of the Ministry's Plant Pathology Laboratory and £2,750 for grants to fox destruction societies. Vote 4 covers the net annual cost of maintaining the strategic stock of foodstuffs, and Vote 5 the various activities of the Fisheries Department described in Chapter XII, including in particular the white fish and herring subsidies and the grants and loans for new boats and engines.

The Finance Department is in the charge of the Principal Finance Officer with rank of Under Secretary and comprises two main sections, Finance Division, which deals with policy matters and general financial control, and the Accountant General's Group, which deals with accounting matters, audit and data processing.

All proposals for new expenditure are subject to the scrutiny of the Finance Division which also examines and approves the Estimates of administrative divisions for submission to the Treasury, and is the formal channel for putting to the Treasury all financial proposals (other than staffing questions, which are the responsibility of the Establishment Departments).

Accounts Division maintains the central accounting records of the Ministry and prepares the Appropriation Accounts and Trading Accounts (such as those for the Agricultural Machinery and Drainage services and for the National Stud). The division is also generally responsible for any costing investigations. During the control period this was an important part of the Ministry of Food's activities, but the only remaining continuing costing responsibility of any magnitude is now that of milk distributors' margins. The Supplies Unit, which co-ordinates arrangements for the purchase of stores and equipment forms part of this Division.

Internal Audit Division undertakes a continuous test audit of the transactions of the Ministry, both at headquarters and in the regions, including the examination of internal control systems and procedures. It examines the accounts of marketing boards, companies and other agencies who operate on behalf of the Ministry, and also carries out regular investigations of the books and records of traders, in verification of the claims for subsidies and other payments. These investigations cover auctioneers, bacon factories and other certifying centres under the Fatstock Guarantee Scheme, egg packers (as agents for the operation of the Egg Guarantee Scheme), potato merchants (whose record of prices are the basis for the compilation of the average realized price for potatoes for the purpose of the Potato Guarantee Scheme), and lime suppliers in connection with the lime subsidy payments.

DATA PROCESSING DIVISION

The work of the remaining division in the Accountant General's Group, the Data Processing Division, is of sufficient general interest to warrant a section of its own.

Many of the functions of the Ministry, including in particular the calculation and payment of the various grants and subsidies and the compilation and analysis of the agricultural census, involve a considerable volume of routine clerical operations, and in recent years increasing use has been made of specialized electro-mechanical and electronic equipment to enable this work to be done more quickly and economically. This work is now concentrated in the Data Processing Division at Guildford.

The work of the division at present falls into four parts. First of all, with the aid of electronic computers, it calculates and pays two of the biggest centrally administered subsidies, namely the Fatstock Guarantee Payment (roughly 1,800,000 payments a year, totalling

Q

some £40,000,000 or more) and the Fertilizer Subsidy (some 850,000 payments a year, totalling about £30,000,000).

The second task of the division is the calculation and payment of a number of the Agricultural Production Grants such as the Ploughing Grant and the Calf Rearing Subsidy which are administered by the Divisional Offices. The details relating to individual grant applications, after they have been checked locally, are recorded in the divisional offices on punched paper tapes produced by special electric typewriters. The tapes are posted to Guildford, where the information is automatically transferred to punched cards which are used for the production of payable orders and associated documents and statistical analyses. In the busiest season of the year the division makes about 12,000 payments each week. The division also undertakes various other payments such as compensation for animals slaughtered for foot-and-mouth disease.

Thirdly, the division calculates and pays, with the assistance of electro-mechanical punched card equipment, wages and salaries of some 10,500 monthly paid staff and 2,500 weekly paid staff involving total payments of the order of £14,000,000 a year.

Finally, with the assistance of a large electronic computer and punched card equipment, the division now undertakes the compilation of the agricultural census and the analysis of the data derived therefrom, as mentioned in Chapter XIV above.

The monthly account prepared by the division already covers over a half of the Ministry's total Votes and is made available to the Accounts Division, fully analysed under subheads, five days after the end of the month.

THE LEGAL DEPARTMENT

The Ministry's Legal Adviser and Solicitor, who also acts for the Forestry Commission, has a professional staff of about forty, all qualified barristers or solicitors and non-professional staff of about the same number. All are stationed in London, though the professional staff from time to time have to travel to any part of England and Wales for such tasks as the conduct of cases in County and Magistrates' Courts or the holding of inquiries.

The work undertaken by the Legal Department is extremely varied. Parliamentary work includes instructing Parliamentary Counsel for the preparation of Bills, the drafting of Statutory Instruments, the conduct of proceedings if such instruments become subject to 'special parliamentary procedure', and dealing with Private or Hybrid Bills in which the Ministry has a particular interest. Work arises under numerous Statutes relating to commons, land drainage, sea and freshwater fisheries, animal health, minimum agricultural wages, safety, health and welfare, milk and dairies, the agricultural price guarantees and many other subjects. There is from time to time litigation in the High Court and much advocacy in County and Magistrates' Courts, including a number of prosecutions on such matters as obtaining payments by fraud.

There is also a large volume of conveyancing and advisory work arising from the ownership of land by the Minister, including land held for the Forestry Commission.

THE WELSH DEPARTMENT

The Ministry has a separate Welsh Department with offices at Aberystwyth in the charge of the Welsh Secretary, who holds the rank of Under Secretary.

Wales is a country with its own problems, language and national sentiments, and the Minister and the department need an adviser with a close knowledge of the Principality and of its agriculture. The Welsh Secretary, who is consulted on all matters of policy affecting Wáles, is responsible for liaison with the Welsh Offices of other government departments, the Welsh Sub-Commission of the Agricultural Land Commission, local authorities and other public bodies in Wales.

The Welsh Department is responsible for a number of matters which in England are dealt with at London headquarters, including functions in respect of land tenure, allotments and county council smallholdings; relations with the Welsh Agricultural Organization Society (the central organization for agricultural co-operation in Wales), bull and boar licensing and other livestock improvement schemes; and land use (including forestry). The Welsh Department, under the direction of the Welsh Secretary, also carries out in Wales the functions of Regional Controller described in the next chapter.

INFORMATION DIVISION

'Public Relations' and 'Press Officer' are terms which in recent years have tended to be regarded as rather dirty words. However it is now generally accepted that since government departments nowadays have perforce to intervene in so many ways in the lives and activities of individuals they need an adequate organization both to make known and explain what the Department is doing and also to deal with the many requests for information on all aspects of the department's work that are received from the Press.

It is the job of Information Division, and in particular of the Ministry's Press Officer, to ensure that not only farmers but the public are given the fullest information about the Ministry's activities. This means understanding the nature and capabilities of the different media of publicity and the manner in which they require information to be presented. It also means maintaining personal contact with an ever widening circle of Press, radio and television correspondents who report or comment on matters of agricultural, fishery or food interest.

The means adopted for publicizing any new development may vary from the simple issue of a Press notice with the routine weekly announcement of the current rates of guarantee payments for fatstock to a major information exercise for the annual price review announcements. On the latter occasion it is usual for the Minister to make a statement in the House of Commons, to meet the Lobby correspondents at the House, to hold a Press conference attended by up to 150 representatives of the national and farming Press and the broadcasting authorities, to meet personal representatives of the leading farming papers, and record interviews for radio and television: in addition, a white paper and a Press notice are issued to correspondents and distributed throughout the regional organization. Each occasion such as this calls for a plan of campaign to settle the timing, taking care to avoid any breach of Parliamentary privilege. Especial care has to be taken to consult other government departments when appropriate, and, in questions affecting international relations—as is often the case for example with fisheries matters—to observe agreements for simultaneous release of news throughout the world.

Newspapers and periodicals are studied for any references that have a bearing on the Department's activities, and representatives of the division attend the Press conferences held by the Farmers' Unions and other outside bodies. The staff of the Press Office deal with technical and policy enquiries from the Press and broadcasting authorities on the basis of information supplied by the division concerned with the subject, or arrange an interview for the enquirer with the division. They deal also with personal and telephone enquiries from the general public, and are liable outside office hours to receive enquiries at their homes through the duty officer.

A great proportion of the division's work is devoted to assisting and supplementing the work of the technical advisory services in promoting the efficiency of the agricultural industry by encouragement, advice and the dissemination of the knowledge gained from research. This has always been one of the primary objectives of the Department; indeed, when the Board of Agriculture was established in 1889 a government spokesman said that he was able to hold out little hope that the depression from which the agricultural industry had long been suffering could be cured by Parliament or by a government department; the Government, however, intended to provide farmers with the necessary knowledge by which they could work out their own salvation.

The agricultural shows which are held throughout the summer provide one effective way of getting over advice to farmers. In addition to the national and regional shows, every county has its own. At major shows such as the 'Royal', the 'Royal Welsh' or the 'Bath and West', the Ministry has an exhibit on a site of up to one acre, with sections devoted to various aspects of farming, particularly those of local interest and including demonstrations of the working of the Ministry's grant schemes or safety regulations, together with a bookstall selling the Ministry's advisory publications. Live animals demonstration plots of grass or crops and practical building, drainage, etc. demonstrations form the main items of the exhibit, and a booklet 'handout' is available to explain or elaborate on the exhibits. At other shows exhibits are staged on a less ambitious scale, whilst even at a district show there is usually at least a caravan bookstall.

From its earliest days the Ministry has relied to a considerable extent on the printed word for getting over technical information to farmers. The publication and distribution of such information in a form suited to the needs of the practical farmer is an integral part of the work of the advisory services; a leaflet on weedkillers or a 'typical plan' of a milking parlour, for example, may suffice to answer a farmer's queries or provide him with a permanent record of the advice received which he can study at his leisure.

Some hundreds of leaflets are available dealing with all aspects of agriculture, horticulture and estate management; crop and animal husbandry, diseases, pests, machinery, farm buildings and other fixed equipment all find their place.

More detailed treatment is given in the Ministry's technical bulletins, of which about a hundred are normally in print. The great majority are addressed to farmers, but some of them, such as *Domestic Preservation of Fruit and Vegetables* and *The Manual of Nutrition* have a wider appeal and for many years have been among the best sellers in the Ministry's publications. A Technical Publications Committee keeps under review the whole range and subject matter of the Ministry's publications.

By far the oldest of the Ministry's publications is the monthly journal *Agriculture* with articles of interest to all connected with agriculture. It was first issued in September, 1894, as the quarterly *Journal of the Board of Agriculture*. On a higher technical level there is the *NAAS Quarterly Review* intended for officers of the National Agricultural Advisory Service and for more scientifically inclined farmers, whilst the quarterly *Plant Pathology* deals with plant pests and diseases.

A 'house journal' is issued each month with the object of keeping all the headquarters and regional staff in touch with the numerous activities of the Ministry. Movements among staff, promotions and the like are included as a regular feature.

Libraries

The Ministry has always collected books and all manner of publications of interest and value to its work. The aim has been to provide for the technical staff a library service comparable to that of a university, for by the very nature of their duties they need access to all available published information on their field of activities and need especially to keep in touch with the constant technological advances of research.

In collecting over the years for its own needs all current publications, the central library in London has achieved the status of a national reference library for agriculture; its collection of the publications of other governments, obtained by exchange for the Ministry's own, is probably unequalled in this country and it is now a depository library for FAO publications. One or two university libraries may be comparable in scope, but these are not usually available to the public, whereas the Ministry is prepared to lend, through the National Central Library and the normal nation-wide network of inter-library co-operation, to any college, municipal or other library, and individual members of the public are at liberty to study in the library during office hours. Regional and other local offices also have similar branches adequate for the needs of the technical staff.

CHAPTER XVIII

Regional and Local Organization

THE Ministry could not hope to discharge effectively from Whitehall all the Department's present day functions, many of them requiring direct contact with the individual farmer. Extensive decentralization is essential.

Before the war the number of staff of the Ministry of Agriculture and Fisheries stationed away from headquarters was comparatively small. Apart from the staff of the Welsh Department they consisted for the most part of the professional and technical staff needed for various Ministry services—the veterinary staff, education, wages and drainage inspectors, land commissioners, livestock officers, fishery officers and the like. Generally each service followed a different pattern in the distribution and grouping of its officers throughout the country.

At the outbreak of war a temporary war agricultural executive committee was established in each county with wide executive responsibility for the local conduct of the food production campaign as described briefly in Chapter II; with a few exceptions the staff were employees of the committee, and not of the Ministry. Unlike most other departments dealing with the home front in war-time the Ministry had no regional organization; headquarters and the county committees dealt direct with each other on day to day questions, whilst on policy matters the Minister and his senior officers maintained contact with the counties by personal visits to committees and through the Minister's Liaison Officers. The Ministry's Land Commissioner attached to the committee had a fair amount of authority delegated to him which helped to avoid excessive to-ing and fro-ing between a committee and headquarters on day to day questions.

The Agriculture Act, 1947, reconstituted the county agricultural executive committees as permanent bodies to whom the Minister could delegate any of his functions relating to agriculture, and they continued to be responsible for a wide range of executive tasks, such as the administration of various agricultural grants and trading services. As a corollary to the permanent status now given to the committees, the Act provided that their staffs should be civil servants employed by the Minister; in this way it became possible to offer to many of the 'war ag' staff permanent posts as established civil servants, and to give them opportunities for promotion within the Ministry as a whole. At the same time as these changes were being made in the constitution of the CAEC's the Ministry's technical staffs in the country were being reorganized. First there was the establishment in 1946 of the National Agricultural Advisory Service (NAAS). This was organized in eight 'provinces' whose boundaries did not coincide with the standard government regions of other departments but were based rather on the areas previously covered by the advisory services of the various university agricultural departments and agricultural colleges, largely on the principle of dealing with areas of similar farming types.

The Agricultural Land Service, when it was established in 1948, adopted the same provincial boundaries as the NAAS and over the next few years a number, though not all, of the Ministry's other technical agricultural services were regrouped within the same boundaries. At each provincial headquarters there was the chief officer for each technical service (such as the Provincial Director of the NAAS and the Provincial Land Commissioner of the Agricultural Land Service) but no administrative officer.

Although county agricultural executive committees were grouped into Ministry provinces for some purposes, such as periodic local conferences of committee chairmen, for the most part Ministry headquarters continued to deal direct with committees and their staff instead of through any regional organization.

Much of the Ministry of Food's local organization was based on the standard regional and local government boundaries, but many of the commodity organizations (e.g. meat and livestock) did not conform to this standard pattern. By the time of the amalgamation in 1955 much of the local organization of the Ministry of Food was in process of liquidation. The largest continuing service was the Fatstock Marketing Organization which had recently been brought into being for local administration of the scheme of guarantee payments to fatstock producers (including supervising the grading of live animals and carcases).

THE WILSON COMMITTEE ON THE PROVINCIAL AND LOCAL ORGANIZATION AND PROCEDURES

In the summer of 1954 the Select Committee on Estimates of the House of Commons presented a report on the Regional Organizations of Government Departments[1] in which they drew attention to the complicated and unusual nature of the Department's local

[1] Parliamentary Paper 233, Session 1953/54.

organization, saying that it was so complicated that it might be called not one organization but several and that they feared that this complexity might result in overlapping, inefficiency and waste. In view of this the Minister appointed a committee under the chairman-ship of Sir Arton Wilson (a former Permanent Secretary of the Ministry of Pensions) to review the provincial and local organization of the Ministry of Agriculture and Fisheries and also (in view of the amalgamation then impending) the remaining similar organizations of the Ministry of Food.

The committee in their report of April, 1956,[1] recommended that the local executive work of the Ministry, and in particular the administration of the various agricultural grants and subsidies and the remaining trading services (such as field drainage and machinery), should be organized not in 60 county units but in some 35 to 40 divisional offices, each covering one or more administrative counties and of a size to provide an optimum work load. They also recom-mended that the Ministry should appoint a Regional Controller in each of the government regions, and that he should be responsible for the effectiveness of all the Ministry's work in the region (including that of divisional offices) and for the general direction of staff (subject to technical staff having direct access to their superiors at headquarters on technical matters). The committee also advised that county agricultural executive committees should cease to participate in the routine administration of grants, subsidies and trading services or to supervise civil servants engaged on this work (which in any case would not have been practicable for a division covering two or more counties).

These recommendations were accepted by the Minister and are the basis of the present organization described below.

THE REGIONAL CONTROLLER

Since April, 1957, the Ministry's local organization in England has been based on seven regions, each with a Regional Controller holding the rank of Assistant Secretary as the Ministry's chief administrative officer and representative and as such responsible for the co-ordination and general efficiency of all the Ministry's work in the region. For Wales the functions of Regional Controller are carried out at the Welsh Department under the control of the Welsh Secretary.

The work of the Regional Controller falls roughly into four parts. First of all he is responsible for the administration of the grants and subsidies and other activities dealt with in the divisional offices (see

[1] Cmd. 9732.

below). He also has certain delegated authority from the Establishment Department to settle questions of complements, discipline and accommodation, for Ministry staff in the region.

The second main function of the Regional Controller is to co-ordinate the Ministry's work in the region and to infuse into the various separate parts of the organization the sense of belonging to a team. He is the recognized spokesman and representative of the Ministry in dealing with public and other organizations in his region and with the regional heads of other government departments and the county agricultural executive committees. He is also responsible for local defence planning and for co-ordinating arrangements for the maintenance of essential food and other supplies in a peace-time emergency such as severe flooding or a transport strike.

Thirdly, the Regional Controller is the Department's eyes and ears in the region and through his contacts with local personalities, particularly the Minister's Liaison Officers and chairmen and members of the county agricultural executive committees, must be able to give advance warning of any development of which the Department should be aware. To do this effectively he may have to raise or look into any matter concerning the activities of the Department in the region.

Finally he keeps headquarters informed of developments in his region, and advises on the formulation of new policy in the light of his practical knowledge of how things will work out on the spot.

The regional heads of the National Agricultural Advisory Service, Agricultural Land Service and the Veterinary, Drainage and other services are responsible for technical efficiency of their staffs and for the development of technical work in the region. It is, however, vitally important that the Regional Controller and the heads of the technical services should maintain close working relations with one another. So much of the work of the technical services nowadays is geared to or arises from the administration of the grant and subsidy and other statutory work for which the Regional Controller is responsible in his region that consultation with his professional colleagues on any related technical matters of importance is both natural and frequent. For example, he would be approached about any important issue arising out of the application of the economic tests under the Farm Improvement Scheme or from the application of technical standards in the administration of the Slaughter-house Regulations. The Regional Controller takes a lead in co-ordinating advice and help on matters not primarily the concern of any one of the technical services such as the staging of the Ministry's exhibit at major agricultural shows in the region or arrangements for county committee members to take part in technical development work.

The Regional Controllers also, of course, have to keep in close touch with headquarters. They meet in London, for example, once a month under the chairmanship of one of the Deputy Secretaries of the Ministry. These meetings are attended by the Principal Establishment Officer and also as necessary by other senior officers when questions in which they are interested are being discussed. Apart from this there are constant interchanges by letter, visit and telephone between Regional Controllers and headquarters, and it is the normal practice to include a representative from the regions in any departmental committee which may be set up to consider matters in which regions have an interest.

DIVISIONAL AND AREA OFFICES

In accordance with the recommendations of the Wilson Committee the work previously done in some 60 county offices is now concentrated in 32 divisional offices. Counties which do not contain a divisional office have an area office and the larger counties may have one or more area offices as well as the divisional office. A chart showing the organization of typical regional and divisional offices is given at Appendix I.

The executive, field and clerical staff come under the Divisional Executive Officer who, under the Regional Controller, is responsible for administering various agricultural grants and subsidies dealt with locally and the remaining trading services.

The Divisional Executive Officer is the chief officer of the county agricultural executive committees in his division. As such he is responsible for seeing that the committees are supplied with all the information that they need for discharging their functions, and in particular that they are kept fully informed of developments in the Minister's policy and the reasons for them and equally that the views thereon of the committee are conveyed back to headquarters through the Regional Controller. He provides the committee with secretarial and clerical services and in consultation with his technical colleagues and the chairman prepares the agenda and the papers for the committee's meetings and ensures that all the necessary officials are present at each meeting to assist the committee in dealing with all the items on the agenda. He is also responsible for the proper running of field work other than that of the three major technical services, that is to say, the work of the drainage and water supply officers, pests officers and the other field officers required for operating the various grant and subsidy schemes and trading services etc. He thus has important managerial functions, having under him some 100 staff in the smaller offices and 200 in the larger, and he accounts for expenditure that may run to more than a million pounds annually.

The Divisional Executive Officer is also responsible to the Regional Controller for the administration of such measures as the Milk and Dairies Regulations and of the legislation relating to minimum rates of agricultural wages and to the health, safety and welfare of agricultural workers. When there are any local controversies arising from any of the activities of the Ministry it is the Divisional Executive Officer who will generally deal in the first place with questions and criticisms.

All the executive work in connection with the grants and subsidies is done at the divisional office. The area office is in essence a *pied-à-terre* for technical officers when it is more convenient for them to be based on an area office rather than the divisional office. The area office also acts as a local inquiry bureau and (in counties without a divisional office) is also the local centre for meetings of the county agricultural executive committee.

COUNTY AGRICULTURAL EXECUTIVE COMMITTEES

The war agricultural executive committees whose work was briefly described in Chapter II were a unique piece of government machinery, in so far as the Minister's executive powers in relation to an industry were exercised not by officials but by a body of men drawn from the industry and chosen by the Minister. In agriculture there is a very large number of relatively small production units, occupied by men with a healthy distrust of officialdom and of theory and engaged in operations in which local knowledge and experience can count for so much in view of the very wide range of conditions of soil and climate that can be met within the boundaries of a single county, let alone over the country as a whole. In such circumstances the great war-time increase in agricultural production in the face of all sorts of shortages could only have been secured by the work of the local progressive farmers on the 'war ags' and their district committees in guiding, encouraging and cajoling their fellows.

In war-time and the immediate post-war years it was a question of securing maximum production almost irrespective of quality or cost, with powers of compulsion and dispossession which could be invoked as a last resort when all attempts at securing co-operation had failed. The picture today is very different. The successful farmer needs to produce at low cost and to study the requirements of the market, and the economic incentive has replaced government compulsion to grow particular crops or to reach a minimum level of technical efficiency.

In these new circumstances county agricultural executive committees still have an important role though the range of their duties and responsibilities has changed, and the emphasis is now very much less on executive functions. The Agriculture Act, 1947, defined the primary duty of county committees as that of 'promoting agricultural development and efficiency'. Following a review of the work of county agricultural executive committees by a committee of county chairmen and officials under the chairmanship of the then Joint Parliamentary Secretary, Lord St Aldwyn, the Minister reaffirmed this view in August, 1958, when he added that the committees' wide knowledge of local conditions would be of great value to him in the working out of policy in its detailed application and in the work of technical development.

A county agricultural executive committee as now constituted under the Agriculture Act, 1947, has a total of twelve members, all appointed by the Minister, who also selects the chairman and deputy chairman. One-third of the members retire every year, being eligible for reappointment. Three members of the committee are drawn from lists submitted by the National Farmers' Union and two each from lists submitted by the trade unions of the agricultural workers' and by the Country Landowners' Association respectively. When vacancies occur for such members these organizations are asked to submit a sufficient number of names to give the Minister a real freedom of choice; these members are not on the committees as representatives of the nominating organizations, and as committee members they owe allegiance solely to the Minister. There are not more than five other members, chosen directly by the Minister, one of them being a member of the county council appointed after consultation with the council.

Committees normally appoint a number of district committees, consisting for the most part of some of the best and most progressive farmers in the district who are naturally in much closer touch with their neighbours than the main committee can hope to be. A typical district nowadays might contain about 2,000 farms, although the number can vary quite a lot according to conditions in the county.

One of the main tasks of county committees today is co-operation not only with the National Agricultural Advisory Service but with all the other technical services of the Department in everything that involves advice and help for the farming community, such as the advice offered by the drainage service on the improvement and maintenance of farm drains or the pests service in encouraging the formation of rabbit clearance societies. The intimate knowledge which district committee members have of the farming conditions of their district can be of particular value to a District Officer of the NAAS more especially when he is transferred to a district from another area and even more so when a young officer takes over a district for the first time. District committees moreover are the local representatives of the county committee, who would consult them on any question requiring a personal knowledge of conditions on particular farms.

The Minister is empowered to delegate to county committees any of his statutory functions relating to agriculture. For example, as mentioned in Chapter XI, the Minister has delegated to committees a number of his responsibilities in the enforcement of the Milk and Dairies Regulations, and the Special Designation Regulations on farms. Other powers at present delegated include a number under the legislation for the control of land pests, such as granting authority to enter and inspect land, and the serving of notices on occupiers of land requiring them to take steps to destroy or reduce breeding places or cover for rabbits.

The Arton Wilson Committee had recommended, firstly, that county agricultural executive committees should cease to participate in the routine administration of grants and subsidies and in any way to supervise the civil servants engaged on this work and, secondly, that each committee should provide an independent court of appeal to which an aggrieved farmer could state his case against a decision of officials on his application for a grant or subsidy.

These recommendations were accepted. In addition the Minister decided that officials should consult appropriate members of county or district committees in difficult or doubtful cases involving matters of local knowledge and agricultural practice, and before rejecting or reducing any claim. This procedure was designed not only to avoid the wrong sort of relationship that could arise if members of county committees were given the formal task of sitting in judgement on the decisions of officials, but at the same time to take full advantage of the valuable help committee members could give to officials on questions which involved an intimate knowledge of local conditions and agricultural practice and of the confidence of farmers in their judgement on such matters.

On questions involving a discretionary interpretation of matters of local agricultural practice the Department is normally content to accept the advice of the committee after it has heard the farmer's representations. In the few cases where no agreement can be reached between the Regional Controller and the committee, the matter is referred to the Minister for a final decision. Experience has shown that in practice it is very seldom indeed that the committee fail to reach agreement with the Regional Controller and his staff and, again, that there are relatively few cases where the applicant shows himself seriously dissatisfied with the final decision taken on his application.

Finally, the committee members as men with practical local experience are available to advise the Ministry's technical officers and other officers on local problems on such matters as land use and pest destruction. More generally committees are consulted on the development of policy and on its local application.

LIAISON OFFICERS

During the war contact between county committees and the Minister were maintained largely by the Minister's Liaison Officers. These appointments came to an end after the war but they were revived in 1952.

There are now fourteen Liaison Officers, each of whom covers a group of up to half a dozen counties forming the whole or part of one of the Ministry's regions. A Liaison Officer is invariably a prominent local agricultural figure and is not infrequently chairman of one of the county agricultural executive committees in his area. In any event he needs to be a person of considerable local standing in agricultural circles.

The main functions of a Liaison Officer are to interpret the Minister's policy to chairmen and members of county agricultural executive committees and to keep the Minister informed of agricultural opinion on developments in his area and of any local problems. In particular, he acts as the unofficial channel through which the Minister can transmit the 'feel' of the Government's policy to county agricultural executive committees and obtain an impression of the response to that policy in the country. On the other hand he is not normally concerned with day to day business between county committees and the Ministry. The Minister has meetings in London with his Liaison Officers three or four times a year which are attended also by the Parliamentary Secretaries and senior officers of the Department. This gives the Minister the opportunity of informing Liaison Officers personally of current developments and Liaison Officers in their turn report to the Minister on matters in their own areas and may raise any subjects they wish. Information Division who are responsible for arranging these meetings also supply the Liaison Officers with a monthly report on developments in the activities of the department and day to day information on other current happenings of which they should be aware.

The Liaison Officer's role as a personal link between the Minister and county committees is, therefore, quite different from that of the

Regional Controller who is rather the Department's chief official local representative in dealings on day to day matters not only with county committees but all sorts of other organizations, official and unofficial, in his region. The Regional Controller, of course, keeps in close touch with the Liaison Officers.

Appendixes

APPENDIX I

ORGANIZATION OF TYPICAL REGIONAL AND DIVISIONAL OFFICES

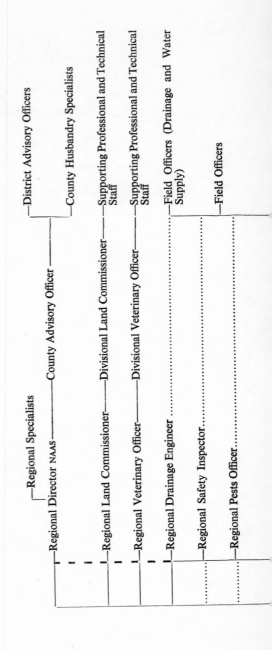

Regional Specialists

Regional Director NAAS —— County Advisory Officer —— District Advisory Officers
                                                   —— County Husbandry Specialists

Regional Land Commissioner —— Divisional Land Commissioner —— Supporting Professional and Technical Staff

Regional Veterinary Officer —— Divisional Veterinary Officer —— Supporting Professional and Technical Staff

Regional Drainage Engineer .... —— Field Officers (Drainage and Water Supply)

Regional Safety Inspector...............

Regional Pests Officer............... —— Field Officers

HEADQUARTERS

REGIONAL CONTROLLER

Divisional Executive Officer ———
- Sections dealing with
  - i. Grants and Subsidies
  - ii. Finance Control
  - iii. Common Services
  - iv. Servicing CAEC's
- Area Offices
- Supporting Technical and Laboratory Staff
- Supporting Staff

Regional Lime Officer

Divisional Milk Officer

Divisional Fatstock Officer

Regional Milk Officer

Regional Fatstock Officer

Regional Office Staff (Defence Plans Food Stocks Information Advisory Aids)

Divisional Level

Regional Level

LEGEND
—————— Direct Control
·············· Technical Advice
▬ ▬ ▬ Co-ordination

Ministers, Parliamentary Secretaries and Permanent Secretaries

A. MINISTRY OF AGRICULTURE AND FISHERIES
(1889–1903 BOARD OF AGRICULTURE; 1903–1919 BOARD OF AGRICULTURE AND FISHERIES)

Ministers

1889–1892	Rt Hon Henry Chaplin (later Viscount Chaplin)
1892–1895	Rt Hon Herbert Gardner (later Lord Burghclere)
1895–1900	Rt Hon Walter Long (later Viscount Long)
1900–1903	Rt Hon R. W. Hanbury
1903–1905	Rt. Hon. the Earl of Onslow
1905	Rt Hon Ailwyn Fellowes (later Lord Ailwyn)
1905–1911	Rt Hon Earl Carrington (later Marquis of Lincolnshire)
1911–1914	Rt Hon Walter Runciman
1914–1915	Rt Hon Lord Lucas
1915–1916	Rt Hon the Earl of Selbourne
1916–	Rt Hon the Earl of Crawford
1916–1919	Rt Hon Rowland Prothero (later Lord Ernle)
1919–1921	Rt Hon Lord Lee of Fareham
1921–1922	Rt Hon Sir Arthur Griffith Boscawen
1922–1924	Rt Hon Sir Robert Sanders
1924	Rt Hon Noel Buxton (later Lord Noel-Buxton)
1924–1925	Rt Hon Edward Wood (later Lord Irwin)
1925–1929	Rt Hon Walter Guinness (later Lord Moyne)
1929–1930	Rt Hon Noel Buxton (later Lord Noel-Buxton)
1930–1931	Rt Hon Dr Christopher Addison (later Lord Addison)
1931–1932	Rt Hon Sir John Gilmour
1932–1936	Major the Rt Hon Walter Elliott
1936–1939	Rt Hon W. S. Morrison (later Lord Dunrossil)
1939–1940	Rt Hon Sir Reginald Dorman-Smith
1940–1945	Rt Hon R. S. Hudson (later Lord Hudson)
1945–1951	Rt Hon Tom Williams (later Lord Williams)
1951–1954	Major the Rt Hon Sir Thomas Dugdale (later Lord Crathorne)
1954–1958	Rt Hon Derick Heathcoat Amory (later Lord Amory)

Parliamentary Secretaries

1909–1911	Sir Edward Strachey (later Lord Strachie)
1911–1914	Lord Lucas
1914–1915	Sir Harry Verney
1915–1916	Francis Acland (later Rt Hon Sir Francis Acland)
1916–1917	Sir Richard Winfrey
1917–1918	The Duke of Marlborough
1918	Rt Hon Viscount Goschen
1918–1919	Rt Hon Lord Clinton
1919–1921	Rt Hon Sir Arthur Griffith Boscawen
1921–1924	The Earl of Ancaster
1924	Walter Smith
1924–1925	Rt Hon Lord Bledisloe, KBE
1925–1929	The Earl of Stradbroke, KCMG, CB, CVO, CBE
1929–1930	Dr the Rt Hon Christopher Addison (later Lord Addison)
1930–1935	Rt Hon the Earl De La Warr
1935–1936	Rt Hon H. E. Ramsbotham, OBE, MC (later Lord Soulsbury)
1936–1939	The Earl of Feversham, DSO, DL
1939–1940	Lord Denham, MC

Parliamentary Secretaries (Lords)

1940–1941	Rt Hon Lord Moyne, DSO
1941–1945	Rt Hon the Duke of Norfolk, KG, GCVO
1945–1950	The Earl of Huntingdon
1950–1951	Rt Hon the Earl of Listowel
1951–1954	Rt Hon Lord Carrington, MC
1954–1955	The Rt Hon Earl St Aldwyn, TD

Parliamentary Secretaries (Commons)

1940–1945	Rt Hon Tom Williams (later Lord Williams)
1945	R. Donald Scott
1945–1947	P. Collick
1947–1951	George A. Brown
1951	Arthur J. Champion
1951–1955	G. R. H. Nugent (later Rt Hon Sir Richard Nugent, BT)

Permanent Secretaries

1889–1891	Sir George Leach, KCB
1892–1913	Sir Thomas Elliott, KCB
1913–1917	Sir Sydney Olivier, KCMG (later Lord Olivier)
1917–1919	Sir Alfred Daniel Hall, KCB, FRS

1919–1927	Sir Francis Floud, KCB
1927–1936	Sir Charles Howell Thomas, KCB, KCMG
1936–1945	Sir Donald Fergusson, KCB
1945–1952	Sir Donald Vandepeer, KCB, KBE
1952–1955	Sir Alan Hitchman, KCB

B. MINISTRY OF FOOD

Ministers

1939–1940	Rt Hon W. S. Morrison, MC, KC (later Lord Dunrossil)
1940–1943	Rt Hon the Earl of Woolton, CH, DL, LL.D
1943–1945	Col the Rt Hon J. J. Llewellin, CBE, MC, TD (later Lord Llewellin)
1945–1946	Rt Hon Sir Ben Smith, KBE
1946–1950	Rt Hon John Strachey
1950–1951	Rt Hon Maurice Webb
1951–1954	Major the Rt Hon Gwilym Lloyd George (later Lord Tenby)
1954–1955	Rt Hon Derick Heathcoat Amory (later Lord Amory) (Combined the separate posts of Minister of Agriculture and Fisheries and Minister of Food pending the merger of 1955)

Parliamentary Secretaries

1939–1940	Rt Hon Alan Lennox-Boyd
1940	Robert Boothby (later Lord Boothby)
1941–1942	Major the Rt Hon Gwilym Lloyd George (later Lord Tenby)
1942–1945	Rt Hon William Mabane
1945	Rt Hon Dame Florence Horsbrugh, CBE
1945–1950	Dr the Rt Hon Edith Summerskill
1950	Stanley Evans
1950–1951	F. T. Willey
1951–1955	Dr the Rt Hon Charles Hill

Permanent Secretaries

1939–1945	Sir Henry L. French, KCB, KBE
1946	Sir Frank Tribe, KCB, KBE
1946–1948	Sir Percivale Liesching, KCMG
1949–1951	Sir Frank Lee, KCB, CMG
1951–1955	Sir Henry D. Hancock, KCB, KBE, CMG

c. MINISTRY OF AGRICULTURE, FISHERIES AND FOOD

Ministers

1955–1958	Rt Hon Derick Heathcoat Amory (later Lord Amory)
1958–1960	Rt Hon John Hare, OBE
1960–	Rt Hon Christopher Soames, CBE

Parliamentary Secretaries (Lords)

1955–1958	The Rt Hon Earl St Aldwyn, TD
1958–	The Earl Waldegrave, TD

Parliamentary Secretaries (Commons)

1955–1957	G. R. H. Nugent (later Rt Hon Sir Richard Nugent, BT)
1957–1960	J. B. Godber
1960–	W. M. F. Vane, TD

Permanent Secretaries

1955–1959	Sir Alan Hitchman, KCB
1959–	Sir John Winnifrith, KCB

INDEX